Hath God Said?
Emergent Church Theology

ELLIOTT NESCH

Acknowledgements

Above all I want to thank my wife, Harmony, for her help in our home and in ministry.

I want to thank my brothers in Christ, especially David Valderrama and Dennis Maloy, who offered wise counsel and helpful suggestions for the content of this book.

I would like to express my gratitude to Linda VonBergen for editing this third edition.

Thanks to Bob DeWaay, Gary Gilley, Phil Johnson, Robert LeBus, Eric Ludy, Jay Peters, Chris Rosebrough, Joe Schimmel, James Sundquist, Ray Yungen for their research and participation in my documentary film *The Real Roots of the Emergent Church.*

David Bercot's *A Dictionary of Early Christian Beliefs* has been a very useful tool of reference for the writing of this book.

Thanks to Mark Karis for designing the book cover.

CONTENTS

Preface

This book was written out of a growing burden for the professing and visible church which is emerging into something new. And emergence this is nothing new. The professing church has been emerging out of and into various heresies and apostasies throughout the centuries. But one of the primary deceptions of our day is the Emergent movement. It is my desire to lead people back to the Jesus of the Bible who is to be loved, believed and obeyed by true Christians.

In 2012, I released a documentary film on the Emergent Church movement. Prior to producing the film, I read Emergent books and blogs, listened to Emergent sermons and podcasts, and watched Emergent videos. I was inspired and helped by many of the men I traveled to interview for the film who shared my concern with the Emergent movement. Along the way, I have met many who would call themselves postmodern Christians and have dialogued with them extensively in person and online about what they call Emergence Christianity.

The film was dismissed as a "Mockumentary" by leaders within the movement because they argued that the subjects of the film were not directly contacted. Thankfully, I was able to respond that the subjects *were* contacted for direct interviews. For instance, I contacted Brian McLaren, Tony Jones, Doug Pagitt and other prominent leaders within the movement, but there was no response. At a *Love Wins* book signing, Rob Bell told me he would be willing to do an interview and to contact

i

his church which I did several times with no response. I'm not going to fault them for that; I know they are all probably very busy people. The only person that ever got back to me was Shane Claiborne who spoke with me over the phone about a number of issues including community, social justice, and homosexuality. Prior to producing this second edition, I contacted the leaders of the movement once again in January of 2014 and asked them to review the film and respond if their views have changed, have been taken out of context or misrepresented. Tony Campolo and I corresponded by e-mail on a number of topics, but he asked not to be quoted. Doug Pagitt replied, "Good luck on your next edition." Others did not respond.

Nevertheless, the books, articles, sermons, podcasts, videos, and public statements of those leading the movement are plenty descriptive and sufficient for a critique such as the film and this book. These are my ways of joining the Emergent conversation. This book includes much of the research which could not be included into a two-hour feature film.

Introduction

Jesus said, "I am come that they might have life, and that they might have it more abundantly" (John 10:10). Satan, on the other hand, came "to steal, and to kill, and to destroy" (John 10:10). Satan "is a liar, and the father of it" (John 8:44). Today, Satan is repeating the lie told from day one in the Garden of Eden: "Yea, hath God said?" (Genesis 3:1). Before this conversation there were no questions or dilemmas. "Ye shall not surely die" (Genesis 3:4), the serpent told the woman, "then your eyes shall be opened, and ye shall be as gods, knowing good and evil" (Genesis 3:5). The attack and lie of the Serpent comes against God's Word. The Serpent suggests that people can disobey the Word of God without consequence, that people's eyes can be opened with some higher mystical experience and that people can be as gods. In other words, the Serpent would have us do what is right in our own eyes though it be contrary to God's commandments. Satan seeks to give the creature the right to sit in judgment against the Creator and His word.

"He was a murderer from the beginning, and abode not in the truth, because there is no truth in him. When he speaketh a lie, he speaketh of his own: for he is a liar, and the father of it" (John 8:44). The weapon of choice in Satan's murdering and stealing and destroying is a lie. It is not a dagger, not a sword, neither guns nor bombs, but a lie that Satan has designed for inflicting spiritual and eternal damage in the lives of people. "The devil, as a roaring lion, walketh about, seeking whom he may devour" (1 Peter 5:8). Today, many people are being devoured, swallowed up, murdered spiritually, and destroyed for eternity by the lies of Satan; little do they know what they are being told and preached by professing Christian leaders. They speak lies.

We live in a time so similar to the days of the prophet Jeremiah, just prior to the Babylonian captivity, that it's frightening. "Mine heart within me is broken because of the prophets; all my bones shake; I am like a drunken man, and like a man whom wine hath overcome, because of the LORD, and because of the words of his holiness. . . For both prophet and priest are profane; yea, in my house have I found their wickedness, saith the LORD. . . I have seen also in the prophets of Jerusalem an horrible thing: they commit adultery, and walk in lies" (Jeremiah 23:9,11,14). It was the prophet and priest of Jeremiah's day, the spiritual leadership of the people *who spoke lies*.

It is the church that Satan has targeted because Washington DC and Hollywood are already convinced that the devil doesn't exist. It is the profane pastors, teachers, leaders and authors within Christianity today that demonstrate how the lies of Satan are being propagated in the church. "For such are false apostles, deceitful workers, transforming themselves into the apostles of Christ. And no marvel; for Satan himself is transformed into an angel of light" (2 Corinthians 11:13,14). R.A. Torrey wrote:

> When Satan gets into the pulpit, or the theological chair, and pretends to teach Christianity, when in reality he is corrupting it; pretends to be teaching Christian evidences when in reality he is undermining the very foundations of faith; pretends to be teaching Biblical Introduction, when in reality he is making the Bible out to be a book that is not worthy of being introduced — then look out for him; he is at his most dangerous work.[1]

As the Serpent was in the Garden, so he is now behind the pulpit

---

1   R.A. Torrey, *What the Bible Teaches* (New Kensington, PA: Whitaker House, 1996), 517.

preaching another gospel, within the house of God, on the pages of Christian books and on the screens of computers. Satan's goal is to rob the faith in and application of a single verse or word from the Living God. "Yea, hath God said?" (Genesis 3:1).

Of these false and profane pastors, teachers, leaders and authors, we are told to beware because they "come to you in sheep's clothing, but inwardly they are ravening wolves" (Matthew 7:15). Thus these profane, ferocious and wild wolves are in the church masquerading as sheep. Sheep's clothing suggests that outwardly these false prophets look like Christians. They are in our midst of worship and fellowship, attending our gatherings and meetings. They look and smell like sheep but inwardly they are ravening wolves. Speaking to the church at Ephesus, Paul warned of false elders, "For I know this, that after my departing shall grievous wolves enter in among you, not sparing the flock" (Acts 20:29). They look and act and sound like Christians, but inwardly they are liars and workers of iniquity. They speak and prophesy in the name of Christ; they do many wonderful works in His name. Jesus said, "Many will say to me in that day, Lord, Lord, have we not prophesied in thy name? and in thy name have cast out devils? and in thy name done many wonderful works? And then will I profess unto them, I never knew you: depart from me, ye that work iniquity" (Matthew 7:22,23).

"But I fear, lest by any means, as the serpent beguiled Eve through his subtlety, so your minds should be corrupted from the simplicity that is in Christ. For if he that cometh preacheth another Jesus, whom we have not preached, or if ye receive another spirit, which ye have not received, or another gospel, which ye have not accepted, ye might well bear with him" (2 Corinthians 11:3,4). These false prophets come into the church subtly polluting the body with their damnable heresies. They speak with cunning and crafty wisdom of men, but not according to the foolishness of the Gospel of Jesus Christ. These ministers of Satan are often unaware of the havoc they are wreaking and remain ignorant of the devastating nature and catastrophic effect of their lies because they themselves are also deceived "according to the course of this world, according to the prince of the power of the air, the spirit that now worketh in the children of disobedience" (Ephesians 2:2). Evil men and seducers shall wax worse and worse, deceiving, and being deceived (2 Timothy 3:13).

They have crept into the church, and they have broadened the narrow way which leads to life. These are "certain men crept in unawares, who were before of old ordained to this condemnation, ungodly men, turning the grace of our God into lasciviousness, and denying the only Lord God, and our Lord Jesus Christ" (Jude 1:4). Likewise, Peter warned of false teachers "who privily shall bring in damnable heresies, even denying the Lord that bought them, and bring upon themselves swift destruction" (2 Peter 2:1). We are exhorted to depart from such false prophets as these that pose themselves as Christians but pervert the teachings of Christ. Paul said, "Now I beseech you, brethren, mark them which cause divisions and offenses contrary to the doctrine which ye have learned; and avoid them" (Romans 16:17).

How do we discern a wolf which outwardly looks and sounds like a sheep? Jesus said, "By their fruits ye shall know them" (Matthew 7:20). What is in the heart of these false prophets will manifest their true allegiance. The fruit of the Spirit is "love, joy, peace, longsuffering, gentleness, goodness, faith, meekness, temperance" (Galatians 5:22,23). Even these fruits and deeds of the Spirit may be counterfeited and will be forged by these false prophets. Jesus also taught, "Either make the tree good, and his fruit good; or else make the tree corrupt, and his fruit corrupt: for the tree is known by his fruit. O generation of vipers, how can ye, being evil, speak good things? for out of the abundance of the heart the mouth speaketh. A good man out of the good treasure of the heart bringeth forth good things: and an evil man out of the evil treasure bringeth forth evil things. But I say unto you, That every idle word that men shall speak, they shall give account thereof in the day of judgment. For by thy words thou shalt be justified, and by thy words thou shalt be condemned" (Matthew 12:33-37). Thus, you will know false prophets not only by their deeds but also by the things they say and teach. Their words and deeds may be tested by the doctrines of the Bible. Jesus said, "For a good tree bringeth not forth corrupt fruit; neither doth a corrupt tree bring forth good fruit" (Luke 6:43).

A true prophet of God, Jeremiah exclaims, "And the LORD hath given me knowledge of it, and I know it: then thou shewedst me their doings. But I was like a lamb or an ox that is brought to the slaughter; and I knew not that they had devised devices against me, saying, Let us destroy the tree with the fruit thereof, and let us cut him off from the land of the living, that his name may be no more remembered" (Jeremiah 11:8,9). Jeremiah was a docile lamb, a tree with fruits of the Spirit and the testimony of Jesus. But the false prophets sought to destroy him. Just as the entire nation of Israel in Jeremiah's day accepted the false prophets as true prophets of God, so Satan still has his pastors, teachers, leaders and authors within the church today. Just as the wolf has camouflaged itself in sheep's wool, so these leaders fit into mainstream Christianity with their smooth, crafty and subtle words, even Scriptural words. It is time the Church prays for spiritual discernment between fleece and fur.

Notice how Satan quoted the Word of God in his brutal attack of temptation against Christ: "If thou be the Son of God, cast thyself down: for it is written, He shall give his angels charge concerning thee: and in their hands they shall bear thee up, lest at any time thou dash thy foot against a stone" (Matthew 4:6). This then, the Word of God, is the first thing to be diluted, undermined and sabotaged in the attack of Satan against the church of God. "Yea, hath God said?" (Genesis 3:1). The enemy knows that the Word of God is our only armor and offensive weapon. If he can disarm us by spoiling the truth of God, then the Christian is defenseless and unable to retaliate.

Christ responded to Satan's attack with the Sword of the Spirit, which is the Word of God: "It is written again, Thou shalt not tempt the Lord thy God" (Matthew 4:7). Thus the Sword of the Spirit which is the Word of God (Ephesians 6:17) is our only offensive weapon against these lies of Satan, against these devious and cunning strategies of manipulation that have crept into the Church through the sermons, books, videos, and blogs of false prophets.

In this book, much of the Emergent Church movement will be exposed as a lie. This book will equip the the Christian reader with the knowledge to preach against it using the Sword of the Spirit. Whether the leaders of this movement are consciously sowing deception into the body of Christ or are doing it ignorantly is complicated to discern based on their sincerity and devotion to good principles. True Christians do help the poor, feed the hungry, clothe the naked, care for the sick and help widows and orphans. But we cannot water down the Gospel message in the process of "loving" people and building relationships. This is about Jesus Christ and the glory due His name.

We are told to "reprove, rebuke, exhort with all longsuffering and doctrine" (2 Timothy 4:2). In doing so, it is important to expose these men by name as the Apostle Paul did similarly telling Timothy of Hymenaeus, Alexander and Philetus: "Holding faith, and a good conscience; which some having put away concerning faith have made shipwreck: Of whom is Hymenaeus and Alexander; whom I have delivered unto Satan, that they may learn not to blaspheme. . . . Study to shew thyself approved unto God, a workman that needeth not to be ashamed, rightly dividing the word of truth. But shun profane and vain babblings: for they will increase unto more ungodliness. And their word will eat as doth a canker: of whom is Hymenaeus and Philetus; Who concerning the truth have erred, saying that the resurrection is past already; and overthrow the faith of some. . . . Alexander the coppersmith did me much harm. May the Lord repay him according to his works. You also must beware of him, for he has greatly resisted our words" (1 Timothy 1:19,20; 2 Timothy 2:15-18; 4:14-15). These men were named of Paul because they were enemies of the truth. And the Apostle John to Gaius wrote: "Diotrephes, who loveth to have the preeminence among them, receiveth us not" (3 John 1:9). It is my hope that those being led astray along with the leaders of the Emerging movement will repent and find the true mercy of our Lord Jesus Christ unto eternal life according to the word of God.

In providing the following quotations and criticisms in this book, I do not intend to slander these personalities aligned with the Emergence Christianity but to expose the underlying spiritual deception. The purpose is not to personally attack them, but to confront and rebuke what they are teaching. Our battle is not against flesh and blood. The battle is not against Rob Bell or Brian McLaren, but against the spiritual principalities, powers, rulers of darkness of this world, against the spiritual wickedness in high places behind the scenes (Ephesians 6:12). "For though we walk in the flesh, we do not war after the flesh (2 Corinthians 2:3). This is a raging and bloody spiritual battle for the souls of men. The kingdom of light against the kingdom of darkness. The truth of Jesus Christ against the lies of the enemy.

"Thus saith the LORD of hosts, Hearken not unto the words of the prophets that prophesy unto you: they make you vain: they speak a vision of their own heart, and not out of the mouth of the LORD. . . . Behold, I am against them that prophesy false dreams, saith the LORD, and do tell them, and cause my people to err by their lies, and by their lightness; yet I sent them not, nor commanded them: therefore they shall not profit this people at all, saith the LORD." (Jeremiah 23:16,32).

1

The "New Christians"

"Beloved, when I gave all diligence to write unto you of the common salvation, it was needful for me to write unto you, and exhort you that ye should earnestly contend for the faith which was once delivered unto the saints."
– Jude 1:3

Postmodern Christians

The Emergent Church, also known as the Emerging Church or Emergence Christianity, is a movement within Christendom that crosses a number of theological boundaries. Emergence "Christianity" is practiced by a wide spectrum of circles including Protestant, Catholic, Evangelical, Anabaptist, Reformed, and Charismatic. The movement is predominantly in North America, Western Europe, Australia, New Zealand, and Africa.

Because Emergence Christianity is literally all over the place, any critique which presents the Emergent movement as having consistent theology is erroneous and should not be taken seriously. Obviously, this makes the movement hard to define. Nevertheless, this book will demonstrate many of the predominant views of the movement which are all consistent with the expressions of postmodern culture. Consider the shifting worldview among today's young Evangelicals:

A 2014 Public Religion Research Institute survey found that 43 percent of young Evangelical Protestants support same-sex marriage. According to Relevant magazine, nearly 80 percent of born-again Millennials have had sex and 2/3 have been active in the last year. Even more worrisome is that The Christian Post reported that 1 in 3 Evangelical young people do not believe Jesus Christ is the only path to God.[2]

At the heart of the Emerging reformation is a perception of major changes in contemporary culture. Most Emerging pleas for reformation in Christendom are rooted in their understandings of postmodernism. They believe that the modern era and culture, which began with the Enlightenment, have been replaced by a counter-enlightenment worldview known as postmodernism. These ministers believe that the only way to be effective is to adapt to the postmodern culture by changing Christianity to make it relevant and palatable postmodern generations.

While defining the movement has been likened to nailing jello to a wall, it is clear that postmodernism is a key component of the Emergent movement. Scot McKnight says, "[E]merging Christians are as diverse as the universal Church. Some are simply evangelicals with a missional slant, while others are postmodernists with a Christian hangover."[3]

Eddie Gibbs and Ryan K. Bolger define Emerging churches as "communities that practice the way of Jesus within postmodern cultures."[4] Emerging leader Dan Kimball says, "The term 'the emerging

---

2   Chelsen Vicari, "Thinking the 'Emergent Church' Was Ineffective? Think Again,"   *Christian*   *Post*,   November   21,   2014, http://m.christianpost.com/news/thinking-the-emergent-church-was-ineffective-think-again--130084/

3   Scot McKnight, "What is the Emerging Church?" (presented at Fall Contemporary Issues Conference for Westminster Theological Seminary, October 26-27, 2006), 30, http://www.vanguardchurch.com/mck_ec.pdf.

4   Ryan K. Bolger and Eddie Gibbs, *Emerging Churches: Creating Christian Community in Postmodern Cultures (*Grand Rapids, MI: Baker Academic of Baker Publishing Group, 2005), 44.

church' simply meant churches who were focusing on the mission of Jesus and thinking about the Kingdom in our emerging culture. It meant churches who were rethinking what it means to be the church in our emerging culture."[5] Thus, the Emerging Church speaks of a movement which is emerging from the traditional understanding of Christianity into a postmodern expression. Therefore, in order to grasp what's being embraced in Emergent congregations, we must have a clear understanding of postmodern culture.

In the next chapter, we will look at the postmodern worldview more in depth by comparing it with a biblically Christian worldview. Prior to that, some may find it helpful to know the origin of Emergent Church and its status today.

Leadership Network

While the Emergent Church movement seems to be a reaction against the large, plastic, church growth phenomenon, both movements have in common a lineage that can be traced back to business management guru Peter Drucker. The genesis of Emergent can be traced back to an organization called Leadership Network. This organization was introduced as a resource to help leaders of innovative postmodern churches to connect. These efforts were aided by Harold Myra and Paul Robbins of *Christianity Today*.

In an article in the *Criswell Theological Review,* former Emergent leader Mark Driscoll, co-founder and preaching pastor of Mars Hill Church in Seattle, recalls the initiation of the Emerging Church movement:

> In the mid-1990's I was a young church planter trying to establish a church in the city of Seattle when I got a call to speak at my first conference. It was hosted by Leadership Network and focused on the subject of Generation X. . . . Out of that conference a small team was formed to continue conversing about post-modernism. . . .

---

5   Dan Kimball, "Origin of the terms 'Emerging' and 'Emergent' church - Part 1," *Dan Kimball,* April 20, 2006, http://dankimball.com/origin_of_the_t/

By this time Leadership Network hired Doug Pagitt to lead the team and organize the events. He began growing the team and it soon included Brian McLaren. . . . Pagitt, McLaren, and others such as Chris Seay, Tony Jones, Dan Kimball, and Andrew Jones stayed together and continued speaking and writing together as friends. . . .

McLaren, a very gifted writer, rose to team leader in part because he had an established family and church, which allowed him to devote a lot of time to the team. That team eventually morphed into what is now known as Emergent.[6]

Brian McLaren himself explains how this whole Emerging Church got started:

Well, back in the early 1990s there was an organization called Leadership Network funded by an individual in Texas, and Leadership Network was bringing together the leaders of megachurches around the country. By the early and mid-'90s, they noticed, though, that the kinds of people that were coming to their events were getting a year older every year, and there wasn't a [group of] younger people filling in. They were one of the first major organizations to notice this.

They started realizing that there was a sentence that was being said by church leaders of all denominations across the country, and that was, "You know, we don't have anybody between 18 and 35."

After a couple of years some of these young Gen X guys

---

6   Mark Driscoll, "A Pastoral Perspective on the Emergent Church." pp.87-89,
http://bobfranquiz.typepad.com/bobfranquizcom/files/32_apastoralperspectiveon theemergentchurchdriscoll.PDF

said, "You know, it's not really about a generation. It's really about philosophy; it's really about a cultural shift. It's not just about a style of dress, a style of music, but that there's something going on in our culture. And those of us who are younger have to grapple with this and live with this." The term that they were using was the shift from modern to a postmodern culture. And so what began to happen — and as this thing had a life of its own, they said, "If it's not just about Gen X, then we have to make sure that we get some older people who aren't just in that age frame to talk about this.[7]

Just who was this "individual in Texas" who funded the Leadership Network organization? It was Bob Buford, an owner of a successful cable television company in Texas at the time. Buford happens to have a lot in common with influential megachurch pastors Rick Warren (Founder and Senior Pastor of Saddleback Church) and Bill Hybels (Founder and Senior Pastor of Willow Creek Community Church). Some have referred to these three men as the Druckerite trinity for their relationships with business management guru Peter Drucker.

Apologist and Pirate Christain Radio host Chris Rosebrough interviewed Emergent leader Doug Pagitt regarding the beginnings of the Emergent Church. Rosebrough concludes that without the Druckerites there may have never been an emerging church. He goes on to state that the Druckerites (Bob Buford, Bill Hybels, and Rick Warren) "formed, bankrolled and promoted the Emerging Church much the same way a music marketing company might form and promote a boy band like the Backstreet Boys or N Sync."[8]

Peter Drucker was born in 1909 in Austria and immigrated to America in 1937. He was a writer, management consultant, and self-described "social ecologist." Drucker had taught at California's Claremont Graduate School for more than 30 years, where the

---

7" Interview: Brian McLaren." Religion and Ethics. PBS. July 15, 2005, http://www.pbs.org/wnet/religionandethics/week846/interview.html

8 Chris Rosebrough, "The Druckerites Must Issue a Safety Recall For Their 'Emerging Church' Product Line," http://www.extremetheology.com/emergent-church/

Management Center carries on his name. He published over thirty books in addition to articles for the *Wall Street Journal, Harvard Business Review*, and *Forbes*. His books and popular scholarly articles explored how people are organized across the business, government, and nonprofit sectors of society.

Drucker's writings were characterized by a focus on relationships among people rather than number crunching. Before his death in 2005, he rose to a position of great esteem for his contributions to business and management. In fact, he had a worldwide reputation as "the father of modern management." When it comes to management theory and practice, Drucker is one of the most widely influential thinkers and writers on the subject.

Drucker made time to consult with business leaders as well as government and nonprofit organizations. Leadership Network has noted:

> Drucker "devoted much of his energy to analyzing and advising" nonprofits, including church leaders, with a particular 'prescience about the growing role of megachurches in American society.'

> Both Drucker and Buford recognized the potential of these churches to re-energize Christianity in this country and address societal issues that neither the public nor private sectors had been able to resolve. Drucker was quoted in Forbes magazine as saying, "The pastoral megachurches that have been growing so very fast in the U.S. since 1980 are surely the most important social phenomenon in American society in the last 30 years."[9]

Those leading the organizations of the Emerging Church, the Purpose Driven Network and the Willow Creek Association also happen to be the most influential organizations in evangelical Christianity. *Time* magazine named Brian McLaren, the "elder statesman" of the Emerging Church, Bill Hybels, senior pastor at Willow Creek, and Rick Warren, the Purpose Driven pastor of Saddleback Church, as three of the most

---

9 Leadership Network feature. November 14, 2005, http://www.pursuantgroup.com/leadnet/advance/nov05o.htm

influential evangelicals in America.[10] Have these men become so influential within Evangelical Christianity because they are following the commandments of Jesus or because they are following best business management practices of Peter Drucker?

It is certainly peculiar that these movements have become so popular and well-received within Christendom when the Lord said to His disciples, "Woe unto you, when all men shall speak well of you! for so did their fathers to the false prophets" (Luke 6:26), and "ye shall be hated of all men for my name's sake" (Luke 21:17). How have these organizations become so prominent when "narrow is the way, which leadeth unto life, and few there be that find it" (Matthew 7:14)?

Though the organizations of Leadership Network, the Purpose Driven Network, and the Willow Creek Association are uniquely divided, they are intimately connected to one another. These three organizations are businesses that sell products to the target market of church leaders and pastors based on Peter Drucker's business and management ideas. All of these organizations have designed products that appeal to their consumers (be it baby boomers or Generation X). It is no coincidence that these three successful and influential men in Christendom were all mentored by the late business management guru Peter Drucker.[11] One *Christianity Today* article explains:

> Over the last 20 years Drucker has had a good deal of interaction with what he calls "pastoral" churches. These include megachurches like Bill Hybels's Willow Creek or Rick Warren's Saddleback Community. Bob Buford's Leadership Network has invited Drucker to speak to conferences of large-church leaders and has linked him to many pastors seeking advice.

---

10 "The 25 Most Influential Evangelicals in America." *Time,* http://www.time.com/time/covers/1101050207/photoessay/17.html
11 An entire book could be written on the relationships of Bob Buford, Rick Warren and Bill Hybels with business management guru Peter Drucker. For a detailed synopsis, see my article, "Drucker's Discipleship," *Holy Bible Prophecy,* July 27, 2011, http://www.holybibleprophecy.org/2011/07/27/druckers-discipleship-by-elliott-nesch/#more-277

Drucker calls these pastoral churches because their size is not nearly so significant to him as their orientation around meeting needs. They find their guiding light not from church tradition or doctrine so much as their analysis of their target audience. Hybels is a leading example: before beginning Willow Creek, he went door-to-door asking unchurched people why they didn't attend church, and then built Willow Creek around their answers. Pastoral churches waste no time regretting a changing world, but see change as their opportunity for ministry. This is precisely the approach that Drucker has urged on businesses and nonprofits for decades. In many ways, pastoral churches echo the management thinking that Drucker has long emphasized.[12]

Before Leadership Network began, its founder Bob Buford was consulting with business management guru Peter Drucker. Buford not only founded Leadership Network but also founded the Peter F. Drucker Foundation for Nonprofit Management.[13] Buford stated, "Peter Drucker who's Bill [Hybels]'s friend and mine, and I think one of the wisest men alive."[14] Often expressing his deep admiration for Drucker, Bob Buford notes, "Peter Drucker is the 'intellectual father' of most all that guides my approach to philanthropy. I've long since ceased trying to determine what thoughts are mine and which come from Peter."[15]

Four years after the beginning of the Leadership Network, we read from Bob Buford's official website: "Bob Buford convinced Peter

12   Tim Stafford, "The Business of the Kingdom," Christianity Today, November 15, 1999, http://www.christianitytoday.com/ct/1999/november15/9td042.html?paging=off
13   http://foundationcenter.org/pnd/ontheweb/otw.jhtml?id=5900005
14   "Willow Creek Community Church Creating A Volunteer Revolution Conference." Active Energy.net. October 28 & 29, 2004, http://activeenergy.net/217047
15   "Drucker's Influence on Leadership Network" Leadership Network Advance, November 19, 2005, http://www.pursuantgroup.com/leadnet/advance/nov05o.htm

Drucker to lend his name, his great mind, and occasionally his presence to establish an operating foundation for the purpose of leading social sector organizations toward excellence in performance."[16] In the aftermath of Drucker's death on November 11, 2005, Leadership Network had a press release reiterating this very information by their own admission. This feature describes how Drucker was a close friend and mentor of Bob Buford and "Drucker was instrumental in the forming of Leadership Network and its development over the years." It goes as far as saying that the organization might not exist as all "were it not for Peter Drucker." Leadership Network continues:

> In 1997, *Atlantic Monthly* magazine editor Jack Beatty interviewed Buford for two hours for a book titled, *The World According to Peter Drucker*. The entire volume contained only six words from Buford: 'He's the brains, I'm the legs' . . .

> Their friendship grew over the years as they talked about management, the "Halftime" phenomenon of successful business people looking for significance in the second half of their lives, and other common interests-including the phenomenon of the large pastoral churches emerging in the United States since 1980.[17]

In a nutshell, Bob Buford borrowed the best business practices of Peter Drucker and incorporated them into Leadership Network, much like megachurch leaders Rick Warren and Bill Hybels. Emergent leader Doug Pagitt was hired by Leadership Network to lead the team and organize events. Pagitt handpicked the postmodern leaders, most of whom are now at the forefront of the Emergence movement today. Former Emergent Mark Driscoll continued,

> By this time Leadership Network hired Doug Pagitt to

---

16   http://www.activeenergy.net/templates/cusactiveenergy/details.asp?id=29646&PID=207602

17   Leadership   Network   feature.   November   14,   2005, http://www.pursuantgroup.com/leadnet/advance/nov05o.htm

lead the team and organize the events. He began growing the team and it soon included Brian McLaren. The speaking team continued the conversation about the interface between postmodern America, the gospel, and the church for perhaps a year or so until the group disbanded for a variety of reasons. Most of us were in the middle of planting young churches and were struggling with the time it took to meet as a group, travel, and tend to our young churches and young families. Some of the men in the group spun out to start their own organizations and host their own conferences. Still others who were connected in varying degrees to the small team sadly disqualified themselves from ministry due to immorality.[18]

Driscoll says that Doug Pagitt, Brian McLaren, Chris Seay, Tony Jones, Dan Kimball and Andrew Jones continued speaking and writing together. This original team "emerged" into what is now known as Emergent. But Driscoll makes the distinction between what is Emergent and what is Emerging. Driscoll says that the Emerging Church "is a broad category that encompasses a wide variety of churches," including, "Europeans and Australians who are having the same conversation as their American counterparts."[19]

While some critics of the movement have primarily focused on the leadership of the Emergent movement, I have found the broader Emerging Church movement leadership to be equally problematic. Driscoll classified the Emerging Church into three categories. First, he describes the Emerging *Relevants* as "theologically conservative evangelicals who are not as interested in reshaping theology as much as updating such things as worship styles, preaching styles, and church leadership structures." Driscoll says their goal is to be more relevant appealing to postmodern-minded people. Relevant leaders look to people

---

18   Mark Driscoll, "A Pastoral Perspective on the Emergent Church." p. 89, http://bobfranquiz.typepad.com/bobfranquizcom/files/32_apastoralperspectiveon theemergentchurchdriscoll.PDF
19   Ibid.

like Dan Kimball, Donald Miller and Rob Bell as "like-minded leaders."[20] He added. "Within the Relevants there is also a growing group of outreach-minded Reformed Relevants, which look to men like John Piper, Tim Keller, and D. A. Carson for theological direction."[21]

Secondly, he noted the Emerging *Reconstructionists,* who are, according to Driscoll, "generally theologically evangelical and dissatisfied with the current forms of church (e.g. seeker, purpose, contemporary)."[22] This category can be characterized by more informal church forms such as house churches. He identifies Neil Cole, Australians Michael Frost and Alan Hirsch as influential voices for the Reconstructionists.

Thirdly are the Emerging *Revisionists,* the theological "liberals" who, "question key evangelical doctrines," by "critiquing their appropriateness for the emerging postmodern world."[23] Reconstructionists look to such influential leaders as Brian McLaren, Doug Pagitt and other Emergents. Driscoll says that while the Emerging camps may disagree on what is faithful Christian doctrine and practice, they all agree that the result of doctrine and practice remaining constant is "dead orthodoxy."[24]

Is the Emergent Church Dead?

Many prominent evangelical leaders have dismissed the Emergent movement as being dead. But Emergent leader Tony Jones recently said, "Some people say the Emerging Church is dead, other people say the Emerging Church has spread so far it's just been absorbed into the fabric of the American church."[25] I agree with the latter part of Jones' statement.

Perhaps as you read through this book, you will notice many

---

20   Ibid. pp. 89-90.
21   Ibid. p. 90.
22   Ibid.
23   Ibid.
24   Ibid.
25   Sarah Pulliam Bailey, "Values Voter Summit Session Claims Emergent Church, Satan, And Islam Are Bringing Down America," *Huffington Post,* August 28, 2013, http://www.huffingtonpost.com/2013/08/28/values-voter-summit-emergent-church_n_3829356.html

Emergent trends within your own church. Many denominations and sectors of the professing Church have unknowingly adopted Emergent ideas even though they do not label themselves Emergent. Brian McLaren said:

> The conversation continues to grow, not by creating a new slice of the pie, but by seasoning nearly all sectors of the pie. Even where the word "emergent" is not used, ideas from emergence leaders are being considered and adopted, leading to new experimentation and openness.[26]

No, the Emerging Church is not dead, and the recent CANA Initiative is evidence of this fact. In May 2013, Emergent guru Brian McLaren sent out a donation plea for a mysterious project. On his blog McLaren said,

> Readers of my books and blog know that I am a movement person. . .

> I'm looking for some people to join in this initiative. . .

> If you believe in the kinds of things I write, say, and do, and would like to join me in making a significant financial investment over the next three years – to help a broad-based, diverse, and deep Christian movement rise to the next level, I am hoping we can come together in a joint project.

> You might be able to give in the four, five, six, or seven figures. Or you might know a person, foundation, or other donor who can. Or you might be willing to start giving a smaller amount on a regular basis for the long term.[27]

26   Brian McLaren, "More on the Emergent Conversation," *brian d. mclaren* blog,   http://brianmclaren.net/archives/blog/more-on-the-emergent-conversatio.html
27   Brian McLaren, "A Request for Help," *brian d. mclaren* blog,

Seven figure donations? What kind of "initiative" requires millions of dollars? This CANA Initiative is now up and running and the "initiators" include participants of the typical Emergent cast of Brian McLaren, Rob Bell, Spencer Burke, Tony Jones, Doug Pagitt, and Phyllis Tickle among many others. The homepage reveals other participants:

> The CANA Initiative is comprised of Roman Catholic, Evangelical, Mainline Protestant, Orthodox, and other Christians who believe the future for Christian life and mission will be different in many ways from the past and present.

> The CANA Initiative brings together innovative leaders from all streams of the faith to collaborate in the development of new ways of being Christian...new ways of doing theology and living biblically, new understandings and practices of mission, new kinds of faith communities, new approaches to worship and spiritual formation, new integrations and conversations and convergences and dreams.[28]

Brian McLaren elaborated in the following e-mail response when asked about his request for large sums of money for the CANA Initiative. He said,

> For some time I (along with many others) have been seeing the need for some kind of small, non-competitive hub to serve – not control – the many networks that are spontaneously forming and developing in this general space we've all been opening but haven't figured out how to name yet ... Emergence Christianity, Convergence Christianity, a new kind of Christianity, Christianity for the rest of us, missional Christianity, progressive Christianity, generous orthodoxy, Red-Letter

http://brianmclaren.net/archives/blog/a-request-for-help.html
28   http://www.canainitiative.org/

Christianity, Just Faith, etc.

I believe that for this conversation to develop and mature towards being a lasting and effective movement leading to concrete action for the common good, we now need some coordination, facilitation, and behind-the-scenes encouragement and support. I want to continue doing what I'm doing – writing and speaking and networking, and I don't want to run anything. But I want to find some ways to help others use their gifts to help all of us move forward with more intentional synergy, shared positive identity, and joyful collaboration.[29]

So apparently this million-dollar initiative is to bring together a global third party network of Emergence Christianity. This global hub will bolster the Emerging Church movement through media exposure, a global network, new generations of trained Emerging leaders and a sustainable financial base to support the movement. It intends to meet the needs of Emergent organizations and leaders and to generate their desired outcomes. The website lists the following desired outcomes:

- Encourage new, expanding, generative and meaningful expressions of Christianity in North America
- Create exposure for media and other practitioners to learn about and access the movement
- Highlight more attractive public opinion of Christianity, spirituality and faith
- Connect with and inspire new generation of leaders
- Generate a collaborative environment for shared participation among leaders
- Network with parallel networks globally
- Create pathways for a new kind of interaction between faith traditions
- Generate pathways for faith-based organizations to

---

29 "Donation Plea: Brian McLaren Responds," *Stand Up for the Truth,* http://standupforthetruth.com/2013/05/donation-plea-brian-mclaren-responds/

collaborate with non-faith focused endeavours of Collective Action
- Support systems that generate new innovative initiatives – communities, churches, learning centers, media organizations, causes, etc.[30]

The Emergent Church is not dead but *thriving,* and the CANA Initiative intends to capitalize on its growth by strengthening this progressive movement, and bring it together. They believe it is time to make their movement visible at the national level. The CANA Initiative "will serve as a 'network of networks' building this ecosystem and seeking the common good. Together, all of these networks will be able to embody a new Christian ethos leading to constructive collective action in the United States."[31]

In his blog, Brian McLaren noted the emergent's target of youth:

> Key next steps may include the creation of a national, trans-denominational campus ministry, collaborative and transdenominational church planting and "branding," new approaches to theological and ministry education, and the development of a new genre of progressive Christian worship music.[32]

As this book will demonstrate in detail, the logical implications of Emergence Christianity intentionally set aside all religious difference (not only in Christian camps but also in non-Christian ones) in the name of common good and social justice. The end result is a global religion rallying around a powerless social gospel. In the words of CANA:

> we are eager to collaborate with people of other faiths, and those seeking the common good. Our networks of dialogue and action thus extend beyond Christian communities to persons of all faiths, as well as to

---

30   http://www.canainitiative.org/outcomes.html
31   http://www.canainitiative.org/the-need.html
32   Brian McLaren, "A Request for Help," *brian d. mclaren* blog, http://brianmclaren.net/archives/blog/a-request-for-help.html

communities that are not themselves faith-based.[33]

Much of contemporary Christianity is apostate. The answer to this widespread apostasy is not a "new Christianity," but the old Christianity revealed in the New Testament and by the "old Christians" of the primitive Church. We don't need to redefine Christianity, but rediscover Christianity. The CANA Initiative says nothing of Jesus Christ and nothing of repentance and forgiveness of sins. This is another gospel.

Faith Once Delivered To The Saints

Our only infallible source of authority is the Bible. Jesus said to the apostles, "Howbeit when he, the Spirit of truth, is come, he will guide you into all truth" (John 16:13). Jesus told *the apostles* that the Spirit would guide *them* into all truth. In other words, the apostles had been guided into all truth through the Holy Spirit when they wrote Scripture.

John the Apostle wrote, "Let that therefore abide in you, which ye have heard from the beginning. If that which ye have heard from the beginning shall remain in you, ye also shall continue in the Son, and in the Father" (1 John 2:24). Continuing in the Son and the Father is dependent upon the apostolic truth remaining in us. There was an established faith which was taught by the apostles "from the beginning." Deviation from that apostolic faith to something new is a departure from the faith.

Paul the Apostle said, "But though we, or an angel from heaven, preach any other gospel unto you than that which we have preached unto you, let him be accursed" (Galatians 1:8). The faith was complete by this early time in Christian history. The Church of God is "built upon the foundation of the apostles and prophets, Jesus Christ himself being the chief corner stone" (Ephesians 2:19,20). The church does not continue to be the giver of new revelation. God has preserved the teachings of Jesus and the apostles as the once for all foundation of the Church, "the pillar and ground of the truth" (1 Timothy 3:15). In the New Jerusalem, "the wall of the city had twelve foundations, and in them the names of the twelve apostles of the Lamb" (Revelation 21:14). Once again, the

---

33   http://www.canainitiative.org/

doctrine of Jesus and the apostles is the foundation of the Church.

Paul the Apostle had received the Gospel from Jesus and the apostles. He wrote to the Church at Corinth: "Moreover, brethren, I declare unto you the gospel which I preached unto you, which also ye have received, and wherein ye stand; By which also ye are saved, if ye keep in memory what I preached unto you, unless ye have believed in vain. For I delivered unto you first of all that which I also received" (1 Corinthians 15:1-3). Thus, Paul received the Gospel and delivered it to the Church.

Paul wrote to Timothy: "And the things that thou hast heard of me among many witnesses, the same commit thou to faithful men, who shall be able to teach others also" (2 Timothy 2:2). At this early time, the Holy Spirit had already guided the apostles into all truth and the complete faith. The faith had already been delivered to the saints by the apostles. Timothy was supposed to pass on that apostolic faith to faithful men. The Holy Spirit was not going to give Timothy special revelation like the apostles had received. Rather, Timothy was to pass on the apostolic faith which he had received from the Apostle Paul. From generation to generation, the authority of the apostles is passed on to the Church from the writings of the apostles, that is, the New Testament Scriptures.

Finally, "Beloved, when I gave all diligence to write unto you of the common salvation, it was needful for me to write unto you, and exhort you that ye should earnestly contend for the faith which was once delivered unto the saints" (Jude 1:3). The faith was *once for all delivered* by the apostles to the saints. Conversely, the faith is not an emerging or progressive thing which evolves over the centuries. It was not an unfinished faith that needed to be completed by successive generations. The faith had been *once for all delivered* to the saints by the apostles! On this basis alone, the Emerging Church is not the true Church, and New Christianity is not Christianity at all.

What we need in our day is not a *re-invention* of Christianity as the Emergent Church has done, but a *rediscovery* of the old apostolic faith! What did the early Christians believe as opposed to the emerging Christians? How did their beliefs compare to the new Christians? To answer this question, we should reference the early Christian writings. This I will do for the remainder of the book as we explore various

Emergent doctrines. By the term "early Christians," I am referring primarily to Christians who lived within the first three centuries. This is not including the heretics of that period such as the Gnostics.

Certainly the early Christian disciples were in a much better place than we are today to imitate true Christianity. Like the apostles, many of the early Christians spoke in the ancient Greek language of the original New Testament. Not only did they fluently speak ancient Greek, but they also lived within the same Greek culture as the apostles. They were not inspired like the apostles, but they were direct recipients of the faith once delivered to the saints. These men believed and practiced an unchanging and historic faith which was delivered to them by the apostles.

For example, Irenaeus (130-202 AD) was a very respected bishop in the early church and a direct disciple of Polycarp (80-167 AD). Also a respected bishop, Polycarp was a personal disciple of the Apostle John. So Irenaeus, a pupil of Polycarp, was only one human link removed from the Apostle John. Irenaeus wrote:

> The Church, though dispersed through our the whole world, even to the ends of the earth, *has received from the apostles and their disciples this faith*: [She believes] in one God, the Father Almighty, Maker of heaven, and earth, and the sea, and all things that are in them; and in one Christ Jesus, the Son of God, who became incarnate for our salvation; and in the Holy Spirit, who proclaimed through the prophets the dispensations of God, and the advents, and the birth from a virgin, and the passion, and the resurrection from the dead, and the ascension into heaven in the flesh of the beloved Christ Jesus, our Lord, and His [future] manifestation from heaven in the glory of the Father "to gather all things in one," and to raise up anew all flesh of the whole human race, in order that to Christ Jesus, our Lord, and God, and Saviour, and King, according to the will of the invisible Father, "every knee should bow, of things in heaven, and things in earth, and things under the earth, and that every tongue should confess" to Him, and that He should execute just

judgment towards all; that He may send "spiritual wickednesses," and the angels who transgressed and became apostates, together with the ungodly, and unrighteous, and wicked, and profane among men, into everlasting fire; but may, in the exercise of His grace, confer immortality on the righteous, and holy, and those who have kept His commandments, and have persevered in His love, some from the beginning [of their Christian course], and others from [the date of] their repentance, and may surround them with everlasting glory.

As I have already observed, the Church, *having received this preaching and this faith*, although scattered throughout the whole world, yet, as if occupying but one house, carefully preserves it. She also believes these points [of doctrine] just as if she had but one soul, and one and the same heart, and she proclaims them, and teaches them, and hands them down, with perfect harmony, as if she possessed only one mouth. For, although the languages of the world are dissimilar, yet the import of the tradition is one and the same. For the Churches which have been planted in Germany do not believe or hand down anything different, nor do those in Spain, nor those in Gaul, nor those in the East, nor those in Egypt, nor those in Libya, nor those which have been established in the central regions of the world. But as the sun, that creature of God, is one and the same throughout the whole world, so also the preaching of the truth shineth everywhere, and enlightens all men that are willing to come to a knowledge of the truth. Nor will any one of the rulers in the Churches, however highly gifted he may be in point of eloquence, teach doctrines different from these (for no one is greater than the Master); nor, on the other hand, will he who is deficient in power of expression inflict injury on the tradition. For the faith being ever one and the same, neither does one who is able at great length to discourse regarding it, make any addition to it, nor does one, who can say but little diminish it.[34]

According to Irenaeus, nobody could make any addition to the apostolic faith because it was already complete. Surely Polycarp and Irenaeus would have known about how the apostolic faith progresses or emerges over time if that were truly the case. But any emergence from the apostolic faith is a corruption, not an improvement. Even among the churches of different countries and cultures, they taught nothing new or different than that which was delivered by the apostles. Anybody who deviates from the teaching of Jesus Christ and the apostles is a heretic.

Much like the Emergent Church, the heretical sect called Gnosticism claimed that the apostles did not have a perfect or complete knowledge. Irenaeus continued:

> We have learned from none others the plan of our salvation, than from those through whom the Gospel has come down to us, which they did at one time proclaim in public, and, at a later period, by the will of God, handed down to us in the Scriptures, to be the ground and pillar of our faith. *For it is unlawful to assert that they preached before they possessed "perfect knowledge," as some do even venture to say, boasting themselves as improvers of the apostles.* For, after our Lord rose from the dead, [the apostles] were invested with power from on high when the Holy Spirit came down [upon them], were filled from all [His gifts], and had perfect knowledge: they departed to the ends of the earth, preaching the glad tidings of the good things [sent] from God to us, and proclaiming the peace of heaven to men, who indeed do all equally and individually possess the Gospel of God.[35]

Like the Gnostics, the Emergents seeks to improve upon the faith once delivered from the apostles to the saints. Irenaeus could prove that the historic faith was first preached by the apostles and committed to a

---

34 Irenaeus, *Ante-Nicene Fathers*, volume 1, 330,331, *emphasis added.*
35 Irenaeus, *Ante-Nicene Fathers*, volume 1, 414, *emphasis added.*

succession of faithful men.

> The blessed apostles, then, having founded and built up the Church, committed into the hands of Linus the office of the episcopate. Of this Linus, Paul makes mention in the Epistles to Timothy. To him succeeded Anacletus; and after him, in the third place from the apostles, Clement was allotted the bishopric. This man, as he had seen the blessed apostles, and had been conversant with them, might be said to have the preaching of the apostles still echoing [in his ears], and their traditions before his eyes. Nor was he alone [in this], for there were many still remaining who had received instructions from the apostles. In the time of this Clement, no small dissension having occurred among the brethren at Corinth, the Church in Rome despatched a most powerful letter to the Corinthians, exhorting them to peace, renewing their faith, and declaring the tradition which it had lately received from the apostles. . . . From this document, whosoever chooses to do so, may learn that He, the Father of our Lord Jesus Christ, was preached by the Churches, and may also understand the apostolical tradition of the Church, since this Epistle is of older date than these men who are now propagating falsehood, and who conjure into existence another god beyond the Creator and the Maker of all existing things. To this Clement there succeeded Evaristus. Alexander followed Evaristus; then, sixth from the apostles, Sixtus was appointed; after him, Telesphorus, who was gloriously martyred; then Hyginus; after him, Pius; then after him, Anicetus. Soter having succeeded Anicetus, Eleutherius does now, in the twelfth place from the apostles, hold the inheritance of the episcopate. *In this order, and by this succession, the ecclesiastical tradition from the apostles, and the preaching of the truth, have come down to us. And this is most abundant proof that there is one and the same vivifying faith, which has been preserved in the*

21

Church from the apostles until now, and handed down in truth.[36]

I must stress that the early Christians provide *information,* not *inspiration.* Irenaeus provides historical proof that the apostolic faith from the beginning was handed down to faithful men just as the apostles had instructed. He confirms what Jesus and the apostles had said earlier. Irenaeus' argument about succession was valid in his day because the heretical Gnostics could produce no apostolic lineage of their false gospel. There are many churches today claiming to be able to historically prove their existence from the time of the apostles. Yet they do not practice the apostolic faith. For instance, the Emergent Church embraces many ancient practices from the Roman Catholic Church and the Eastern Orthodox Church but does not hold to the more ancient apostolic faith. Authenticity is proven by holding to the ancient apostolic faith, not by having an ancient church or doing ancient practices. Jude spoke about *the faith* which was once delivered unto the saints, not *the church* which was once delivered unto the saints. Those who believe and practice *the faith* which was once delivered unto the saints are the true Church of Jesus Christ.

The main point is that the apostolic faith is once for all delivered within the Scriptures. The apostolic faith is the complete doctrine of Jesus and the apostles; it is based upon the totality of the New Testament Scriptures. Irenaeus agrees:

> *True knowledge is [that which consists in] the doctrine of the apostles,* and the ancient constitution of the Church throughout all the world, and the distinctive manifestation of the body of Christ according to the successions of the bishops, by which they have handed down that Church which exists in every place, and has come even unto us, *being guarded and preserved without any forging of Scriptures, by a very complete system of doctrine,* and neither receiving addition nor [suffering] curtailment [in the truths which she believes];

---

36   Irenaeus, *Ante-Nicene Fathers,* volume 1, 416, *emphasis added.*

and [it consists in] reading [the word of God] without falsification, *and a lawful and diligent exposition in harmony with the Scriptures*, both without danger and without blasphemy; and [above all, it consists in] the pre-eminent gift of love, which is more precious than knowledge, more glorious than prophecy, and which excels all the other gifts [of God].[37]

Once again, the apostolic faith was a very complete system of doctrine, not an emerging or progressive system. The historic faith does not progress or emerge into something new, but it is in harmony with the New Testament Scriptures. The early Christians show that the historic Christian faith was complete by the time of the apostles' death. When discussing the heretical Gnostic faith, Tertullian (208 AD) elaborated on the term apostolic:

For if, even at that time, the tradition of the gospel had spread everywhere, how much more now! Now, if it is our gospel which has spread everywhere, rather than any heretical gospel, much less Marcion's, which only dates from the reign of Antoninus, then ours will be the gospel of the apostles. But should Marcion's gospel succeed in filling the whole world, it would not even in that case be entitled to the character of apostolic. For this quality, it will be evident, can only belong to that gospel which was the first to fill the world.[38]

Emergence Christianity is filling the whole world. But the first gospel to fill the entire ancient world is the true Gospel. Tertullian talked about the principle of time in relation to the apostolic faith versus the heretical faith which emerged at a later date. He said:

We must follow, then, the clue of our discussion, meeting every effort of our opponents with reciprocal vigor. I say that my Gospel is the true one; Marcion, that his is. I

---

37   Irenaeus, *Ante-Nicene Fathers*, volume 1, 508, *emphasis added.*
38   Tertullian, *Ante-Nicene Fathers,* volume 3, 470.

affirm that Marcion's Gospel is adulterated; Marcion, that mine is. Now what is to settle the point for us, except it be that principle of time, which rules that the authority lies with that which shall be found to be more ancient; and assumes as an elemental truth, that corruption (of doctrine) belongs to the side which shall be convicted of comparative lateness in its origin. For, inasmuch as error is falsification of truth, it must needs be that truth therefore precede error. A thing must exist prior to its suffering any casualty; and an object must precede all rivalry to itself. . . . So that, whilst he amends, he only confirms both positions: both that our Gospel is the prior one, for he amends that which he has previously fallen in with; and that that is the later one, which, by putting it together out of the emendations of ours, he has made his own Gospel, and a novel one too.[39]

Not only is Emergence theology heretical in light of the Scriptures, but also in its comparative lateness in origin. Even the labels "Emergent" and "New Christianity" characterize the progressive and late nature of the movement. But truth precedes error. If Christianity does not evolve, then the only way Emergence Christianity could possibly be valid is by emerging from a false faith to the original apostolic faith. Is this the case? Was Emergence Christianity taught in antiquity or is it an addition like Gnosticism? If Emergence is progressive and innovative, then it is by its very nature a spurious faith and false gospel. According to the primitive church, innovation is unlawful. In the words of Tertullian,

You lay down a prescription that this faith has its solemnities "appointed" by the Scriptures or the tradition of the ancestors; and that no further addition in the way of observance must be added, on account of the unlawfulness of innovation. Stand on that ground.[40]

---

39 Tertullian, *Ante-Nicene Fathers,* volume 3, 348-349.
40 Tertullian, *Ante-Nicene Fathers,* volume 4, p. 111

It is evident from the Scriptures and early church criteria that the Christian faith is not progressive. Based upon this fact alone, Emergence Christianity is not Christianity at all. A disciple of Christ should receive nothing new in doctrine. As the writer of Hebrews puts it: "Jesus Christ the same yesterday, and to day, and for ever" (Hebrews 13:8). There is no new special revelation after the apostles. Nevertheless, we will hereafter analyze Emergence theology in light of the Scriptures and prove it spurious.

A meaningful analysis of Emergence Christianity must be a comparison to the original apostolic Christianity. Training in identifying counterfeit currency begins with studying genuine money. We must recognize the original, apostolic faith before detecting a counterfeit. Until we fully grasp the apostolic faith, we will never be able to recognize the apostolic Church or identify counterfeits. Concerning counterfeits, Irenaeus had this to say:

> Error, indeed, is never set forth in its naked deformity, lest, being thus exposed, it should at once be detected. But it is craftily decked out in an attractive dress, so as, by its outward form, to make it appear to the inexperienced (ridiculous as the expression may seem) more true than the truth itself. One far superior to me has well said, in reference to this point, "A clever imitation in glass casts contempt, as it were, on that precious jewel the emerald (which is most highly esteemed by some), unless it come under the eye of one able to test and expose the counterfeit. Or, again, what inexperienced person can with ease detect the presence of brass when it has been mixed up with silver?" Lest, therefore, through my neglect, some should be carried off, even as sheep are by wolves, while they perceive not the true character of these men,—because they outwardly are covered with sheep's clothing (against whom the Lord has enjoined us to be on our guard), and because their language resembles ours, while their sentiments are very different, —I have deemed it my duty . . . to unfold to thee, my friend, these portentous and profound mysteries, which

do not fall within the range of every intellect, because all have not sufficiently purged their brains.[41]

Emergence Christianity or New Christianity is not true Christianity. It is in a similar spirit to that of Irenaeus in his *Against Heresies* (quoted above) that I am writing this book. The early Christian Irenaeus exposed the false teachings of a heretical Christian sect called the Gnostics in his day. This group spoke with Christian-sounding language and even used the name of Jesus, but they were preaching another Gospel entirely. If there is in existence today an apostolic Church, it will be teaching and practicing the apostolic faith contained in the Scriptures from the beginning. But those who teach or practice something "new" are heretics. Tertullian explained:

> Paul who, in his Epistle to the Galatians, counts "heresies" among "the sins of the flesh," who also intimates to Titus, that "a man who is a heretic" must be "rejected after the first admonition," on the ground that "he that is such is perverted, and commits sin, as a self-condemned man." Indeed, in almost every epistle, when enjoining on us (the duty) of avoiding false doctrines, he sharply condemns heresies. Of these the practical effects are false doctrines, called in Greek heresies, a word used in the sense of that choice which a man makes when he either teaches them (to others) or takes up with them (for himself). For this reason it is that he calls the heretic self-condemned, because he has himself chosen that for which he is condemned. . . . In the Lord's apostles we possess our authority; for even they did not of themselves choose to introduce anything [new], but faithfully delivered to the nations (of mankind) the doctrine which they had received from Christ. If, therefore, even "an angel from heaven should preach any other gospel" (than theirs), he would be called accursed by us.[42]

---

41   Irenaeus, *Ante-Nicene Fathers,* volume 1, 315.
42   Tertullain, *Prescription Against Heretics*, chapter VI.

2

The Postmodern Rejection of Absolute Truth

"I am the way, the truth, and the life: no man cometh unto the Father, but by me."
– Jesus (John 14:6)

Truth is Subjective, Therefore Relative

The postmodern and Emergent view of truth is incompatible with a Christian worldview. Postmodern Emergents have not claimed to be seekers of truth and found it, but seekers of truth who question it and cannot attain it through logic or rationality. While not all Emergents accept all the premises of postmodernism, they all are greatly influenced by it.

For example, addressing the issue of truth, Emergent leaders Tony Jones, Doug Pagitt, Spencer Burke, Brian McLaren, Dan Kimball, Andrew Jones and Chris Seay have responded to critics:

> [W]e would like to clarify, contrary to statements and inferences made by some, that yes, we truly believe there is such a thing as truth and truth matters – if we did not believe this, we would have no good reason to write or speak; no, we are not moral or epistemological relativists any more than anyone or any community is who takes

hermeneutical positions – we believe that radical relativism is absurd and dangerous, as is arrogant absolutism; yes, we affirm the historic Trinitarian Christian faith and the ancient creeds, and seek to learn from all of church history – and we honor the church's great teachers and leaders from East and West, North and South; yes, we believe that Jesus is the crucified and risen Savior of the cosmos and no one comes to the Father except through Jesus; no, we do not pit reason against experience but seek to use all our God-given faculties to love and serve God and our neighbors; no, we do not endorse false dichotomies – and we regret any false dichotomies unintentionally made by or about us (even in this paragraph!); and yes, we affirm that we love, have confidence in, seek to obey, and strive accurately to teach the sacred Scriptures, because our greatest desire is to be followers and servants of the Word of God, Jesus Christ. We regret that we have either been unclear or misinterpreted in these and other areas. [43]

Emergence leaders affirm truth, but in their truth claims they deny absolute truth. Postmodernism may be characterized by the rejection of objective truth (relativism), rejection of exclusive truth (pluralism) and the rejection of objective meaning (conventionalism). Brian McLaren, leading speaker, author, and activist in the Emergent movement, insists: "Arguments that pit absolutism versus relativism, and objectivism versus subjectivism, prove meaningless or absurd to postmodern people."[44] To the postmodern mind, truth is subjective and therefore relative.

Emergents' postmodern tactic of literary deconstruction denies objective interpretation by attacking language itself as a carrier of

---

43   Tony Jones, Doug Pagitt, Spencer Burke, Brian McLaren, Dan Kimball, Andrew Jones, Chris Seay, "Response to Recent Criticism," http://tallskinnykiwi.typepad.com/tallskinnykiwi/files/response2critics.pdf.
44   Brian McLaren and Duane Litfin, "Emergent Evangelism." *Christianity Today,* November 1, 2004, http://www.christianitytoday.com/ct/2004/november/14.42.html.

transcendent truth (We will cover deconstruction in more depth below). While the general postmodern deconstructionists are literary critics, the Emergent Church applies deconstruction to the Bible. Though this critical concept may be useful in reassessing many false evangelical traditions, deconstruction ultimately allows the Bible to mean whatever the reader, critic or community wants it to mean.

For instance, Rob Bell, founder of Mars Hill Bible Church in Grandville, Michigan, defines binding and loosing as "the authority to make new interpretations of the Bible"[45] and says that these interpretations must be done in community.[46] The biases of the community will overrule the ultimate authority of God who communicated supernaturally and directly through His Word. Bell acknowledges that "the implications are endless"[47] for a community that follows his instructions to make new interpretations of the Bible. Of course the possibilities are endless when people can suddenly make the Bible say whatever they want it to mean. This is the ultimate absurdity of postmodernism because the Bible can mean whatever people want it to mean as Bell essentially acknowledges.

Though people can clearly understand Jesus Christ and His word irrespective of culture, biases, or community, the Emergent Church is anti-objective. Emergence adopts the postmodern worldview that absolute and objective truth is just a characteristic of the modern era and the Enlightenment. Stan Grenz, based at Carey Theological College in Vancouver, Canada, writes, "We ought to commend the postmodern questioning of the Enlightenment assumption that knowledge is objective and hence dispassionate."[48]

"Nobody is objective," says Bell.[49] Rather than fighting for the faith once delivered to the saints, he contends for the viewpoint that taking the Bible for what it really says is "warped and toxic."[50] It is irrational and self-refuting to make an objective claim that there are no

---

45   Rob Bell, *Velvet Elvis* (Grand Rapids, MI: Zondervan, 2005), 50.
46   Ibid., 52.
47   Ibid., 50.
48   Stanley Grenz, *A Primer on Postmodernism.* (Grand Rapids, MI: Wm. B. Eerdmans Publishing Co.), 166.
49   Bell, *Velvet Elvis,* 53.
50   Ibid., 53.

true objective claims. Rob Bell adds: "Our words aren't absolutes. Only God is absolute, and God has no intention of sharing his absoluteness with anything, especially words people have come up with to talk about him."[51] Bell says, "Our words aren't absolutes." Are we absolutely sure about that? The irony is that Bell is making an absolute statement and is again demonstrating the logical fallacy of postmodern thought that two contradicting claims can be simultaneously true.

One *Christianity Today* interview with Brian McLaren says:

> Making absolute truth claims—so important to evangelism in the modern era—becomes problematic in the postmodern context. Instead, he said, we can focus on recruiting people who follow Jesus by faith (without claims of certainty or absolute knowledge) with the goal of being transformed and participating in the transformation of the world. "Our lack of example in speech, behavior, love, faith, and purity may also explain why we must rely so heavily on arguments, many of them making claims that appear to postmodern people to be coercive and colonial, and therefore immoral, heavily laced with adjectives like absolute and objective to modify the noun truth," McLaren said.[52]

Bell's book *Velvet Elvis* is also full of postmodern rejections of absolute truth. For instance, Bell describes faith as a trampoline in contrast to traditional Christianity being more like a wall of bricks. Unlike a brick wall, a trampoline is springy; it can be stretched or flexed. He criticizes that a "brick is fixed in size," and "It can't flex or change size."[53] While the postmodern and Emergent "truth" can bend or adapt to the next culture, God says, "I am the LORD, I change not" (Malachi 3:6). The truth cannot be stretched as the spring of a trampoline.

Bell finds fault with a faith built with bricks because "Brickianity" will "inevitably keep people out."[54] Though God's truth is

---

51   Ibid., 23.
52   McLaren, "Emergent Evangelism."
53   Bell, *Velvet Elvis*, 27.
54   Bell, *Velvet Elvis,* 28.

not described as a brick, it is characterized by a Rock which is much *like* a brick. A rock doesn't change. Rocks do not adapt to environment or climate as postmodernity adapts to the customs and social institutions of the times. Jesus Christ is our Rock and He said, "Therefore whosoever heareth these sayings of mine, and doeth them, I will liken him unto a wise man, which built his house upon a rock: And the rain descended, and the floods came, and the winds blew, and beat upon that house; and it fell not: for it was founded upon a rock" (Matthew 7:24,25).

Season after season, through winds and storms and waves, we can always expect a rock to be the same solid, unchanging and unmovable mass. Winds and waves of false doctrines have been hurled at the church throughout the centuries, but God's truth remains the same. From now on, we should be no more like children tossed to and fro, and carried about with every wind of doctrine, by the sleight of men, and cunning craftiness, whereby they lie in wait to deceive; but speaking the truth in love, may grow up into him in all things, which is the head, even Christ (Ephesians 4:14,15).

The exceeding great and precious promises contained in Scripture are based on the following two principles: God has promised and He cannot lie. But if God can change and "emerge" from generation to generation, then He can also change His mind. If He can change His mind and break His promise, then we are left with no assurance whatsoever upon which to base our hope of salvation. But the Bible says: "Wherein God, willing more abundantly to shew unto the heirs of promise the immutability of his counsel, confirmed it by an oath: That by two immutable things, in which it was impossible for God to lie, we might have a strong consolation, who have fled for refuge to lay hold upon the hope set before us" (Hebrews 6:17,18).

Rather than Scripture having the preeminence and authority as God intended, *experience ultimately becomes the basis for Emergent knowledge.* Thus, there is no absolute truth or ultimate reality in the Emergent movement because reality is subjective and progressive. Tony Jones, Emergent blogger, author and speaker, affirms this view:

> Emergent doesn't have a position on absolute truth, or on anything for that matter. Do you show up at a dinner party with your neighbors and ask, "What's this dinner

31

party's position on absolute truth?" No, you don't, because it's a non-sensical question.[55]

Actually, Jones' statement is "non-sensical" because the New Testament speaks of a certain dinner party that does have a position on absolute truth. It is that blessed marriage supper of the Lamb: "And he saith unto me, Write, Blessed are they which are called unto the marriage supper of the Lamb. And he saith unto me, *These are the true sayings of God*" (Revelation 19:9).

In sum, postmodernists and the Emergent Church claim to know that we cannot know absolute and objective truth. This irrational mode of thinking is inconsistent with itself. They refute themselves by claiming they know that we cannot know absolute truth. If it's not absolute, then it's obsolete.

Pluralism

When we consider some of the Emergent truth claims, it is no wonder why there is such confusion. For instance, Doug Pagitt, the pastor of Solomon's Porch in Minneapolis, Minnesota, says this about the truth:

> When we talk about truth, we're really considering two concepts: reality (the way things are) and truth (a person's perspective of that reality). . . . No one has access to all reality in such a way that he can conclusively call his experience and understanding the truth.[56]

Notice how Pagitt defines truth as a person's perspective on reality, not actual reality. Pagitt is essentially saying that truth is whatever a person believes. Postmodernism asserts that all truth is based on

---

55   Tony Jones, "National Youth Workers Convention," *Theoblogy Weblog,* November 21, 2005, http://theoblogy.blogspot.com/2005/11/national-youth-workers-convention.html.

56   Doug Pagitt, *Preaching Re-Imagined,* (Grand Rapids, MI: Zondervan, 2005), 136.

perspective: "It's true for you but not true for me." The top postmodern virtue is tolerance or an open mind. This worldview teaches that everybody's truth is true . . . except for Bible-believing Christians. While Jesus taught that the Spirit of truth "will guide you into all truth" (John 16:13), the Emergent movement uses a postmodern argument that the truth can have different meaning at different times:

> [T]he beauty of the Spirit controlling the text is that it can, indeed, have different meaning in different times . . . and that the Spirit can use our own experiences and viewpoints to enlighten us to the meaning of the Word.[57]

The problem with postmodern open-mindedness is that people are opening themselves up to every other contradicting worldview or religion. But the Christian worldview is one of displacement. Jesus is acknowledged as truth and lies are rejected. Jesus comes in, that means Buddha and Muhammad have to go. By definition, truth is the quality or state of being true regardless of a person's perspective. Truth is that which is true. Truth is fact that is accepted as true and corresponds to reality. The Bible tells us that ultimate truth is found in Jesus Christ. But Pagitt's definition that truth depends on a person's perspective of reality presents the postmodern dilemma. In reality, the truth which corresponds to reality is true for all whether they believe it or not. If something is true, it is true for all and must therefore exclude everything else that contradicts.

But Emergent is anti-exclusive. The postmodern claim is that no view is exclusively true. Again, this is a self-refuting argument because it asserts that its view (that no view is exclusively true) *is* exclusively true. For instance, McLaren states:

> Missional Christian faith asserts that Jesus did not come to make some people saved and others condemned. Jesus did not come to help some people be right while leaving

---

57   Scott R. Smith, *Truth and the New Kind of Christian: The Emerging Effects of Postmodernism in the Church* (Wheaton, IL: Crossway Books. 2005), 70.

everyone else to be wrong. Jesus did not come to create another exclusive religion.[58]

But Scripture is exclusive by making distinction between believers and unbelievers. The Apostle John couldn't have been any more exclusive when he said, "He that hath the Son hath life; and he that hath not the Son of God hath not life" (1 John 5:12). And in his Gospel he writes, "He that believeth on the Son hath everlasting life: and he that believeth not the Son shall not see life; but the wrath of God abideth on him" (John 3:36). Some consider the statements made by Jesus to His followers too extreme in their exclusivity. This is one perspective, yet the message of the Gospel is inclusive to all who receive it through an obedient, love, faith relationship with God through Jesus Christ. "He that honoureth not the Son honoureth not the Father which hath sent him" (John 5:23). Jesus Himself said when sending out His disciples, "He that receiveth you receiveth me, and he that receiveth me receiveth him that sent me" (Matthew 10:40).

Anti-exclusivity leads to pluralism, inter-spirituality and universalism. Eddie Gibbs and Ryan K. Bolger are co-authors of *Emerging Churches: Creating Christian Community in Postmodern Cultures*. On the back cover of the book is the claim, "The Best Book Yet on the Emerging Church." Brian McLaren agrees with this evaluation by saying, "If you want to be truly conversant with the emerging churches, this is the book to read," and "It recognizes the essential theological emphases of emerging churches, and it is based on actual conversations with over 50 people."[59] Gibbs and Bolger describe Spencer Burke's Emergent community called The Ooze:

> Burke's community is prepared to learn from faith traditions outside the Christian fold. There is a Buddhist family in their church. As a community, the church visited a Buddhist temple. They participated in guided meditation with this family. Burke celebrates the many ways God is revealed. He recognizes that the Spirit has

---

58   Brian McLaren, *A Generous Orthodoxy* (Grand Rapids: Zondervan, 2004), 109.
59   Bolger and Gibbs, *Emerging Churches,* back cover.

been with these people all along. The community celebrates other traditions. They reach out to other traditions, and see them as beloved children of God. With a focus on kingdom rather than on church, people find that their relationship with other faiths changes."[60]

Refusing to accept Jesus as the exclusive truth, Emergent leaders, such as Spencer Burke, defend and even celebrate false religions such as Buddhism, Hinduism and Islam. Similarly, Brian McLaren states:

I don't believe making disciples must equal making adherents to the Christian religion. It may be advisable in many (not all!) circumstances to help people become followers of Jesus and remain within their Buddhist, Hindu, or Jewish contexts.[61]

This position works both ways. Not only does McLaren believe that ex-Buddhist/Hindu/Jewish/Muslim converts to Christianity can remain within their religions as followers of Jesus, but he also believes that Christians can incorporate false religious practices into their form of Christianity. For instance, McLaren celebrates the Muslim holiday of Ramadan. He says,

Ramadan is the Muslim holy month of fasting for spiritual renewal and purification. It commemorates the month during which Muslims believe Mohammed received the Quran through divine revelation, and it calls Muslims to self-control, sacrificial generosity and solidarity with the poor, diligent reading of the Quran, and intensified prayer.

This year, I, along with a few Christian friends . . . will be joining Muslim friends in the fast which begins August 21. We are not doing so in order to become Muslims: we are deeply committed Christians. But as

---

60   Bolger and Gibbs, *Emerging Churches*, 132.
61   McLaren, *Generous Orthodoxy*, 293.

Christians, we want to come close to our Muslim neighbors and to share this important part of life with them. Just as Jesus, a devout Jew, overcame religious prejudice and learned from a Syrophonecian woman and was inspired by her faith two thousand years ago (Matthew 15:21 ff, Mark 7:24 ff), we seek to learn from our Muslim sisters and brothers today.[62]

The Syrophonecian woman worshipped Jesus (Matthew 15:25) and had great faith in Jesus (Matthew 15:28), not like Buddhists, Hindus or Muslims who reject Jesus as the divine Son of God. We cannot be inspired by an uninspired false religious expression. On the contrary, Christians are inspired by the Holy Ghost to inspire the uninspired to Christ. Here we see the influence of postmodern relativism which, in the end, makes the fatal mistake of allowing two contradictory truth claims to exist at once. Both the Bible and the Qur'an cannot be inspired by divine revelation because they contain contradictory truth claims about reality and salvation. The idea that a person can be a follower of Jesus without becoming a Christian or being a part of the Christian church is false. Jesus said, "No servant can serve two masters" (Luke 16:13). A disciple of Jesus cannot hold the Christian traditions taught by word or epistle as the Apostle Paul exhorted (2 Thessalonians 2:15) while simultaneously celebrating the reception of the Qur'an with the Muslim holiday of Ramadan. When Jesus truly enters a person's life, He displaces everything that is against Him and His nature. Thus, Christians cannot call themselves Muslims that follow Jesus. Given the blasphemous beliefs of Islam, such a profession is false. There is no such thing as a Buddhist Christian or a Hindu disciple of Christ because these various religious expressions are in themselves antithetical to Christianity.

Foundationalism describes the view that there are self-evident principles at the basis of all thought:

1. The Law of Identity (A is A).

---

62   Brian McLaren, "Ramadan 2009: Part 1 What's going on?" *Brian D McLaren*,   http://www.brianmclaren.net/archives/blog/ramadan-2009-part-1-whats-going.html.

2. The Law of Non-Contradiction (A is not non-A).
3. The Law of Excluded Middle (Either A or non-A).
4. The Laws of rational inference.

A foundational inference may occur in several forms. For example, any given individual is either saved from his sins, or he is lost. If a person is not saved, then he is lost. In The Emergent Church Postmodern Spirituality Debate, author and speaker Bob DeWaay offered the following foundational inferences: "Either there are boundaries for religious activities to approach God, or there are no boundaries for religious activities to approach God and we can come to Him freestyle," and "Either God determines the terms and means of salvation and sanctification, or we are free to come to God for salvation and sanctification on our own terms and by creating pathways to God from our own imagination." To this, Emergent leader Doug Pagitt responded, "That's what I refer to as binary reductionistic reasoning. Either, or; it's either this *or* that. Binary means you have two choices and only two choices. . . . it makes it very difficult to really go somewhere."[63]

The Emergent Church in practice embraces a third alternative to either/or foundational inferences by accepting every worldview as valid. Stan Grenz wrote an entire anti-foundationalism book called *Beyond Foundationalism*. Similarly, Brian McLaren states:

> For modern Western Christians, words like authority, inerrancy, infallibility, revelation, objective, absolute, and literal are crucial. . . . Hardly anyone knows . . . Rene Descartes, the Enlightenment, David Hume, and Foundationalism—which provides the context in which these words are so important. Hardly anyone notices the irony of resorting to the authority of extra-biblical words and concepts to justify one's belief in the Bible's ultimate authority.[64]

---

63 The Emergent Church Postmodern Spirituality Debate between Bob DeWaay and Doug Pagitt (Part II), Twin City Fellowship, Minneapolis, Minnesota, January 20, 2006.
64 McLaren, *Generous Orthodoxy*, 164.

Though Donald Miller professes to be a Christian, it is not on the basis of truth and reality. In fact, he believes Christianity is a contradiction of reality:

> There are many ideas within Christian spirituality that contradict the facts of reality as I understand them. A statement like this offends some Christians because they believe if aspects of their faith do not obey the facts of reality, they are not true.[65]

The postmodern irrationality of Emergent rejects foundationalism and claims that opposites and contradictions (A is non-A) can both be true. Thus, Brian McLaren can make two antithetical truth claims that both the Bible and the Qur'an are divinely inspired. This position may be politically correct, but both cannot be true because the two texts contradict. Emergents actually made up a term called "orthoparadoxy" which suggests that contradictory views can be held simultaneously. Dwight J. Friesen explains:

> The theological method of orthoparadoxy surrenders the right to be right for the sake of movement towards being reconciled one with the other, while simultaneously seeking to bring the fullness of convictions and beliefs to the other. Current theological methods that often stress agreement/disagreement, win/loss, good/bad, orthodoxy/heresy, and the like set people up for constant battles to convince and convert the other to their way of believing and being in the world.[66]

It is this type of irrational thinking that rejects absolute truth. In fact, it is a core belief of the Emerging Church that Biblical matters are uncertain rather than absolute. Certainty is not helpful for Emergent communities because it divides people, they say. But to surrender doctrine for unity is irrational. But McLaren says that "people seem to

---

65   Donald Miller, *Blue Like Jazz* (Nashville, TN: Thomas Nelson, 2003), 201.
66   Dwight J. Friesen, "Orthoparodoxy" in *An Emergent Manifesto of Hope,* eds. Tony Jones and Doug Pagitt (Grand Rapids, MI: Baker Books, 2007), 208.

think that since modernity was rationalistic, postmodernity must be either antirational or irrational." He says, "No, that's antimodernity, not postmodernity." McLaren says that postmodernity seeks to integrate rationality with things "beyond rationality" like imagination, intuition, and faith."[67]

Donald Miller admits to irrationalism by saying, "My belief in Jesus did not seem rational or scientific, and yet there was nothing I could do to separate myself from this belief."[68] Emergent postmodernism exalts itself against the knowledge of truth, logic and rationality which flow from God's nature. Truth is both knowable and rational but Emergents reject these attributes of truth even though they have denied doing so. Miller also says,

> My most recent faith struggle is not one of intellect. . . .
> I don't believe I will ever walk away from God for
> intellectual reasons. Who knows anything anyway? If I
> walk away . . . I will walk away for social reasons,
> identity reasons, deep emotional reasons.[69]

Who knows anything anyway? This certainly doesn't sound like the Apostles who claimed that God gave *the knowledge* of His glory in the face of Jesus Christ (2 Corinthians 4:6), that God's will is that all men come *to the knowledge of the truth* (1 Timothy 2:4), and that God has given to us all things that pertain to life and godliness, *through the knowledge* of Him that has called us to glory and virtue (2 Peter 1:3). Anti-rationalism is also self-refuting because the Emergents claim to know (or have the knowledge) that we can't have the luxury of knowledge when it comes to absolute truth.

I believe these types of illogical ideas are stepping stones to a global religion in which everything is "true" as long as it's "true for you." Rock music group U2's frontman Bono used the epitomizing postmodern message of "COEXIST." On U2's 2005 Vertigo tour, Bono sought to bridge all faiths into a global religion. The word "COEXIST" appeared

---

67   Tony Campolo and Brian McLaren, *Adventures in Missing the Point* (Grand Rapids, MI: Zondervan. 2003), 278.
68   Miller, *Blue Like Jazz*, 54.
69   Miller, *Blue Like Jazz,* 103.

on a giant screen—the "C" in the symbol of the Islamic crescent, the "X" as the Jewish star of David, and "T" as the Christian cross. Bono led their fans in a chant singing, "Jesus, Jew, Mohammed—It's True."[70] While Mohammed would be considered a false prophet and Islam a false religion to a Christian, the postmodern young person can chant with Bono, "Jesus, Jew, Mohammed—It's True." Emergent leader Doug Pagitt speaks favorably of the COEXIST message:

> Through an email I read an article on the Relevant website of one person's experience at a concert. I can't find the article on the website, but I read it in the email. It is called "How to Dismantle an Idolized Bono." She was disturbed by Bono's call to Coexist (which is as much a marketing effort of a line of products as anything else, it seems to me). But the article's author raises concerns about Bono not being what she thought because of his call for "oneness" and his use of the Coexist logo which included the Crescent Moon, Star of David, and Cross. The article makes statements that made me groan aloud, and yell in frustration a couple of times. It drove me to Bono's side, to come to his defense, to join the Coexist crowd. So, here's to you my man Bono.[71]

What is Truth?

Thankfully, we don't have to be like the Emergents who essentially echo the question of Pilate who said, "What is truth?" (John 18:38). God's character and His truth are absolute and unchangeable. The Emergent movement must be challenged with the fact that Jesus Christ is the same yesterday, and today, and for ever (Hebrews 13:8). There was no debate about absolute truth in the primitive Church. For example,

---

70 "U2 Bono Co-Exist New York MSG," YouTube video, 0:01-0:26, posted by "damopants," January 27, 2007, http://www.youtube.com/watch?v=HVoemrstxbI.
71 Doug Pagitt, "Bono My Man," *Pagitt Blog*, December, 2005, http://pagitt.typepad.com/pagittblog/2005/12/bono_my_man.html.

Justin Martyr (160 AD) wrote:

> The word of truth is free, and carries its own authority,
> disdaining to fall under any skilful argument, or to
> endure the logical scrutiny of its hearers. But it would be
> believed for its own nobility, and for the confidence due
> to Him who sends it. Now the word of truth is sent from
> God; wherefore the freedom claimed by the truth is not
> arrogant. For being sent with authority, it were not fit
> that it should be required to produce proof of what is
> said; since neither is there any proof beyond itself,
> which is God. For every proof is more powerful and
> trustworthy than that which it proves; since what is
> disbelieved, until proof is produced, gets credit when
> such proof is produced, and is recognised as being what
> it was stated to be. But nothing is either more powerful
> or more trustworthy than the truth; so that he who
> requires proof of this is like one who wishes it
> demonstrated why the things that appear to the senses do
> appear. For the test of those things which are received
> through the reason, is sense; but of sense itself there is
> no test beyond itself. As then we bring those things
> which reason hunts after, to sense, and by it judge what
> kind of things they are, whether the things spoken be
> true or false, and then sit in judgment no longer, giving
> full credit to its decision; so also we refer all that is said
> regarding men and the world to the truth, and by it judge
> whether it be worthless or no. But the utterances of truth
> we judge by no separate test, giving full credit to itself.[72]

God's word instructs us not to accommodate the spiritual expectations and values of any nation, culture, or competing worldview. Christians are called to boldly proclaim the Gospel of the Kingdom that Jesus Christ is Lord and He will save His people from their sins. Postmodernity assumes that objective truth is unknowable. This is

---

[72]   Justin Martyr, *Fragments of the Lost Work of Justin on the Resurrection*, ANF, volume 1, 294.

incompatible with the bold and clear proclamation that Jesus is "the way, the truth, and the life" (John 14:6).

Therefore, viewing Christianity through the lens of postmodernity can only lead to heresies and compromise, such as religious pluralism and redefining essential doctrines of the Christian faith. Tying postmodernism to Christianity is only another lost battle in the age-old war for truth in which Satan is the ultimate conspirator. Emergent is fighting against Christ by attacking the validity of the Scriptures: "Yea, hath God said?" (Genesis 3:1).

We will soon see that Emergents depend upon interpretation and opinion when it is convenient for their arguments against biblical doctrine and transcendent morality. But when it comes to their own assertions that "God has no intention of sharing his absoluteness with anything" or that "Jesus is the best possible way to live," or that the Bible can "have different meaning in different times," they are making their own truth claims and demonstrate the self-destructive irrationality of postmodern thought.

Such fatal statements that God "has no intention of sharing his absoluteness with anything" fly in the face of biblical verses: "And God said" (Exodus 3:14); "And God spake unto Moses" (Exodus 6:2); "Thus speaketh the LORD" (Jeremiah 28:2). The Bible gives its own tests of divine inspiration. Though the Bible is a compilation of writers over thousands of years, the Bible's completeness, fullness and holiness of its teachings taken as a whole trace back to the Divine authorship of God's Holy Spirit, not merely the men who physically wrote it.

Just as a school teacher, who is far more intelligent and advanced than a classroom of kindergardeners, can prepare lessons and instruction for her students in a way that can be easily communicated and clearly understood, surely the Almighty Creator can cut through the interpretive grids of His created beings in order to reveal truth directly to them. God would not be limited in any way from communicating absolute truth through human language in a way that is meaningful and understandable to all people, regardless of their time and culture.

Pilate asked Jesus the postmodern question, "What is truth?" (John 18:38). Little did Pilate know that he was staring truth in the face. Jesus Himself is the proof of Himself as the truth. Jesus said, "My doctrine is not mine, but his that sent me. If any man will do his will, he shall know of the doctrine, whether it be of God, or whether I speak of myself" (John 17:16,17). Peter the Apostle said, "God now commandeth all men every where to repent: Because he hath appointed a day, in the which he will judge the world in righteousness by that man whom he hath ordained; whereof he hath given assurance unto all men, in that he hath raised him from the dead" (Acts 17:30,31). The early Christian, Justin Martyr (160 AD), said:

> And God, the Father of the universe, who is the perfect intelligence, is the truth. And the Word, being His Son, came to us, having put on flesh, revealing both Himself and the Father, giving to us in Himself resurrection from the dead, and eternal life afterwards. And this is Jesus Christ, our Saviour and Lord. He, therefore, is Himself both the faith and the proof of Himself and of all things. Wherefore those who follow Him, and know Him, having faith in Him as their proof, shall rest in Him.[73]

Emergents continue to stare at the face of Truth when they read of the Word of God, but only to deconstruct it of its clear meaning. It reminds us of the Pharisees to whom Jesus said, "Search the scriptures; for in them ye think ye have eternal life: and they are they which testify of me. And ye will not come to me, that ye might have life" (John 5:39,40). In order to come to Jesus, we must come to Jesus as He is in reality revealed by the testimony of the Scriptures and not our own imaginations or favorite interpretations.

Furthermore, the Bible says, "Study to shew thyself approved unto God, a workman that needeth not to be ashamed, rightly dividing the word of truth" (2 Timothy 2:15). God has revealed objective truth through His Word, but the Emergent subjective definitions confuse the Bible and ultimately endanger eternal souls. After rejecting truth as an absolute, *anything goes!* Thus, the postmodern generation of Christians finds itself in a time like that recorded in the book of Judges: "When also all that generation were gathered unto their fathers: and there arose another generation after them, which knew not the Lord, nor yet the

---

73   Justin Martyr, *Fragments of the Lost Work of Justin on the Resurrection,* ANF, volume 1, 294.

works which He had done for Israel" (Judges 2:10).

Postmodernism is idolatry because it submits to culture rather than the word of the Lord Jesus. They have changed the truth of God into a lie, and worshipped and served the culture more than the Creator, who is blessed forever. Nothing is more relevant to a lost and hopeless culture held captive as slaves to sin than the good news that Jesus is Lord. "My son, fear thou the LORD and the king: and meddle not with them that are given to change" (Proverbs 24:21).

Deconstruction

One of the most popular postmodernist tendencies within aesthetics is deconstruction. Deconstruction is a postmodern and Emergent tactic of textual analysis, typically literary critique, that questions presuppositions, ideological underpinnings, hierarchical values and power structures within any given text. Deconstructive approaches apply techniques of close reading of the text without reference to information outside of the text or an authority over the text such as the author. One famous deconstructionist famously wrote, "There is nothing outside of the text."[74]

Deconstruction ultimately questions all objective meaning and authority. Although deconstructions can be developed using various methods, the process typically involves demonstrating multiple possible readings of a text (the Bible in this case). For instance, as a postmodern deconstructionist, Eric English of Emergent Village rails against the Bible: "The bible is not the WORD OF GOD." Notice the lower case letter "b" in "bible." When speaking of the Church's use of the Bible in terms of power structures and oppression, English epitomizes postmodern deconstruction:

> The bible is not the WORD OF GOD. However, our elevation of the bible to almost divine status has seemingly resulted in the Church believing it is to be the moral authority over the world – as though they speak for God. We have equated the language of the bible with

---

74 Jaques Derrida, *Of Grammatology,* trans. Gayatri Chakravorty Spivak (Baltimore: John Hopkins University Press, 1967), 159.

the Words of God. This has seemingly resulted in the bible being used as a weapon of power to oppress others. Incredibly, the Church's oppression has not been limited to the secular world, but has even been used as a weapon to oppress its own people.[75]

This statement goes to show how deconstructionists can find anything they want to in the text they are deconstructing. The Holy Spirit, the ultimate Author behind the writers of Scripture, intended for the Bible to be called the Word of God since this definitive title is within the text itself. Paul thanked God for the Thessalonians who received the Apostles' words "not as the word of men, but as it is in truth, *the word of God*" (1 Thessalonians 2:13). Notice, Eric English does not quote from the Bible in order to present his argument. He concludes, "The bible is not the WORD OF GOD. The WORD OF GOD is Jesus Christ."[76] True, the Word of God is Jesus Christ. Jesus is the Word of God made flesh (John 1:1-14; Revelation 19:13). But this is not always the case and context we find in the Bible.[77]

In the Emergent movement, postmodernism emphasizes the role of language. Hence, the Emergent movement is often referred to as a conversation. Language appeals to the intellect but images (candles,

---

75   Eric English, "The Bible is NOT the WORD OF GOD: a polemic against Christendom." Emergent Village, April 9, 2013. available: http://www.patheos.com/blogs/emergentvillage/2013/04/the-bible-is-not-the-word-of-god-a-polemic-against-christendom/.

76   Ibid.

77   For instance, in the Parable of the Sower, Jesus said, "Now the parable is this: The seed is the word of God" (Luke 8:11). "The Seed" referred to the preaching of the Word of God. In other words, the sower sowing seed is a preacher preaching the Word of God. Furthermore, Paul referred to the Old Testament Scriptures as "the Word of God" (Romans 9:6). Jesus also referred to the Old Testament Law and Prophets as the Word of God. Jesus said: "Full well ye reject the commandment of God, that ye may keep your own tradition. For Moses said, Honour thy father and thy mother; and, Whoso curseth father or mother, let him die the death: But ye say, If a man shall say to his father or mother, It is Corban, that is to say, a gift, by whatsoever thou mightest be profited by me; he shall be free. And ye suffer him no more to do ought for his father or his mother; Making *the word of God* of none effect through your

45

incense, icons) appeal to the emotions. For this reason, language is deconstructed as a carrier of transcendent truth. Doug Pagitt takes on the role of the deconstructionist on his radio program when he attacks language in order to question the doctrine of hell. Pagitt says, "One of the reasons we have such a chronic argument about the issues of heaven and hell is that we don't have a very effective way or set of language by which we can talk about these issues." His co-host responds, "And we can only have the existing language which is faulty and inadequate to describe this big topic." Pagitt concludes, "The language doesn't allow us to convey a solution to the problem that our language creates."[78]

Once language is deconstructed of its clear meaning, "truth" becomes experiential and subjective so that mystical practices are taught in the place of sound biblical doctrine. Since Emergents consider words to be inadequate to convey truth and meaning, mysticism provides for them an experienced truth rather than an understood truth.

This philosophy epitomized Fascist ideology and the Nazi worldview. In *The Deconstruction of Literature: Criticism After Auschwitz*, David Hirsch devotes an entire chapter linking postmodern deconstruction to the Nazi SS special police force. He writes:

> Although postmodernists claim to be critical of the social ills of contemporary life . . . their ideology carries with it, inevitably, the less desirable tendencies of their patron saint, Heidegger. Their attack on the Cartesian human subject and on reason itself; their contempt for the values of liberalism, of human and individual rights, and of constitutional democracy; their elevation of abstract terminology above affective speech; their cultivation of an obscure vocabulary accessible only to

---

tradition, which ye have delivered: and many such like things do ye." (Mark 7:9-13); "It is written, That man shall not live by bread alone, but by *every word of God*." (Luke 4:4); "Is it not written in your law, I said, Ye are gods? If he called them gods, unto whom *the word of God* came, and the scripture cannot be broken; Say ye of him, whom the Father hath sanctified, and sent into the world, Thou blasphemest; because I said, I am the Son of God?" (John 10:34-36)

78   "Doug Pagitt Radio | 3/6/11 | Heaven & Hell," YouTube video, posted by Doug Pagitt, March 6, 2011,,http://www.youtube.com/watch?v=d_i_fyuQVpE.

votaries of the movement; their inability to hear voices other than their own . . . and their mocking of any notion of "transcendence," while at the same time elevating their own ideas into a religion with a priesthood and a resurrected god . . .

The tendency among contemporary literary theorists . . . who are critical of postmodernist cliches, is to treat postmodernist literary theory in isolation from history as a movement grounded (either correctly or mistakenly) in a philosophical continuum stretching, essentially, from Kant through Hegel and Nietzsche to Marx and Heidegger and their followers. . . [P]ostmodernist literary theory and criticism does not make sense outside the context of what happened at Auschwitz.[79]

The intellectual influence of the Emerging Church comes from these postmodern philosophers such as Martin Heidegger, Jacques Derrida, Michel Foucault and Richard Rorty. In *The Routledge Companion to the Christian Church*, the authors acknowledge that the academic influence on the Emerging Church movement includes the work of postmodern deconstructionists such as Michel Foucault and Jacques Derrida.[80] Tony Jones also writes about how the Emergents are being influenced by these philosophies of Rorty, Derrida and Foucault.[81]

Jaques Derrida was a French philosopher of the 20th century. Among some of those who influenced Derrida were Friedrich Nietzsche, Soren Kierkegaard, Martin Heidegger and Karl Marx. Derrida developed the critical theory known as deconstruction associated with postmodernity. Derrida gave the following definition of deconstruction: "One of the definitions of what is called deconstruction would be the effort to take this limitless context into account, to pay the sharpest and

---

79   David Hirsch, *The Deconstruction of Literature. Criticism After Auschwitz* (Brown University Press, 1991), 161,164.

80   *The Routledge Companion to the Christian Church* (New York, NY: Routledge, 2008), 269.

81   Tony Jones, *The New Christians* (San Francisco, CA: Jossey-Boss, 2008), 41,43.

broadest attention possible to context, and thus to an incessant movement of recontextualization.[82]

Deconstruction encourages people to question everything. It asserts that we cannot know what the author had in mind when he or she wrote. To deconstructionist philosophers like Derrida, there is no inherent meaning, and the meaning is left to the interpretation of the reader. We must keep in mind with the Bible that the Holy Spirit inspired the text through God's prophets and apostles with a clear message in mind, not of any private interpretation. Peter says, "Knowing this first, that *no prophecy of the scripture is of any private interpretation. For the prophecy came not in old time by the will of man: but holy men of God spake as they were moved by the Holy Ghost*" (2 Peter 1:20,21). Just as God spoke through these prophets of the Old Testament to communicate precisely what was on His heart and not their own private interpretations or origin, God's word has an objective meaning that was intended by the Author. When deconstruction is applied to the Bible, it becomes confusion. But "God is not the author of confusion" (1 Corinthians 14:33).

Martin Heidegger, one of the most influential philosophers of the 20th century, was famous for deconstruction. Again demonstrating that deconstruction cannot be understood outside of the context of the Jewish Holocaust, Heidegger was also an ideologically dedicated Nazi.[83] Paul de Man, another deconstructionist and intellectual friend of Derrida, wrote over 100 articles in a pro-Nazi newspaper called *Le Soir*, including several articles which were antisemitic.[84] Deconstruction must be understood in this light because the Bible tells us that the strong delusion and reprobation of nations (as with Nazi Germany or other totalitarian fascist dictatorships) begins with the rejection of truth.[85] Deconstruction,

---

82   Jaques Derriada, *Afterword* in *Limited Inc* (Evanston, IL: Northwestern University Press, 1988), 136.

83   See Victor Farias. *Heidegger and Nazism* (Philidelphia, PA: Temple University Press), 1989.

84   James Atlas, "The Case of Paul De Man," *The New York Times*, August 28, 1988,   http://www.nytimes.com/1988/08/28/magazine/the-case-of-paul-de-man.html?pagewanted=all&src=pm.

85   2 Thessalonians 2:10,11 says, "because they received not the love of the truth, that they might be saved. And for this cause God shall send them strong

especially when applied to the Scriptures, results in a casting off of all transcendent morality and inevitably leads to utter rebellion and unrestrained evil.

Though Emerging leader and author Leonard Sweet admits Heidegger's "anti-Semitic and Nazi sympathies,"[86] he writes of Heidegger in numerous books such as *11 Indispensable Relationships You Can't Be Without, A is for Abductive, Nudge, Soultsunami, The Church in Emerging Culture, I am a Follower*, and *Postmodern Pilgrims*. Leonard Sweet states:

> I collect Black Forest carvings and stories. Above the door to my study is a carved sign that reads, in German, "Peace and Joy to all who enter." But I almost carved another sign in its place. It was reputedly carved above the front door of an old German schoolmaster: "Dante, Luther, Goethe, Barth, Heidegger live here." None of them live there, of course. But this old schoolmaster had so lived in communion with their ideas and ideals that it seemed as if they all shared his humble home.[87]

Sweet and Brian McLaren devote an entire chapter to postmodern deconstruction in their book *A is For Abductive*. In the chapter entitled "V is for Voice" they quote from Heidegger's essay on Heraclitus and his take on the Logos.[88] The authors state that deconstruction is "one of the most important philosophical/interpretive concepts of postmodernity." They say that deconstruction "begins by

---

delusion." Romans 1:18 states: "For the wrath of God is revealed from heaven against all ungodliness and unrighteousness of men, who hold the truth in unrighteousness."

86   Leonard Sweet. *11 Indispensable Relationships You Can't Be Without* (Colorado Springs, CO: David C Cook, 2008), 197.
87   Leonard Sweet. "A Response to Recent Misunderstandings," *Leonard Sweet,* http://www.leonardsweet.com/response.php.
88   Jerry Haselmayer, Brian McLaren and Leonard Sweet. *A Is For Abductive – The Language of the Emerging Church* (Grand Rapids, MI: Zonderan, 2003), 301.

questioning many of the assumptions of traditional interpretation."[89] They continue:

> Traditional modern interpretation, then, is fond of finding the one "true" meaning in a text, while deconstructionists do not give any one reading privileged status, but rather are interested in hearing the interplay of many interpretations that arise from within many different interpretive communities.[90]

In the end, deconstruction gives the reader the authority over the text. When applied to Scripture, they can make it say whatever they want it to say! Rather than searching out the authorial intent of the Holy Ghost accompanied with the use of grammatical and historical analysis, Emergents write:

> Traditional interpretation generally assumes a logical structure and deep coherence of texts; in other words, the author meant to say something sensible and did so in a coherent way. Deconstruction looks for points of inherent tension, contradiction, and incoherence.[91]

Emerging leader Doug Pagitt includes almost two identical sections in both of his books *Preaching in the Inventive Age* and *Preaching Re-Imagined*. In them he describes a conversation with his friend Michael who described Derrida's words "as if Jesus himself had said these things."[92] Pagitt comments on Derrida saying:

> This is a call to be prophetic in the deconstruction of the systems of power. When we are willing to notice, point out, and name the issues of power in our settings, we're creating a better situation in which the gospel can be

---

89 Ibid., 87.
90 Ibid., 88.
91 Sweet,, *A Is For Abductive*. 87.
92 Doug Pagitt, *Preaching in the Inventive Age,* (Minneapolis, MN: Augsburg Fortress. 2011), 210.

preached.[93]

Tony Jones also says:

> What does this say about what we believe about God? In some ways, it seems, we were following the lead of Derrida and other postmodern deconstructionists in questioning the very premises of the Christianity that we had inherited.[94]

In his book *Adventures in Missing the Point* co-authored with Brian McLaren, Tony Campolo an author, sociologist, pastor and speaker[95] confesses the inherent dangers he sees in Brian McLaren for buying into this postmodern thinking:

> Brian may have bought into postmodern thinking just a little bit too much for me. As I see it, Jacques Derrida, the famous postmodern deconstructionist philosopher, and his followers contend that the text of Scripture has no single interpretation; instead the Bible should be read as though it was a Rorschach test. They tell us to see in the text whatever meaning we want to impose on it. They tell us that no single interpretation should be considered objectively valid.[96]

---

93   Doug Pagitt, *Preaching Re-Imagined.*
94   Tony Jones, *The New Christians* (San Francisco, CA: Jossey-Bass, 2008), 47.
95   In a personal e-mail to me, Campolo stated, "I am not part of the Emergent Church movement, even though you chose to put me there. You are entitled to put me anywhere you want to put me, but you cannot do so without taking into account the following: 1. I believe in each of the doctrines of the Apostles' Creed. 2. I have a very high view of Scripture, believing that the authors were inspired by the Holy Spirit, so that what they wrote became an infallible guide for faith and practice. 3. I believe that salvation comes only through a personal relationship with Jesus." Tony Campolo, "Re: Please respond (if you have time)," January 20, 2014. E-mail.
96   Tony Campolo and Brian McLaren, *Adventures in Missing the Point,* (Grand Rapids, MI: Zondervan, 2003), 89.

Campolo rightly points out the error of postmodern thinking that the Bible does not have a single valid interpretation but multiple interpretations. How could we ever expect to find the valid meaning of the Bible if it is always changing depending on who is reading it and when? Bono says,

> I don't read it as a historical book. I don't read it as, "Well, that's good advice." I let it speak to me in other ways. They call it the rhema. It's a hard word to translate from Greek, but it sort of means it changes in the moment you're in. It seems to do that for me.[97]

Again, even Emergent leader Tony Campolo realizes that postmodern deconstruction is not conducive to objective truth claims. Campolo concludes, "To me, that approach to the Bible has inherent dangers."[98] He is correct. Earlier, this postmodern tactic was an essential part of the fascist worldview which challenged all language as a carrier of transcendent moral truth and later resulted in the Holocaust. But these warnings of the inherent dangers of deconstructionism don't stop Emergents from attacking language. Borrowing LeRon Shults' anti-statement of faith, Tony Jones notes:

> Languages are culturally constructed symbol systems that enable humans to communicate by designating one finite reality in distinction from another. The truly infinite God of Christian faith is beyond all our linguistic grasping, as all the great theologians from Irenaeus to Calvin have insisted, and so the struggle to capture God in our finite propositional structures is nothing short of linguistic idolatry.[99]

In fact, the Emergents are guilty of idolatry by overthrowing the

---

97 Jann S. Wenner, "The Rolling Stone Interview: Bono." *Rolling Stone,* November 3, 2005, http://www.jannswenner.com/Archives/Bono.aspx.
98 Campolo and McLaren, *Adventures in Missing the Point,* 89.
99 Jones, *The New Christians,* 233, 234.

word of God with their own linguistic attack against the clear commands of Scripture. This fascist tactic of deconstruction can be traced even further back from Derrida and Heidegger to the Garden of Eden when the Serpent utilized the same radical questioning of God's word, even by attacking God's language. No doubt this diabolical tactic originated in the Garden of Eden with the Serpent as the first deconstructionist who questioned God's authoritative word: "Now the serpent was more subtle than any beast of the field which the LORD God had made. And he said unto the woman, Yea, hath God said, Ye shall not eat of every tree of the garden?" (Genesis 3:1).

In Emergent philosophy, questioning becomes the highest form of knowledge. The absurdity of deconstruction is that any given text may be given infinite interpretations. Again and again, the Emerging Church is finding ways to give communities more control over the meaning of God's word. The Emergent method of deconstruction seeks to ridicule the ability of God and humans to communicate clearly through language, all the while they expect the readers of their books to understand what they mean through the use of conventional language. In other words, deconstruction is not convenient when applied to Emergent writings. It's only useful to Emergents when applied to the Bible, religion, philosophy and morality. Concepts like deconstruction leave readers with limitless interpretations and questions. Deconstruction leads to "ever learning, and never able to come to the knowledge of the truth" (2 Timothy 3:7).

The serpent questioned God's authoritative and understandable word to which Adam and Eve were to be held accountable: "Of every tree of the garden thou mayest freely eat: But of the tree of the knowledge of good and evil, thou shalt not eat of it: for in the day that thou eatest thereof thou shalt surely die" (Genesis 2:16,17). Just as to Adam, God gave a command. He has spoken understandably and authoritatively in these last days through His Son Jesus Christ (Hebrews 1:1,2) by which we will all be held accountable to repent: "And the times of this ignorance God winked at; but now commandeth all men every where to repent: Because he hath appointed a day, in the which he will judge the world in righteousness by that man whom he hath ordained; whereof he hath given assurance unto all men, in that he hath raised him from the dead" (Acts 17:30,31).

3

Changing the Message

"For I am the LORD, I change not."
− Malachi 3:6

A noteworthy emphasis of the Emerging Church movement is orthopraxy, that is, correct action/activity or right living. They believe that how a person lives is more important than what he believes. Though they endorse ungodly ways of living, they nevertheless believe and emphasize this principle. Most in the Emergent Church movement will agree that we need both orthodoxy and orthopraxy, but the focus has shifted, which has led to unorthodoxy. In turn, orthopraxy has also been compromised. Rather than being reactionary against over-emphasis of doctrine and neglect of holy living by emphasizing holy living to the neglect of sound doctrine, we ought to emphasize both without neglecting one or the other.

It has been difficult for some to determine whether or not the Emergent Church movement is orthodox because of its claim to Christian orthodoxy. In a chapter entitled "Avoiding Heresy" in *Reimagining Spiritual Formation,* Doug Pagitt says that at Solomon's Porch they are committed to

> the guidance of the Holy Spirit" and they, "gently call on
> our Christian traditions to help clarify why a certain kind

54

of thinking isn't really consistent with orthodoxy. . . if someone presents a position that was held in the past but has been rejected by orthodox Christianity, then someone else who knows the issue will provide the necessary context.[100]

Tony Jones appeals to Christian orthodoxy. Recounting a visit to Southern Baptist Theological Seminary, he personally affirmed the historic, physical, bodily resurrection of Jesus which he considered "the pivot point in the entire history of the cosmos."[101] In these statements alone, Pagitt and Jones appear to uphold Christian orthodoxy. However, other statements reveal just the opposite. For instance, in a 2004 seminar entitled "A New Theology for a New World" at the Emergent Convention in San Diego, Jones said:

We do not think this [Emerging Church Movement] is about changing your worship service. We do not think this is about . . . how you structure your church staff. This is actually about changing theology. This is about our belief that theology changes. The message of the gospel changes. It's not just the method that changes.[102]

Tony Jones reveals that the Emergent Church *is* about changing theology and even the message of the Gospel of Jesus Christ. Theology is the study of the nature of God and religious belief. Depending on whose theology he is changing, this may not necessarily be a bad endeavor. But Jones goes on to say that theology *itself* changes and the message of the

---

100 Doug Pagitt, *Reimagining Spiritual Formation* (Grand Rapids: MI: Zondervan. 2003), 90.

101 Tony Jones, "My Day at SBTS." *Theoblogy Weblog,* December 15, 2005, http://theoblogy.blogspot.com/2005/12/my-day-at-sbts.html.

102 Tony Jones. "A New Theology for a New World." A workshop for the 2004 Emergent Convention in San Diego, CA. The audio recording of this seminar can be purchased through PSI, Inc. at 1-800- 808-8273 or via the web at: http://sf1000.registeredsite.com/%7euser1006646/miva/merchant.mv? Screen=BASK&Store_Code=YS- SD&Action=ADPR&Product_Code=NS05-057CD&Attributes=Yes&Quantity=1.

Gospel *itself* changes. Jones is implying that God's nature and message are changeable, not eternal. Thus, Jones is first appealing to Christian orthodoxy as the starting point and then preaching another changed or emerged gospel, "which is not another; but there be some that trouble you, and would pervert the gospel of Christ" (Galatians 1:7).

If doctrine changes, then God changes. But Malachi 3:6 says, "For I am the Lord, I do not change." In the blog post "Doctrine DOES Change," Jones unashamedly states the implications of his faulty premise which he shares with Roman Catholics:

> First, the Catholic church has changed innumerable doctrines, and saying that it's just a change in interpretation is semantics. Second, and more problematic, is the idea that there is some perfect, unchangeable ideal that emanates from an unchangeable God.
>
> But that's not the God of the Bible, not the God of history, and not the church of history. *God changes. Yes She does.*[103]

Earlier, I explained how the faith once delivered to the saints cannot be changed. In the words of the early Christian Tertullian (198 AD): "No further addition in the way of observance must be added, on account of the unlawfulness of innovation."[104] Based upon the fact that the Christian faith is not progressive, Emergence Christianity is not Christianity at all. A disciple of Christ should receive nothing new in doctrine. But, according to Jones, "Doctrine DOES Change," and, "God changes."

Author Spencer Burke, co-founder of the online community The Ooze, has been another recognized leader in the Emergent Church movement. In his aptly named book *A Heretic's Guide to Eternity* (which includes a foreword by Brian McLaren), he makes no mistake in saying, "I am not merely seeking to put a new spin on old beliefs; I am actually

---

103 Tony Jones, "Doctrine DOES Change," Theoblogy, October 20, 2014, http://www.patheos.com/blogs/tonyjones/2014/10/20/doctrine-does-change/#more-10203

104 Tertullian, *Ante-Nicene Fathers,* volume 4, 111.

declaring that there are new ways of believing when it comes to the Christian story."[105]

Rob Bell also makes clear that the Emergent movement is changing more than methodology:

> By this I do not mean cosmetic, superficial changes like better lights and music, sharper graphics, and new methods with easy-to-follow steps. I mean theology: the beliefs about God, Jesus, the Bible, salvation, the future. We must keep reforming the way the Christian faith is defined, lived and explained.[106]

Shane Hipps, former co-pastor and now pastor of Rob Bell's Mars Hill church, demonstrates how the Emergent church is not only changing methodology but also orthodoxy: "That statement, 'The methods change, but the message stays the same' is actually a lie."[107]

Erwin McManus is pastor of a church called Mosaic and is also a popular author and speaker. Though McManus claims not to be Emergent,[108] many have grouped him into the Emergent camp because he is helping to propel the Emergence spirituality:

> My goal is to destroy Christianity as a world religion and be a recatalyst for the movement of Jesus Christ . . . Some people are upset with me because it sounds like I'm anti-Christian. I think they might be right.[109]

---

105 Spencer Burke, *A Heretic's Guide to Eternity* (San Francisco, CA: Jossey-Bass, 2006), xxiv-xxv.

106 Bell, *Velvet Elvis,* 12.

107 "Rob Bell and Shane Hipps Interview." YouTube video, posted by "ziland76," March 9, 2009, http://www.youtube.com/watch?v=D6QiyElRG3c&feature=related.

108 McManus says, "Because people don't know where to put our community [Mosaic] they put us in the 'emergent' category, and we really are a different animal than emergent. We're not against emergent, but we are not like them." Interview by Al Sergel with Erwin McManus. "Soul Cravings, Q&A." *Relevant Magazine,* http://www.relevant magazine.com/god_article.php?id=7241.

109 CE Staff Reporter citing Erwin McManus. "Pastor, noted author takes uncivil approach in new offering." *Christian Examiner,*

From his statement, McManus suggests that Christianity as a world religion and the movement of Jesus are not one and the same. Certainly there are tares amongst the wheat (Matthew 13:25), and Christianity as a world religion has at many times and in many places drifted far from the truth, but there is definitely an overlap between what McManus refers to as the world religion of Christianity and an authentic movement of Jesus (if this is what he means). Even if we perceive a need for major changes within Christendom, one ought to be hesitant to label himself "anti-Christian." The first disciples were called "Christians" (Acts 11:26), and there is nothing wrong with this label. If it was good enough for them, it should be good enough for us to be called Christians.

Brian McLaren also admits to changing not only methodology but also the message. He says, "Our message and methodology have changed, do change, and must change if we are faithful to the ongoing and unchanging mission of Jesus Christ."[110] It's no wonder that *Time* magazine called Brian Mclaren a "paradigm shifter."[111] McLaren presents the Emergent Church view of orthodoxy:

> Ask me if Christianity (my version of it, yours, the Pope's, whoever's) is orthodox, meaning true, and here's my honest answer: a little, but not yet. Assuming by Christianity you mean the Christian understanding of the world and God, Christian opinions on soul, text, and culture. . . I'd have to say that we probably have a couple of things right, but a lot of things wrong, and even more spreads before us unseen and unimagined. But at least our eyes are open! To be a Christian in a generously orthodox way is not to claim to have the truth captured, stuffed, and mounted on the wall.[112]

---

http://www.christianexaminer.com/Articles/Articles %20Mar05/Art_Mar05_09.html.

110 McLaren, *A Generous Orthodoxy*, 214.

111 "The 25 Most Influential Evangelicals in America," *Time,* February 7, 2005, http://www.time.com/time/covers/1101050207/photoessay/17.html.

112 McLaren, *A Generous Orthodoxy,* 293.

The titles of McLaren's books, such as *A New Kind of Christian*, *Everything Must Change*, *The Secret Message of Jesus*, and *A New Kind of Christianity*, demonstrate how McLaren is also changing the message of orthodox Christianity. Thus, McLaren is teaching a dangerous orthodoxy. He says:

> If I seem to show too little respect for your opinions or thought, be assured I have equal doubts about my own, and I don't mind if you think I am wrong. I'm sure I am wrong about many things, although I'm not sure exactly which things I'm wrong about. I'm even sure I'm wrong about what I think I'm right about in at least some cases. So wherever you think I'm wrong, you could be right.[113]

This comment does not absolve him of the great responsibility which comes with teaching the Scriptures. "My brethren, be not many masters, knowing that we shall receive the greater condemnation" (James 3:1). If McLaren is so uncertain about his own beliefs, then he shouldn't be risking "greater condemnation" in the chance that he is wrong and leading astray many souls. Whatever is contrary to orthodoxy is heresy even if it is disguised as a generous orthodoxy. For this reason, Emergent emphasizes orthopraxy. McLaren writes, "We place less emphasis on whose lineage, rites, doctrines, structures, and terminology are right and more emphasis on whose actions, service, outreach, kindness, and effectiveness are good."[114]

On the other hand, the New Testament does not sacrifice doctrine for morality but emphasizes both. Our good deeds are a fruit of salvation, not the cause: "But as many as received him, to them gave he power to become the sons of God, even to them that believe on his name" (John 1:12); "For by grace are ye saved through faith; and that not of yourselves: it is the gift of God: Not of works, lest any man should boast. For we are his workmanship, created in Christ Jesus unto *good works*, which God hath before ordained that we should walk in them" (Ephesians 2:8-10).

In response to McLaren's *A Generous Orthodoxy*, D.A. Carson,

---

113 Ibid., 19,20.
114 Ibid., 12.

evangelical theologian and professor of the New Testament, writes:

> At what point does an "orthodoxy" that is more "generous" than God's become heterodoxy? Not for a moment do I want a vote cast in favor of the narrow-minded, whining, fault-finding, picky, sectarianism with which Christianity has sometimes been afflicted. Rather, what is called for is biblical fidelity. One can be biblically unfaithful by being much narrower than Scripture; one can be biblically unfaithful by being much broader than Scripture. Both sides call it faithfulness; both sides are seriously mistaken. How can we know? By returning to Scripture, again and again, and refusing to be uncomfortable with the categories that God himself has given us, but seeking to learn and digest and believe and obey the whole counsel of God, as far as we see it, without flinching, without faddishness.[115]

Without exception, every major theological movement that has turned from orthodox Christianity began with unbelief of biblical doctrine. While the Emergent Church may be attempting to make constructive changes in regard to Christian behavior, the emerging attitude toward doctrine is of great concern.

By de-emphasizing orthodoxy in favor of orthopraxy, the Emergent movement has allowed the Gospel to be changed in order to accommodate its experiential subjective truth and social gospel. But it is correct belief in the truth of Jesus Christ who said, "I am . . . the truth" (John 14:6) that will set us free. Knowing the truth by abiding in His word (John 8:31) will make us free. Thus, Jesus commanded His disciples in the Great Commission to "teach all nations" (Matthew 28:19) and to go "teaching them to observe all things whatsoever I have commanded you" (Matthew 28:20). Belief influences our experience and behavior. This command is not so in the emerging culture as Dan Kimball admits that "we are seeing a shift to: experience influences

---

115 D.A. Carson, *Becoming Conversant with the Emerging Church* (Grand Rapids: Zondervan, 2005), 208.

belief" and then "belief influences behavior."[116] Biblically speaking, right actions will follow right beliefs. Jesus said, "Ye shall know the truth, and the truth shall make you free" (John 8:32). James also shares about how Abraham's faith and belief led him to behavior or actions: "Seest thou how faith wrought with his works, and by works was faith made perfect?" (James 2:22).

The Emergent leaders are self-professing change-agents of the Gospel of Jesus Christ. The following chapters will demonstrate specifically how the Emergent Church changes Christian doctrine. The writer of Hebrews instructs: "Let us go on unto perfection; not laying again the foundation of repentance from dead works, and of faith toward God, of the doctrine of baptisms, and of laying on of hands, and of resurrection of the dead, and of eternal judgment" (Hebrews 6:1,2). These are the foundational "principles of the doctrine of Christ" (Hebrews 6:1). The Emergent Church has *not laid again*, as the writer of Hebrews instructs us, but *laid aside* the foundational principles of the doctrine of Christ.

From the very beginning, God had a clear message to communicate to mankind. God told Moses, "According to all that I shew thee, after the pattern of the tabernacle, and the pattern of all the instruments thereof, even so shall ye make it" (Exodus 25:9). All of the ceremonial laws of the Old Covenant, such as those pertaining to the tabernacle, feast days and sacrifices, had to be carried out exactly and meticulously in order to not muddle the message which would later be fulfilled in Jesus Christ. Throughout the Bible, there are severe and sobering warnings to those such as the Emergent movement who would seek to change or muddle God's message. Deuteronomy 4:2 tells us, "Ye shall not add unto the word which I command you, neither shall ye diminish ought from it, that ye may keep the commandments of the LORD your God which I command you." Also Revelation 22:19 says, "And if any man shall take away from the words of the book of this prophecy, God shall take away his part out of the book of life, and out of the holy city, and from the things which are written in this book."

"Bono" Fide Christianity

---

116 Dan Kimball, *The Emerging Church* (Grand Rapids: Zondervan. 2003), 189.

Emergent leaders themselves provide further evidence that they are changing the message with book titles such as *The New Christians: Dispatches from the Emergent Frontier* by Tony Jones, *A New Kind of Christian* and *A New Kind of Christianity* by Brian McLaren. Bona fide Christianity is no longer relevant to Emergents who might as well call their movement the "Bono" fide church. Let me explain.

After reading through Emergent books, articles, blogs and after watching Emergent videos and sermons, I am amazed at how often the Emergent Church exalts Bono as its role model. Bono, the Irish singer for the band U2, is arguably the most famous rockstar in the world. He is certainly one the most, if not the most, politically influential celebrities of our time. With his anti-poverty work with DATA, then ONE, then RED, Bono has made many allegiances in the evangelical community as well as meeting with people like the Pope and Billy Graham. In addition, he has been labeled by some to be the icon of the Emerging Church. This is partly due to his humanitarian work in campaigning for third-world debt relief and raising awareness of the AIDS pandemic in Africa. Bono's philanthropy and cool Christianity make him an Emergent Church leader and icon. A summation of his good works and words prove to be an embodiment of what it means to be a new kind of Emerging Christian in postmodern contexts. Bono says, "It's cool to be concerned about the environment and have a political attitude but only if it brings you close to your real job as a firework."[117]

At the 2006 Shepherd's Conference, Phil Johnson, Executive Director of Grace to You, made a stunning statement about the Emergent Church. In his commissioned studies of the movement, he states:

> This may help you more than anything I have said so far to understand the flavor of the "emerging church movement": Bono—the Irish rocker and politico of U2 fame—seems to be the unofficial icon of the movement. If you've been tuned into pop-culture at any time over the past two decades and know anything about Bono, that might help you to grasp something about the look

---

117 Jonathan, "First of All, I Am God," *New Musical Express,* October 21, 1995, http://www.u2station.com/news/1995/10/first-of-all-i-am-god.php.

and feel of the movement. . . .

> Anyway, Emergent types seem to quote Bono all the time. I would say that he sometimes seems to be the chief theologian of the "emerging church movement"[118]

There are many examples of Emergents quoting Bono as if he were a theologian. For instance, in *Listening to Beliefs of Emerging Churches: Five Perspectives* by Robert Webber and Mark Driscoll, we read:

> Bono of the band U2, in a Rolling Stone interview, stated that he sees the Bible as what "sustains" him. He also called the Bible an "anchor" and a "plumb line." I like Bono's anchor analogy. When we are in a boat that is anchored, we have freedom to drift around, but there is a limit to the drifting.[119]

On Emergent spokesperson Brian McLaren's website, one of his readers poses the question, "Why Bother With Church at All?" to which McLaren posted an answer. It is interesting that the reader praises Bono for his version of Christianity, going to the length of proclaiming Bono as the "leader" of the Emergent Church:

> I think of Bono of U2, who has for years lamented the irrelevance of organized religion and yet conducts praise and worship services for 25,000 people all the while creating a commercial and culturally viable perch from which he can model a compelling vision of a social gospel. This guy is the leader of the "emergent church" movement, . . . not a bunch of dissatisfied ex-Jesus movement pastors fawning after a book deal to tell the

---

118 Phil Johnson, "Introducing the ECM." *Pulpit Magazine,* December 4, 2006, http://www.sfpulpit.com/2006/12/04/introducing-the-ecm-part-5/.
119 Mark Driscoll and Robert Webber. *Listening to Beliefs of Emerging Churches: Five Perspectives* (Grand Rapids, MI: Zondervan, 2007), 97.

church world how to do it better.[120]

In *Adventures in Missing the Point*, co-authored with Brian McLaren, Campolo devotes much time in his "Kingdom of God" chapter to praising Bono. He writes, "U2's lead singer Bono is using his wealth and celebrity status to do just that: increase the kingdom of God in the here and now."[121] Campolo elaborates on Bono's good works of going to Ethiopia and performing concerts to aid in famine and work in orphanages. Campolo says of Bono:

> He now works fiercely to change the policies of governments and of organizations like the World Bank and the International Monetary Fund. . . . Politicians with views as diverse as Bill Clinton and Jesse Helms have taken Bono seriously and joined him in successful efforts to reduce Third World debts. . . . However unlikely you think it is for a rock star to be an instrument of God, Bono has the marks of one.[122]

Emergent Church leader Rob Bell remembers the first time he was in "awe of God" at a U2 concert. Bell says:

> I remember the first time I was truly in awe of God. I was caught up the first time in my life in something so massive and loving and transcendent and . . . true. Something I was sure could be trusted. I specifically remember thinking the universe was safe, in spite of all the horrible, tragic things in the world. I remember being overwhelmed with the word *true*. Underneath it all life is somehow . . . good . . . and I was sixteen and at a U2 concert. The Joshua Tree tour. When they started with the song "Where the Streets Have No Name." I thought I was going to spontaneously combust with joy. This was

---

120 Anonymous, comment on Brian D. McLaren, "Why Bother With Church At All," http://brianmclaren.net/archives/faq/why-bother-with.html.
121 Campolo and McLaren, *Adventures in Missing the Point*, 54.
122 Ibid., 54.

real. This mattered. Whatever it was, I wanted more.[123]

An article from *Bangor Daily News* neatly sums it up well. In Bangor Seminary's 2012 convocation called "Evolving World, Emerging Church," Rev. Steven Lewis called it "humanitarian spirituality" and said, "Salvation in the 21st century is being a good human being," and pointed to rock star Bono.[124] What about faith in Jesus Christ? But what the Emergent movement eventually boils down to is that being a good person in individual subjective understandings *is salvation*, regardless of whether one is a Christian or not. It is precisely for this reason that Bono is heralded as a prophet of the movement. On the Emergent Village website, Bono is labeled as a "Prophetic Preacher." His speech at the National Prayer Breakfast on February 2, 2006 was called "his best sermon yet" by Emergent Village.[125]

In the Emergent book called *Get Up Off Your Knees*, several contributing authors including Eugene Peterson, author of *The Message* Bible translation, praise Bono and U2 as a prophetic voice. One contributor, Brian Walsh, believes that U2 lyrics should be taught in seminaries and that U2 concerts demonstrate how worship should be done in a postmodern Emerging culture.[126] In fact, Calvin College offered a class which analyzed U2's influence on Christians.[127] Contributor to the

---

123 Rob Bell, *Velvet Elvis* (Grand Rapids, MI: Zondervan, 2005), 72
124 Judy Harrison. "Worshippers dance in the aisles as spirit fills Bangor seminary's Convocation." Bangor Daily News, January 12, 2012, http://bangordailynews.com/2012/01/12/religion/worshippers-dance-in-the-aisles-as-spirit-fills-bangor-seminarys-convocation/.
125 Emergent CT, "Best Sermon," Emergent CT, April 16, 2006, http://www.emergentct.blogspot.com/2006/04/best-sermon.html.
126 Contributor Brian Walsh states, "Why isn't the U2 catalog integral to the curricula of theological seminaries around the world? Why aren't there courses on biblical interpretation where Bono's lyrics are set side by side with biblical texts and their commentators? Why don't liturgists study concert footage to see how worship really happens in a postmodern world?" Angela Pancella. "Prayer, Prophecy, and Pop Culture - The Hallelujah Mix." @U2, January 21, 2004, http://www.atu2.com/news/prayer-prophecy-and-pop-culture-the-hallelujah-mix.html.
127 Charles Honey, "Calvin College on U2," Christianity Today, February 23, 2005, http://www.christianitytoday.com/ct/2005/februaryweb-only/33.0c.html

book, Brian Walsh states further:

> Why isn't the U2 catalog integral to the curricula of theological seminaries around the world? Why aren't there courses on biblical interpretation where Bono's lyrics are set side by side with biblical texts and their commentators? Why don't liturgists study concert footage to see how worship really happens in a postmodern world?[128]

In the book, Bono is likened to John the Baptist. The authors state of U2: "If they do not explicitly proclaim the Kingdom, they certainly prepare the way for that proclamation in much the same way that John the Baptist prepared for the kerygma of Jesus." They continue by quoting John 1:23 in reference to Bono, "A voice crying in the wilderness not unlike that of John the Baptist we've been hearing throughout the Advent season."[129]

If Bono had a ministry like that of John the Baptist, he would have been beheaded decades ago. But the world loves and receives Bono because he comes as the herald of another kingdom preaching world peace and philanthropy. This false gospel is nothing Bono is going to lose his head over. By the way, Bono said the following about John the Baptist: "Not since John The Baptist has there been a voice like that crying in the wilderness. . . . Every man knows he is a sissy compared to Johnny Cash."[130] What an irreverent comment to make about John the Baptist when Jesus says, "Verily I say unto you, Among them that are born of women there hath not risen a greater than John the Baptist: notwithstanding he that is least in the kingdom of heaven is greater than he" (Matthew 11:11).

---

128 Angela Pancella. "Prayer, Prophecy, and Pop Culture - The Hallelujah Mix." January 21, 2004. available: http://www.atu2.com/news/prayer-prophecy-and-pop-culture-the-hallelujah-mix.html
129 Get Up Off Your Knees, eds. Raewynne Whiteley and Beth Maynard, (Cambridge, MA. 2003), xi,xii,23.
130 "Tributes to Johnny Cash." *CNN Entertainment,* February 26, 2002, http://articles.cnn.com/2002-02-26/entertainment/cash.quotes_1_essential-johnny-cash-musical-boundaries-tributes?_s=PM:SHOWBIZ.

Ironically, as John the Baptist was crying in the wilderness and preparing the way for the Kingdom of God by preaching repentance, Bono is preaching a false social gospel void of repentance in preparation for the New Emergence Christianity. Bono's goal is for Christians, Jews, Muslims and even atheists to set aside doctrine and beliefs in order to come together for the common causes of promoting peace on earth, and abolishing poverty and AIDS. One reporter observed that Bono has been willing to work with any people who will listen whether they be Jewish, Muslim, Catholic or Protestant in order to "harness the power of faith groups to aid the poor."[131]

Thus, the Great Commission given to the Church by Jesus has been changed to suit the Emerging culture. Jesus said, "Go ye therefore, and teach all nations, baptizing them in the name of the Father, and of the Son, and of the Holy Ghost: *teaching them to observe all things whatsoever I have commanded you*: and, lo, I am with you alway, even unto the end of the world" (Matthew 28:19,20). The New Christianity idolizes Bono because he commissions people to go into all the nations and make world peace by working with other religions to help the poor.

Bono is embraced and given the upper-hand in both religious and political spheres of influence. Many are following Bono in social justice but throwing the Gospel out the window. Bono's hip Christianity will inspire many Christians to embrace ecumenism and apostasy in the cloak of philanthropy. His politicized social Gospel which is contrary to the doctrine of Christ and the Kingdom of God.

In contrast to Bono's new Christianity, the early Christians understood the distinction between the kingdom of Christ and the kingdoms of this world, never mixing the two. Unlike Bono, it was unusual for them to be involved with politics and the affairs of the State. Tertullian (198 AD) wrote:

> In us, all ardor in the pursuit of glory and honor is dead.
> So we have no pressing inducement to take part in your
> public meetings. Nor is there anything more entirely

---

131 Kevin Eckstrom. "Bono, After Years of Skepticism, Finds Partner in Religion." *Religion News Service,* February 3, 2006, http://www.atu2.com/news/bono-after-years-of-skepticism-finds-partner-in-religion.html.

foreign to us than affairs of state.[132]

Jesus did not attempt to work with political leaders like Caesar or take public office. In fact, "when Jesus perceived that they were about to come and take Him by force to make Him king, He departed again to a mountain by Himself alone" (John 6:15). Conversely, Bono has met with a variety of influential politicians including President Barack Obama, former U.S. President George W. Bush, former U.K. Prime Minister Tony Blair former Canadian Prime Minister Paul Martin, and former Russian President Dmitry Medvedev. Bono was named the most politically effective celebrity of all time by the National Journal.[133]

Bono's politicized Christianity is certainly an innovation. Followers of Jesus are to see themselves as citizens from heaven (Philippians 3:20), stationed in a foreign land (I Peter 1:17, 2:11), serving a different King and kingdom, with strict orders not to get involved in civil affairs (I Timothy 2:4). All our trust is to be in our king and his kingdom, which alone holds the solution to the world's problems. There is no precedent in the life of Jesus or anywhere in the New Testament for trying to advise Caesar's regime and how he can do things better.

---

132 Tertullian, *Ante-Nicene Fathers*, volume 3, 45-46
133 Ronald Brownstein, "The Most Politically Effective Celebrities of All Time," *The National Journal*, April 28, 2011, http://www.nationaljournal.com/magazine/the-nj-20-the-most-politically-effective-celebrities-of-all-time-20110428

4

Questioning the Scriptures

"So shall my word be that goeth forth out of my mouth: it shall not return unto me void, but it shall accomplish that which I please, and it shall prosper in the thing whereto I sent it."
— Isaiah 55:11

Jesus is Lord, and He has the right to rule our lives through His authoritative teachings and the traditions of His chosen Apostles that have been preserved for us in the New Testament. In the warfare of our generation, the greatest battle taking place is the battle for the Bible. The Scriptures are authoritative and true. But Emergents ultimately question Scripture because they do not have a solid foundation of what truth is. Evidence demonstrates that Emergents are anti-inerrant regardless of what they may say otherwise. Brian McLaren rejects the protestant Christian view that the Bible is the "ultimate authority" and there are "no contradictions in it," and it is "absolutely true and without error in all it says." McLaren then says sarcastically, "Give up these assertions, and you're on a slippery slope to losing your whole faith."[134]

McLaren adds, "Hardly anyone notices the irony of resorting to the authority of extra-biblical words and concepts to justify one's belief in the Bible's ultimate authority."[135] Some of the extra-biblical words that

---

134 McLaren, *Generous Orthodoxy*, 148.
135 Ibid., 182-183.

McLaren believes should not be used to support the Bible are authority, inerrancy, infallibility, objective, and absolute. McLaren rejects these words to describe the Bible because the context of these words originate, he claims, with "Sir Isaac Newton, Rene Descartes, the Enlightenment, David Hume and Foundationalism."[136]

The Bible says, "God is not a man, that he should lie; neither the son of man, that he should repent: hath he said, and shall he not do it? or hath he spoken, and shall he not make it good?" (Numbers 23:19). In fact, the Bible tells us that God cannot lie (Titus 1:2), that it is impossible for God to lie (Hebrews 6:18). God's Word is true. The Bible is not deceptive, but is trustworthy and authoritative. Biblical inerrancy is built upon the solid foundation that God cannot err. For the Emergents to deny this conclusion, they must deny one or both of these claims. To deny either one is to take the path of liberalism and it is indeed a slippery slope. "Yea, let God be true, but every man a liar" (Romans 3:4).

Within the Emergent conversation, there is an understandable hesitancy to the acceptance of systematized doctrinal statements among churches and leaders who claim to have the final say on the interpretation of Scripture. Though we have all witnessed ecclesial leaders abuse the Bible by forcing their program through isolated proof texts and perversions of God's Word, we should nevertheless continuously strive to teach sound doctrine and come to the knowledge of the truth. But the Emergent Church abandons the authority of Scripture by insisting upon subjectivity rather than objectively. This is spiritual anarchy when the authority of God's word is put into the hands of lawless men. Ultimately, they are making a god of their own image.

On the one hand, many Emergent leaders want to affirm the supremacy of the Bible. For instance, McLaren says that a generous orthodoxy affirms "that Scripture itself remains above creeds and that the Holy Spirit may use Scripture to tweak creedal understandings and emphases from time to time."[137] However, those that do defend Scriptural authority are also quick to turn around and speak against the Scriptures. For instance, McLaren describes how the authority of Scripture cannot apply to the postmodern individual:

---

136 Ibid., 183.
137 Ibid., 28.

How do "I" know the Bible is always right? And if "I" am sophisticated enough to realize that I know nothing of the Bible without my own involvement via interpretation, I'll also ask how I know which school, method, or technique of biblical interpretation is right. What makes a "good" interpretation good? And if an appeal is made to a written standard (book, doctrinal statement, etc.) or to common sense or to "scholarly principles of interpretation," the same pesky "I" who liberated us from the authority of the church will ask, "Who sets the standard?" Whose common sense? Whose scholars and why? Don't these appeals to authorities and principles outside the Bible actually undermine the claim of ultimate biblical authority? Aren't they just the new pope?[138]

But Jesus rebuked the Sadducees and said they were in error for not rightly interpreting the Scriptures. Jesus said, "Do ye not therefore err, because ye know not the scriptures, neither the power of God?" (Mark 12:24). It would not be just or fair for God to judge us according to His word (John 12:48) unless we could be expected to understand it and interpret it correctly. While those in the Emergent Church are confused as to how to interpret the Bible, we read in the epistle to the Corinthians that "God is not the author of confusion" (1 Corinthians 14:33), and the Apostle Paul exhorts, "in understanding, be men" (1 Corinthians 14:20). At this point, Brian McLaren may criticize that argument because it is granting Paul the same Scriptural authority as Jesus. McLaren diminishes the Scriptural authority of the Apostle Paul: "We retained Jesus as Savior but promoted the apostle Paul (or someone else) to Lord and Teacher. . . . And/or decided that Jesus' life and teachings were completely interpreted by Paul."[139]

Rob Bell also demotes the Apostle Paul and thereby the authority of Scripture. Bell comments,

Notice this verse from 2 Corinthians: "I am out of my

---

138 Ibid., 148.
139 Ibid., 68.

mind to talk like this." A man named Paul is writing this, so is it his word or God's Word? Is God out of His mind? Is God out of Paul's mind? Is Paul out of God's mind? Or does it simply mean that Paul is out of Paul's mind? And if the verse is simply Paul being out of Paul's mind, then how is that God's word?[140]

God chose *men* to write Scripture. Jesus chose His apostles and He deemed them faithful *men* to write Scripture which later became the New Testament. Thus, Emergents like McLaren and Bell question to the authority of Scripture by emphasizing the human element and suggesting that the Bible is merely a good book written by *men*. Ending the discussion, they insist that the Bible is a narrative of good stories and morals that are endorsed by God. In *The Post-Evengelical*, Dave Tomlinson writes,

> To say Scripture is the word of God is to employ a metaphor. God cannot be thought of as literally speaking words, since they are an entirely human phenomenon that could never prove adequate as a medium for the speech of an infinite God.[141]

According to the Apostle Paul, Scripture and the words spoken by the apostles are indeed "the word of God," not metaphorically but in truth. He says, "For this cause also thank we God without ceasing, because, when ye received *the word of God* which ye heard of us, ye received it not as the word of men, but *as it is in truth, the word of God*, which effectually worketh also in you that believe" (1 Thessalonians 2:13). Let's stop playing with the clear language and believe the Bible for what it simply proclaims to be in truth, the word of God.

For Christians to believe that the Bible is the Word of God is not to disbelieve that it was also written by men. Contrary to Emergents, the Bible teaches that God carried along the writers of Scripture by His Spirit to write precisely what was on his heart: "All scripture is given by

---

140 Bell, *Velvet Elvis*, 42.
141 Dave Tomlinson, *The Post-Evengelical* (Grand Rapids: Zondervan, 2003), 113-14.

inspiration of God, and is profitable for doctrine, for reproof, for correction, for instruction in righteousness: That the man of God may be perfect, throughly furnished unto all good works" (2 Timothy 3:16,17).

In these verses, Paul was referring to the "God-breathed" inspired writings which came to be the Old Testament canon, and in 2 Peter 1:19-21, Peter was referring to Old Testament prophets who were moved by the Holy Spirit. The Apostle Peter also considered the Apostle Paul's letters in the first century to be Scripture as well. Peter said, "And account that the longsuffering of our Lord is salvation; even as our beloved brother Paul also according to the wisdom given unto him hath written unto you; As also in all his epistles, speaking in them of these things; in which are some things hard to be understood, which they that are unlearned and unstable wrest, *as they do also the other scriptures*, unto their own destruction" (2 Peter 3:15,16). To Peter, a Jew who believed in the inspiration of the Old Testament, Paul's writings were on par right alongside them.

Even what Paul writes as a matter of his opinion is not like the opinion of the average Emergent Christian. It doesn't even compare. When Paul says, "I speak this by permission, and not of commandment" (1 Corinthians 7:6), "But to the rest speak I, not the Lord" (1 Corinthians 7:12), and "I give my judgment" (1 Corinthians 7:25), he is nonetheless inspired by the Holy Spirit because Jesus chose this man as an apostle to the Gentiles and filled him with the Holy Spirit. Paul was ordained an apostle not of men, neither by man, but by Jesus Christ, and God the Father (Galatians 1:1). In the very same letter where those phrases in question occur, Paul says, "If any man thinketh himself to be a prophet, or spiritual, let him take knowledge of the things which I write unto you, that they are the commandment of the Lord." (1 Corinthians 14:37). An early Christian Tertullian (198 AD) explains:

> Although Paul did not have a specific commandment of the Lord [to cite], he was accustomed to give counsel and to dictate matters from his own authority, for he possessed the Spirit of God, who guides into all truth. For that reason, his advice has, by the authority of the Divine Word, become equivalent to nothing less than a

divine command.[142]

Once again, Peter says that the Scriptures were not merely written by men, but "holy men of God spake as they were moved by the Holy Ghost" (2 Peter 1:21). The Bible was written by men, as the Emergents readily acknowledge, but it is also one hundred percent God. Notice the parallel: Jesus Christ was a man, but not merely a man. He is also one hundred percent Divine substance. "In the beginning was the Word, and the Word was with God, and the Word was God. . . And the Word was made flesh, and dwelt among us, (and we beheld his glory, the glory as of the only begotten of the Father,) full of grace and truth" (John 1:1,14). When one begins to break Jesus' divinity apart from His humanity, then Jesus becomes merely a prophet, merely a good moral teacher, and the substance of His deity is lost. It is truly tragic and ironic that these professed theologians of the Emerging Church movement are writing books as "Christians," but have undermined the treasured authority of the Christian faith.

Specifically applied to the twelve apostles of Christ, the word "apostle" comes from the Greek word *apostolos* which means a delegate, messenger, one sent forth with orders. The word apostle emphasizes delegated authority whereas the word disciple emphasizes learning and following. A Christian is a disciple. The Bible says, "The disciples were called Christians first in Antioch" (Acts 11:26). What separates the apostles from disciples is that they were sent directly by Jesus Himself, had the authority to write Scripture, and displayed the signs of apostles. Paul said, "Truly the signs of an apostle were wrought among you in all patience, in signs, and wonders, and mighty deeds" (2 Corinthians 12:12). To reject the authority of the Scriptures is to reject the authority of God and Christ because the writers of Scripture were commissioned by Jesus with delegated apostolic authority to write Scripture as the blueprints for His Church.

When we consider that apostle means "sent one," it is amazing that McLaren has said that those who are willing "to grant Jesus no more authority than Paul renders [him] speechless."[143] Paul was directly sent

---

142 Tertullian, *Ante-Nicene Fathers,* 3.95 in David Bercot. *A Dictionary of Early Christian Beliefs* (Peabody, MA: Hendrickson Publishers, 1998), 602.
143 Brian McLaren. *A New Kind of Christianity* (New York, NY: HarperCollins

by Jesus as an apostle. Yet McLaren doesn't want to grant Paul the same authority as Jesus when Jesus specifically said, "Verily, verily, I say unto you, He that receiveth whomsoever I send receiveth me; and he that receiveth me receiveth him that sent me" (John 13:20). If we don't receive Paul in the same manner as we receive Jesus, then we are essentially rejecting Jesus because Jesus sent Paul in His name. Undoubtedly, we must be cautious about interpreting Jesus' teachings through the lens of Paul's epistles as many theologians have done in the past and greatly erred. We must understand Paul through the teachings of Christ, but count them equally authoritative. The same is true for the epistles from Peter, John, or James.

When the Bible teaches that "all Scripture is given by inspiration of God" (2 Timothy 3:16), the word "inspiration" is translated from the Greek compound word *theopneustos*, which means "God-breathed." God does not breathe or communicate in open-ended language wherein the reader may ultimately determine the meaning. The Emergent conversation suggests that all Scripture is based on the interpretation of the reader. But God clearly expects us to understand His word because in the same context it is "profitable for doctrine, for reproof, for correction, for instruction in righteousness." How could it be profitable for such things if it were so open-ended as the Emergent Church would have us believe?

Binding and Loosing

The Emergent Church leaders "loose" Christians from the lordship of Jesus Christ and the apostles as revealed through Scripture. Doug Pagitt believes that the reader determines the meaning of the Scriptures. This belief renders readers loosed from any binding teaching from the Lord and the apostles because they can essentially make it mean whatever they want it to mean. This view of the Bible is entirely unprofitable. Doug Pagitt writes:

The contemporary church makes two mistakes regarding the function and relationship of the Bible. One is to think

Publishers, 2010), 274.

of her [Pagitt calls the Bible "she" and "her"] as a stagnant telling of all the desires of God. The other is to think of her as something from which we extract truth, whether in the form of moral teaching or propositional statements.[144]

When the Lord Jesus said, "I will give unto thee the keys of the kingdom of heaven: and whatsoever thou shalt bind on earth shall be bound in heaven: and whatsoever thou shalt loose on earth shall be loosed in heaven" (Matthew 16:19), Rob Bell comments:

What he is doing here is significant. He is giving his followers the authority to make new interpretations of the Bible. He is giving them permission to say, "Hey, we think we missed it before on that verse, and we've recently come to the conclusion that this is what it actually means."[145]

As Rob Bell points out in *Velvet Elvis*, the Jewish rabbis would often bind and loose, that is, permit or forbid certain activities. Thus, this language would be familiar to all Jews including the disciples. But Bell goes wrong in his interpretation of binding and loosing. "Bound" and "loosed," in the Greek verb form occur in the perfect passive participle. The NASB more accurately translates, "Truly I say to you, whatever you bind on earth shall *have been bound* in heaven; and whatever you loose on earth shall *have been* loosed in heaven." It is not that Christians have the license to initiate procedures on earth which God and heaven will subsequently affirm and honor, as Rob Bell is insisting. Rather, the apostles bound on earth what had already been established in heaven. In other words, Christians will permit on earth what is already permitted in heaven and disallow on earth what is already forbidden in heaven. The apostles' special authority and moral instruction given in the Church on earth was simply an echo of what God had already determined in heaven. Jesus is referring to the enforcing of edicts on earth that are already decreed in heaven. Having been already bound and loosed in heaven,

---

144 Pagitt. *Preaching Re-imagined*, 44.
145 Bell, *Velvet Elvis*, 50.

Christians are guided by the Holy Ghost to accomplish the same binding and loosing on earth as revealed by Christ and the apostles in the New Covenant. There is already an established order in heaven which we are to bring about on earth through our faith, love, conduct and prayers as Jesus taught us to pray, "Thy kingdom come. Thy will be done in earth, as it is in heaven" (Matthew 6:10).

Specifically, the power to bind and loose being given to the apostles is demonstrated in their being named the foundation of the church: "Now therefore ye are no more strangers and foreigners, but fellowcitizens with the saints, and of the household of God; And are built upon the foundation of the apostles and prophets, Jesus Christ himself being the chief corner stone" (Ephesians 2:19,20). Likewise, the New Jerusalem has twelve foundations with the apostles' names on them (Revelation 21:14). Through the ages, the church of Jesus Christ has been built upon the pillars (Galatians 2:9) of the authoritative words of the apostles and the cornerstone of Jesus Christ (1 Corinthians 3:11). God has preserved the teachings of Jesus and the apostles as the once-for-all foundation of the church, the "the pillar and ground of the truth" (1 Timothy 3:15).

In Paul's last letter, he told Timothy, "And the things that thou hast heard of me among many witnesses, the same commit thou to faithful men, who shall be able to teach others also" (2 Timothy 2:2). From generation to generation, the authority of the apostles is passed on to the church from the writings of the apostles, that is, the Scriptures. Irenaeus (180 AD) explains,

> We have learned the plan of our salvation from no one else other than from those through whom the gospel has come down to us. For they did at one time proclaim the gospel in public. And, at a later period, by the will of God, they handed the gospel down to us in the Scriptures—to be "the ground and pillar of our faith.[146]

The authority of Scripture is the authority that binds and looses on earth what has already been determined by God in heaven, not Rob

---

146 Irenaeus, *Ante-Nicene Fathers*, 4.414 in Bercot, *A Dictionary of Early Christian Beliefs*, 599.

Bell or his readers. One of the most prolific writers of the pre-Nicene Church, "father of Christian theology," Origen (185-255 AD) speaks against Rob Bell's viewpoint on the meaning of binding and loosing:

> When one judges unrighteously and does not bind upon earth according to the Word of God, nor loose upon earth according to His will, the gates of Hades prevail against him. . . . And if anyone who is not such a Peter, and does not possess the things spoken of here, yet he still imagines that as a Peter he will so bind on earth that the things bound are bound in heaven . . . he is puffed up, not understanding the meaning of the Scriptures. And being puffed up, he has fallen into the ruin of the devil.[147]

Scriptural authority for the Emergent Christian is no longer needed because the Bible "was written by a man," and God cannot "literally speak words" nor does God "have any intention of sharing his absoluteness." The infrastructure of Christianity is being deconstructed and reconstructed by the postmodern arguments of the Emergent movement. Thus we cannot appeal to the Word of God as the foundation of reasoning with an Emergent Christian without first reestablishing its truth, tradition, authority and power.

Doubting the Word of God

The Bible tells us, "Faith cometh by hearing, and hearing by the word of God" (Romans 10:17). Thus, when the Emergent Church strips God's Word of all authority and power, it should be no surprise that the participants in the movement are plagued with doubt and uncertainty as a direct result.

Dave Tomlinson would have us, "climb out of the little boat of our settled certainties and join Jesus in walking on the waters of uncertainty and vulnerability."[148] However, the passage alluded to by

---

147 Origen, *Ante-Nicene Fathers*, 9.459 in Bercot, A Dictionary of Early Christian Beliefs, 68.
148 Tomlinson, *Post-Evangelical*, 88.

Tomlinson speaks of Peter being rebuked for uncertainty and doubt when Jesus says to him, "O thou of little faith, wherefore didst thou doubt?" (Matthew 14:31). Jesus was not uncertain as He walked on the water but full of faith and power. The consequences of Peter's doubt were immediate: he began to sink and he cried, saying, "Lord, save me!" Doubt is therefore an exceedingly sinful sin that alienates a person from Jesus Christ. Yet doubt is laced all throughout Emergent books. Emergent authors, pastors and teachers are self-professed cynics of God's Word.

This hip uncertainty being advocated by the Emergent Church will only erode our faith, and without faith it is impossible to please God (Hebrews 11:6) or even to be saved (Ephesians 2:5,8). Tony Campolo treats doubt as a virtue and as "absolutely essential."[149] The postmodern tendency of deconstruction causes a person to question everything and doubt any certain meaning or intentions of the inspired writers of Scripture. For instance, Barry Taylor writes:

> We should consider letting go of our obsession with certainty . . . It is hard to claim clarity when shadows linger over what is revealed. The future of faith does not lie in the declaration of certainties, but in the living out of uncertainties.[150]

One well-known author, Philip Yancey, describes himself as "a pilgrim septic with doubt."[151] For those who would not associate Yancey with Emergent, I point you to the fact that he was a key speaker of the 2013 Wild Goose Festival, an Emergent festival for social justice.[152] Yancey goes on to say,

> Doubt is the skeleton in the closet of faith, and I know no better way to treat a skeleton than to bring it into the

149 McLaren and Campolo, *Adventures in Missing the Point*, 244.
150 Barry Taylor, "Converting Christianity," in *An Emergent Manifesto of Hope,* eds. Pagitt and Jones, 168.
151 Philip Yancey, *Reaching for the Invisible God* (Grand Rapids, MI: Zondervan, 2000), p. 18.
152 Official website for the Wild Goose Festival, available: http://wildgoosefestival.org/about/2013festival/speakers/philip-yancey.

open and expose it for what it is: not something to hide or fear, but a hard structure on which living tissue must grow. . . Why, then does the church treat doubt as an enemy? I was once asked to sign *Christianity Today* magazine's statement of faith "without doubt or equivocation." I had to tell them I can barely sign my own name without doubt or equivocation.[153]

Yancey and other Emergents of our day differ with an early Church writer who said,

Consider this doubting state of mind, for it is wicked and senseless, and turns many away entirely from the faith, even though they be very strong. For this doubting is the daughter of the devil, and acts exceedingly wickedly to the servants of God. Despise, then, doubting, and gain the mastery over it in everything; clothing yourself with faith, which is strong and powerful. For faith promises all things, perfects all things; but doubt having no thorough faith in itself, fails in every work which it undertakes. You see, then," says he, "that, faith is from above—from the Lord—and has great power; but doubt is an earthly spirit, coming from the devil, and has no power. Serve, then, that which has power, namely faith, and keep away from doubt, which has no power, and you will live to God. And all will live to God whose minds have been set on these things.[154]

Christians have an obligation to call Emergents to repentance for their sin of unbelief and the fog of uncertainty. "Faith is the substance of things hoped for, the evidence of things not seen. For by it the elders obtained a good report" (Hebrews 11:1,2). When the Word of God is approached with doubt and hidden in darkness and obscurity, Emergents create a desire for subjective experiences or spiritual encounters to fill the void. This desire is exactly what the Emergent Church emphasizes in

153 Ibid., p. 41
154 Hermas, *Ante-Nicene Fathers*, volume 2, 26.

its embrace of mysticism (we will cover this at greater length in chapter 9). Dan Kimball describes it: "The basis of learning has shifted from logic and rational, systematic thought to the realm of experience. People increasingly long for the mystical and the spiritual rather than the evidential and facts-based faith of the modern soil."[155]

When the Bible is rendered impotent and not acknowledged in truth as the Word of God, the Treasure to whom it points is suddenly obscured and lost. There is only one way to find Jesus Christ, and that is by coming to Him as He is revealed in the Bible: "God, who at sundry times and in divers manners spake in time past unto the fathers by the prophets, Hath in these last days spoken unto us by his Son" (Hebrews 1:12). Thus we are not fighting for merely text when we defend the Word of God, but we are fighting for the divine Son of God Jesus Christ.

This Sword of the Spirit which is the Word of God (Ephesians 6:17) is our only weapon to overcome Emergents' attacks against it. No wonder that they will immediately question the authority of that which is "quick, and powerful, and sharper than any two-edged sword, piercing even to the dividing asunder of soul and spirit, and of the joints and marrow, and is a discerner of the thoughts and intents of the heart" (Hebrews 4:12). The very thing attacked by Satan in the beginning was God's Word: "Yea, hath God said?" (Genesis 3:1). The most valuable tool Satan had in tempting Jesus was the Word of God which the devil perverted (Luke 4:1-13). If the Bible is eternal and timeless truth, why does Rob Bell say that the letters of the Bible "aren't first and foremost timeless truths?"[156] Even if Bell believes they are timeless truths, why make such a statement casting doubt in the minds of his young Christian readers?

The words from the early Christians contrast with those teachings of the Emergent Church. In regard to doubting or disbelieving the Scriptures, Clement of Alexandria (195 AD) wrote of heretical "Christians" who sound much like the Emergent Church. Clement said, "The heretics go the length of impiety by disbelieving the Scriptures."[157] He said also, "In fact, the heretics stitch together a multitude of lies and

---

155 Kimball, *The Emerging Church*, 60.
156 Bell, *Velvet Elvis*, 32.
157 Clement of Alexandria, *Ante-Nicene Fathers,* 2.552 in Bercot, *A Dictionary of Early Christian Beliefs*, 600.

figments so that they might appear to be acting in accordance with reason in their not accepting the Scriptures"[158] Clement of Rome (96 AD) does not contest the inspiration of the Scriptures or the Apostle Paul's writings, but says very confidently, "Truly, [Paul] wrote to you under the inspiration of the [Holy] Spirit."[159] He exhorts: "Look carefully into the Scriptures, which are the true utterances of the Holy Spirit."[160]

Attacking the Canon

Another way Emergent attacks the authority of Scripture is by attacking its canonicity. Rob Bell says,

> In reaction to abuses by the church, a group of believers during a time called the Reformation claimed that we only need the authority of the Bible. But the problem is that we got the Bible from the church voting on what the Bible even is.[161]

"God, who at sundry times and in divers manners spake in time past unto the fathers by the prophets, hath in these last days spoken unto us by his Son, whom he hath appointed heir of all things, by whom also he made the worlds" (Hebrews 1:1,2). Hath God said? *God has said.* God *has* spoken to us by His Son Jesus Christ. The final revelation we have from God is the supreme revelation of Jesus Christ. Concerning the New Testament canon, those who were eyewitnesses of Christ were authorized by Him to write for Him. For example, John the apostle wrote, "And he that saw it bare record, and his record is true: and he knoweth that he saith true, that ye might believe" (John 19:35). Likewise, Peter the Apostle wrote, "For we have not followed cunningly devised fables, when we made known unto you the power and coming of our Lord Jesus Christ, but were eyewitnesses of his majesty" (2 Peter 1:16).

Luke was not an apostle, but he was an associate of the Apostle

---

158 Ibid.
159 Clement of Rome, *Ante-Nicene Fathers,* 1.18 in Bercot, *A Dictionary of Early Christian Beliefs*, 601.
160Ibid.
161 Bell, *Velvet Elvis,* 67-68

Paul. As a historian, Luke consulted all of the living eyewitnesses, including the apostles and Paul, when he wrote his gospel and the book of Acts. In the preface of his gospel, we read: "Forasmuch as many have taken in hand to set forth in order a declaration of those things which are most surely believed among us, even as they delivered them unto us, which from the beginning were eyewitnesses, and ministers of the word; it seemed good to me also, having had perfect understanding of all things from the very first, to write unto thee in order, most excellent Theophilus, that thou mightest know the certainty of those things, wherein thou hast been instructed." (Luke 1:1-4)

Contrary to Bell's criticism, the church did not *determine* the canon but *discovered* the canon. The early church followed some important guidelines in order to recognize the canon of Scripture which are still valid for us today:

- **Apostolicity**: Was it written by an authoritative source who knew Jesus, such as an apostle or an associate of an apostle?
- **Antiquity**: Did it come from the first century?
- **Orthodoxy**: Was it consistent with the teachings of Jesus and the Apostle's Doctrine which we know to be true?
- **Catholicity**: Was it widely recognized as Scripture by a broad base of churches within the ancient world?[162]

What about the Old Testament? Jesus placed his stamp of approval on the books of the Old Testament when He said, "These are the words which I spake unto you, while I was yet with you, that all things must be fulfilled, which were written in the law of Moses, and in the prophets, and in the psalms, concerning me" (Luke 24:44). This statement from Jesus in addition to His quotations of the Old Testament establishes the canonicity of the whole Old Testament. Jesus is the highest authority. It is not the authority of the church but the higher authority of Jesus that establishes the authority and inspiration of the

---

162 See Bruce Metzger, *The Canon of the New Testament* (New York, NY: Oxford University Press), 1989.

Scriptures. Jesus said of the Father, "Thy word is truth" (John 17:17).

Most importantly, I believe and trust the Bible as true and authoritative because Jesus believed it. Jesus did not doubt or have any kind of uncertainty toward Scripture. When Jesus and the apostles quoted from the Old Testament, they called it "the word of God" (Mark 7:13; Romans 9:6). When Jesus was being tempted by Satan, He said in reference to the Law, "It is written, Man shall not live by bread alone, but by every word that proceedeth out of the mouth of God" (Matthew 4:4).

In the Sermon on the Mount, Jesus said, "Till heaven and earth pass, one jot or one tittle shall in no wise pass from the Law, till all be fulfilled" (Matthew 5:18). Our only hope with the Emergents is to lead them back to the true and historical Jesus of the Bible who underlined the authority of the Law (Matthew 5:17-19), the message of the prophets (Luke 24:27) and therefore the authority of Scripture. Jesus answered the Jews, "Is it not written in your law, I said, Ye are gods? If he called them gods, unto whom the word of God came, and the scripture cannot be broken; Say ye of him, whom the Father hath sanctified, and sent into the world, Thou blasphemest; because I said, I am the Son of God?" (John 10:34-36) Here, Jesus used the word "Law" to refer to Psalm 82:6, thus declaring not only the Pentateuch as their "Law" but the whole Old Testament.

The Jesus-endorsed Old Testament tells us, "For ever, O LORD, thy word is settled in heaven" (Psalm 119:89); "Thy word is true from the beginning: and every one of thy righteous judgments endureth for ever" (Psalm 119:160); "Every word of God is pure: he is a shield unto them that put their trust in him" (Proverbs 30:5). Jesus reaffirmed these propositional truth claims by saying, "Thy word is truth" (John 17:17).

Though Tony Jones believes that Jesus actually rose from the grave, he does not believe in the historicity of many Old Testament events. Jones said,

> I don't feel the same way about the historic facticity of
> Adam and Eve, the Tower of Babel, Jonah living in the
> belly of a fish, or Job's family and cattle being wiped out
> by God. So it might seem rather arbitrary that I draw the
> line between some accounts in the Hebrew Scriptures,

which I consider mythological.[163]

It seems very odd that the Messiah who actually rose from the dead was not a trustworthy man when He spoke about the history of the Old Testament as fact. As a Jewish teacher of the Tanakh (the Jewish Old Testament), Jesus constantly referred to the Old Testament in His teachings and, in every case, believed in its historic accuracy and divine authority demonstrated in such facts as Jonah was three days and three nights in the belly of a fish (Matthew 12:40; Jonah 1:17), the Queen of Sheba who came to hear Solomon (Matthew 12:42; 1 Kings 10:2), God who created Adam (Matthew 19:4; Genesis 1:27), Elijah who visited the widow where there was no rainfall for three and a half years (Luke 4:25-26; 1 Kings 17), Noah who entered the ark when the flood destroyed all humankind except Noah's family (Luke 17:27; Genesis 7:23), and fire and brimstone that rained on Sodom (Luke 17:29; Genesis 19:24).

Jesus said that the Scriptures testified of Him as the source of eternal life (John 5:39,40). Not only did Jesus endorse the Old Testament, but He also gave the seal of His divine authority to the New Testament in advance. For example, He commissioned His disciples to go into all the nations "teaching them to observe all things whatsoever I have commanded you" (Matthew 28:20). He also promised, "The Comforter, which is the Holy Ghost, whom the Father will send in my name, he shall teach you all things, and bring all things to your remembrance, whatsoever I have said unto you" (John 14:26), and "I have yet many things to say unto you, but ye cannot bear them now. Howbeit when he, the Spirit of truth, is come, he will guide you into all truth: for he shall not speak of himself; but whatsoever he shall hear, that shall he speak: and he will shew you things to come" (John 16:12,13).

Jesus said, "The scripture cannot be broken" (John 10:35). The apostles also often cited the Old Testament to demonstrate that they believed the Scriptures were clear and understandable to the common man. The manner in which Jesus and the apostles reason from the Scriptures presupposes that the meaning of the Bible may be interpreted objectively by the individual. No matter how ruthless the Emergent Church is in its attempt to break the Scriptures, His Word assures us that

---

163 Tony Jones, *A Better Atonement: Beyond the Depraved Doctrine of Original Sin* (The JoPa Group, 2012), Kindle Edition, 342-344.

"the word of the Lord endureth for ever. And this is the word which by the gospel is preached unto you" (1 Peter 1:25). His Word must be defined, defended and exalted once again.

Query of God's word is not from the Holy Ghost but the adversary. Approaching the Bible with such skepticism, Emergents disarm young Christians and render them useless in battle against the strangleholds of sin and principalities of darkness. Emergents dull the victorious Sword of the Spirit into an ineffectual and pointless rubber dagger. This tactic of the enemy will cause the people of God to turn to the world for their defense as Israel did during the period of judges: "Now there was no smith found throughout all the land of Israel: for the Philistines said, Lest the Hebrews make them swords or spears: But all the Israelites went down to the Philistines, to sharpen every man his share, and his coulter, and his axe, and his mattock" (1 Samuel 3:19,20). We have a responsibility as Christians to study the Scriptures, to be sharpened in order to fight the doctrines that are at enmity with God's word.

5

Muddling God's Clarity

"Thine habitation is in the midst of deceit; through deceit they refuse to know me, saith the LORD."
— Jeremiah 9:6

Perspicuity or Ambiguity?

Christian theologians have long held to God's knowability as well as His immensity, His immanence as well as His transcendence.[164] The Bible teaches us the following of the glorious New Covenant of Jesus Christ: "And they shall not teach every man his neighbor, and every man his brother, saying, Know the Lord: for all shall know me, from the least to the greatest" (Hebrews 8:11). The author of Hebrews is quoting from the prophet Jeremiah's description of the New Covenant (Jeremiah 31:34). God also spoke through Jeremiah saying, "And I will give them an heart to know me, that I am the LORD: and they shall be my people, and I will be their God: for they shall return unto me with their whole heart" (Jeremiah 24:7). One of characteristics of New Covenant believers is that they would know God and have a relationship with Him through His Son. The Bible says, "But if any man love God, the same is known of

---

164 For further discussion on the question "Is God knowable?" see chapter one of Kevin DeYoung and Ted Kluck, *Why We're Not Emergent (By Two Guys Who Should Be)* (Chicago, IL: Moody Publoishers, 2008).

him" (1 Corinthians 8:3).

Liberal movements in the past have attacked the authority, sufficiency and priority of the Word of God. The Emergent Church is doing the same by assaulting the Bible's meaning and clarity. They have de-prioritized the place of Scripture and emphasized intuitive and experiential understanding. They set forth a "feeling theology" of Jesus without knowing the truth of Jesus. Emergent writings defend the liberal position that the Bible is ambiguous. Before proceeding, let's consider the words of Irenaeus (180 AD):

> When, however, the Gnostics are confuted from the Scriptures, they turn round and accuse these same Scriptures as if they were not correct, nor of authority. They say that they are ambiguous, and that the truth cannot be extracted from them by those who are ignorant of tradition.[165]

Much like the Gnostics, the Emerging Church is a movement in search of secrecy and hidden mystery rather than the clear and simple truth.[166] This journey for mystery has led many Emergent leaders to dilute, compromise and even deny the words of Jesus. For instance, one *Christianity Today* article reported on Rob Bell and his wife's questioning of the Bible:

> The Bells started questioning their assumptions about the Bible itself—"discovering the Bible as a human product," as Rob puts it, rather than the product of divine fiat. "The Bible is still in the center for us," Rob says, "but it's a different kind of center. We want to embrace mystery, rather than conquer it."
>
> "I grew up thinking that we've figured out the Bible," Kristen says, "that we knew what it means. Now I have

---

165 Irenaeus, *Ante-Nicene Fathers,* 1.415 in Bercot, *A Dictionary of Early Christian Beliefs,* 599.
166 See Brian McLaren, *The Secret Message of Jesus* (Nashville, TN: Thomas Nelson Inc., 2006).

no idea what most of it means. And yet I feel like life is big again—like life used to be black and white, and now it's in color."[167]

Who wants to hear any more from a man who claims to be a teacher of the Bible but has no idea of what it means? This scenario sounds much like the teachers of the Law in Paul's day: "Desiring to be teachers of the law; understanding neither what they say, nor whereof they affirm" (1 Timothy 1:7). He said these men "swerved," and "turned aside unto vain jangling" (1 Timothy 1:6).

Brian McLaren wrote *The Secret Message of Jesus*. In reality, there is no *secret* message of Jesus. Who wants to hear from a man who has the arrogance to say that after more than 2,000 years of church history, the Christians got it all wrong but he figured it out? Are we to believe that Brian McLaren has the true message of Jesus?

We can declare that the revelation from God is certain. Though Paul said, "we know in part," (1 Corinthians 13:9) and "we see through a glass, darkly," (1 Corinthians 13:13), he did not carry on the Athenian view of the unknown God but he said, "Whom therefore ye ignorantly worship, *him declare I unto you*" (Acts 17:23). Yes the Bible speaks about secret things belonging to the Lord, but it also says, "those things which are revealed belong unto us and to our children for ever" (Deuteronomy 29:29). McLaren, however, intentionally promotes obscurity saying:

> A warning: as in most of my other books, there are places here where I have gone out of my way to be provocative, mischievous, and unclear, reflecting my belief that clarity is sometimes overrated, and that shock, obscurity, playfulness, and intrigue (carefully articulated) often stimulates more thought than clarity.[168]

In another one of his books, McLaren continues this irrational

---

167 Scot McKnight. "Five Streams of the Emerging Church." *Christianity Today,* January 19, 2007, http://www.christianitytoday.com/ct/2007/february/11.35.html.
168 McLaren, *A Generous Orthodoxy,* 22, 23.

theme saying, "Drop any affair you may have had with certainty, proof, argument—and replace it with dialogue, conversation, intrigue, and search."[169] In contrast, when Luke the historian was writing his Gospel, one of his motives was so that Theophilus might know "the *certainty* of those things" pertaining to the Gospel of Jesus Christ. Our established certainty should not be replaced with a conversation of obscurity. The Emergents seek to make the Bible a book of confusion rather than illuminating its simplicity. Notice that they seek to draw away Christians from the simplicity of Christ with a conversation just as the Serpent did with Eve in Genesis 3:1 with a similar conversation, "Hath God said?" Paul exhorted, "But I fear, lest by any means, as the serpent beguiled Eve through his subtlety, so your minds should be corrupted from *the simplicity that is in Christ"* (2 Corinthians 11:3).

Rob Bell asks, "Is the Bible the best God can do? With God being so massive and awe-inspiring and full of truth, why is his book capable of so much confusion?"[170] Contrary to Bell, the Bible says, "God is not the author of confusion, but of peace, as in all churches of the saints" (1 Corinthians 14:33). God has spoken in clear terms to His people. The Apostle Peter tells us that God "hath given unto us all things that pertain unto life and godliness, through the knowledge of him" (2 Peter 2:3). The knowability of Jesus Christ and His word is very important because through this knowledge we have all things that pertain to life and godliness. Emergent suggests that we cannot know what God meant when He gave us His word, but the first epistle of John says, "The anointing which ye have received of him abideth in you, and ye need not that any man teach you: but as the same anointing teacheth you of all things, and is truth, and is no lie, and even as it hath taught you, ye shall abide in him" (1 John 2:27).

Mystery Concealed or Revealed?

As we will see, the Bible does use the term "mystery," but it is in a very different context than how the Emergent Church is using it in its writings. Many have defined the Old Testament as the New Testament concealed and the New Testament as the Old Testament revealed. This

169 McLaren and Campolo. *Adventures in Missing the Point*, 84.
170 Bell, *Velvet Elvis*, 45.

mystery of Christ concealed in the Old Testament has been revealed in the New Testament. There do remain some mysterious elements to the apocalyptic literature of the prophets in the Bible, but other than that, the Scriptures clearly spell out the essentials of God's message to humanity in His Son Jesus Christ. But the Emergent Church would cast doubt on that by saying the Gospel is much more mysterious than we think.

Rob Bell quotes Hollywood actor Sean Penn, whom he calls one of the greatest "theologians" of our time: "The mystery is the truth."[171] The mystery is the truth? Yet this perplexing theme is consistent with all Emergents. If the Emergent teachers undermine the authority of God's Word, they subsequently undermine the knowability of the Lord and are instead enamored with mystery. Donald Miller writes in his book *Blue Like Jazz*:

> At the end of the day, when I am lying in bed and I know the chances of any of our theology being exactly right are a million to one, I need to know that God has things figured out, that if my math is wrong we are still going to be okay. And wonder is that feeling we get when we let go of our silly answers, our mapped out rules that we want God to follow. I don't think there is any better worship than wonder.[172]

Brian McLaren virtually concludes his book *A Generous Orthodoxy* with the same concept:

> Consider for a minute what it would mean to get the glory of God finally and fully right in your thinking or to get a fully formed opinion of God's goodness or holiness. Then I think you'll feel the irony: all these years of pursuing orthodoxy ended up like this—in front of all this glory understanding nothing.[173]

This rhetoric is inconsistent with the declarations of Christ and

---

171   Bell, *Velvet Elvis,* 32-33.
172   Miller, *Blue Like Jazz,* 206.
173   McLaren, *A Generous Orthodoxy,* 294.

his apostles. For instance, the Apostle John wrote, "And we know that the Son of God is come, and *hath given us an understanding*, that we may know him that is true, and we are in him that is true, even in his Son Jesus Christ. This is the true God, and eternal life" (1 John 5:20). The Apostle Paul exhorted and prayed for Timothy: "Consider what I say; and the Lord give thee *understanding in all things*" (2 Timothy 2:7). Certainly this wouldn't have been Paul's prayer for Timothy if all along they understood *nothing*. By darkening our understanding, the Emergent Church would have us on a path of being alienated from God. Paul wrote the Ephesians: "This I say therefore, and testify in the Lord, that ye henceforth walk not as other Gentiles walk, in the vanity of their mind, Having *the understanding darkened*, being alienated from the life of God through the ignorance that is in them, because of the blindness of their heart" (Ephesians 4:17,18). In fact, those "without understanding" are those "filled with all unrighteousness" (Romans 1:30,31). Jesus "opened their [the apostles] understanding, that they might understand the scriptures" (Luke 24:45). Paul spoke about how Jesus opened his understanding and gave him revelation of the mystery of Christ so that his listeners would also "understand" this knowledge in "the mystery of Christ" (Ephesians 3:4). But Doug Pagitt writes:

> Mystery is not the enemy to be [conquered] nor a problem to be solved, but rather, the partner with whom we dance—and dance we must. The call for the post-evangelical community is to dance and play the music. But we are also called to show each other the way into mystery. We would certainly be under providing if we didn't offer new ways to enter and live in mystery.[174]

This subterfuge demolishes the very foundation of the Word of God which is simple and clear revelation. This clandestine effort to impress or influence with intrigue rather than clarity and simplicity characterizes the way of the adversary Satan and not of Christ. God gave us the love letters contained in the Bible that we might know Him and come to the Person of Jesus Christ for grace. Again, Emergent attacks

---

174 Doug Pagitt quoted in Tomlinson, *The Post-Evenagelical,* 85.

language as a carrier of God's transcendent truth as Bell states:

> The Christian faith is mysterious to the core. It is about things and beings that ultimately can't be put into words. Language fails. And if we do definitively put God into words, we have at that very moment made God something God is not.[175]

Certainly there will be an unspeakable revelation when we are face to face with God, when we shall know even as we are known (1 Corinthians 13:12). But language is essential for reasoning and rational beings like ourselves created in the image of God. Jesus did not tell His disciples that they understand nothing but "from henceforth ye know him, and have seen him" (John 14:7). We can have confidence that we know God and that He hasn't left us in darkness concerning who He is and what He requires of us. "And hereby we do know that we know him, if we keep his commandments" (1 John 2:3).

Contrary to the Emergent view that we can understand nothing, Jesus said, "All things that I have heard of my Father I have made known unto you" (John 15:15). The language of the Emergent new Christians contrasts to that of the old primitive Christian Tertullian (198 AD) who said: "In order that we might acquire an ampler and more authoritative knowledge of Himself, His counsels, and His will, God has added a written revelation for the benefit of everyone whose heart is set on seeking Him."[176]

Emergents often speak of mystery, but in a very different manner than the biblical writers do. We never find them saying anything like "the mystery is the truth," as Rob Bell parrots from the movie star Sean Penn. On one occasion Paul speaks about the "mystery" of the Rapture. But then he goes on to unveil this mystery in perfect detail, not to leave Christians in darkness and obscurity. "Behold, *I shew you* a mystery; We shall not all sleep, but we shall all be changed, In a moment, in the twinkling of an eye, at the last trump: for the trumpet shall sound, and the dead shall be raised incorruptible, and we shall be changed" (1

---

175 Bell, *Velvet Elvis*, 32.
176 Tertullian, *Ante-Nicene Fathers,* 3.32 in Bercot, *A Dictionary of Early Christian Beliefs,* 600.

Corinthians 15:51,52).

Paul also unveils the "mystery of Christ and the church" in regard to a husband's relationship in loving his wife (Ephesians 5:32). The "mystery of godliness" is also revealed by Paul: "God was manifest in the flesh, justified in the Spirit, seen of angels, preached unto the Gentiles, believed on in the world, received up into glory" (1 Timothy 3:16).

When the Bible makes predictions about the future in uncertain terms conveyed in mysteries and mysterious symbols such as in the prophetic books of Revelation or Daniel, even these are not meant to cloud and cover meaning but rather to unveil and convey meaning when the event comes to pass. For instance, John says, "The mystery of the seven stars which thou sawest in my right hand, and the seven golden candlesticks. The seven stars are the angels of the seven churches: and the seven candlesticks which thou sawest are the seven churches" (Revelation 1:20). Revelation chapter 17 speaks of a woman and on her forehead was written "MYSTERY, BABYLON THE GREAT, THE MOTHER OF HARLOTS AND ABOMINATIONS OF THE EARTH" (Revelation 17:5). John doesn't leave the mystery unsolved but goes on to say, "*I will tell thee the mystery* of the woman. . . ." (Revelation 17:7). The biblical authors speak of mysteries not to confuse meaning of God's word but to convey its meaning by revealing these mysteries.

In fact, in almost all instances that the New Testament uses the word "mystery," it is in reference to God's ancient plans of accepting believing Gentiles as His people along with the remnant of Israel (See Romans 11:25; Ephesians 1:9,10; Colossians 1:26,27). Paul speaks of this mystery concerning the Gentiles' inclusion in the Church and concludes, "Whereby, when ye read, ye may understand my knowledge in the mystery of Christ, Which in other ages was not made known unto the sons of men, as it is *now revealed* unto his holy apostles and prophets by the Spirit; That the Gentiles should be fellow-heirs, and of the same body, and partakers of his promise in Christ by the gospel: Whereof I was made a minister, according to the gift of the grace of God given unto me by the effectual working of his power. Unto me, who am less than the least of all saints, is this grace given, that I should preach among the Gentiles the unsearchable riches of Christ; And *to make all men see* what is the fellowship of the mystery, which from the beginning of the world hath been hid in God, who created all things by Jesus Christ: To the intent that now unto the principalities and powers in heavenly places *might be known* by the church the manifold wisdom of God, According to the eternal purpose which he purposed in Christ Jesus our Lord: In whom we have boldness and access with confidence by the faith of him" (Ephesians 3:4-12, emphasis added).

The Bible is clear that there is no mystery or darkness in God but that He has "made known unto us the mystery of his will" (Ephesians 1:9). The whole and complete counsel of God has been made known in Jesus Christ. "God is light, and in him is no darkness at all" (1 John 1:5). Paul says, "The revelation of the mystery, which was kept secret since the world began," is now "made manifest" and "*made known to all nations* for the obedience of faith" (Romans 16:25,26). Any mystery of God has been revealed in Jesus Christ so that people might obey God. "But we speak the wisdom of God in a mystery, even the hidden wisdom, which God ordained before the world unto our glory: Which none of the princes of this world knew: for had they known it, they would not have crucified the Lord of glory" (1 Corinthians 2:7,8).

The Emergent Church movement cannot be faithful to Scripture if it does not speak of our ability to know absolute truth as confidently as the Bible does. While Emergent regards the Gospel as a mystery that cannot be known with certainty, Paul asked the Ephesians to pray "that utterance may be given unto me, that I may open my mouth boldly, *to make known* the mystery of the gospel" (Ephesians 6:19; see also Colossians 4:3). Jesus tells us, "*Unto you it is given to know* the mystery of the kingdom of God: but unto them that are without, all these things are done in parables" (Mark 4:11). But the Emergents resemble the recipients of the prophet Ezekiel's message; they sought to obscure God's clear warning of judgment when it was convenient for them: "Then said I, Ah Lord GOD! they say of me, Doth he not speak parables?" (Ezekiel 20:49).

In fact, the Emergent leaders incriminate themselves by their craftiness in handling the Word of God deceitfully. The Bible tells us that if the Gospel is hidden or mysterious, it is hid to those who are lost and blinded by Satan: "Therefore seeing we have this ministry, as we have received mercy, we faint not; But have renounced the hidden things of dishonesty, not walking in craftiness, nor handling the word of God deceitfully; but by manifestation of the truth commending ourselves to every man's conscience in the sight of God. *But if our gospel be hid, it is hid to them that are lost*: In whom the god of this world hath blinded the minds of them which believe not, lest the light of the glorious gospel of Christ, who is the image of God, should shine unto them" (2 Corinthians 4:1-4).

The truth is not hidden in ambiguity and obscurity, but it *can* be difficult to find. The broad road which leads to destruction is much easier to travel than the difficult and narrow way which leads to eternal life. Not only must we seek for truth, but we must also lose our lives in order to find it. This is the one teaching of Jesus that is recorded in all four Gospels:

> He that findeth his life shall lose it: and he that loseth his life for my sake shall find it. (Matthew 10:39)

> For whosoever will save his life shall lose it: and whosoever will lose his life for my sake shall find it. (Matthew 16:25)

> For whosoever will save his life shall lose it; but whosoever shall lose his life for my sake and the gospel's, the same shall save it. (Mark 8:35)

> For whosoever will save his life shall lose it: but whosoever will lose his life for my sake, the same shall save it. (Luke 9:24)

> Whosoever shall seek to save his life shall lose it; and whosoever shall lose his life shall preserve it. (Luke 17:33)

> He that loveth his life shall lose it; and he that hateth his life in this world shall keep it unto life eternal. (John 12:25)

6

Women Rule Over Them

"As for my people, children are their oppressors, and women rule over them. O my people, they which lead thee cause thee to err, and destroy the way of thy paths."
– Isaiah 3:12

As the above verse indicates, it seems the only way God would raise up women to rule over and teach men in the church would be to shame them. In the next two chapters, we will examine the slippery slope into liberalism and the manifest judgment of God upon a people who suppress the truth in unrighteousness. Once the Word of God has been deconstructed of its meaning, the spiral down the path of liberalism leads to the compromise and eventual overthrow of God's transcendent morality and patriarchal order. Demonstrated below, Emergents claim that all the Bible verses on gender roles are refuted by recent scholarship, or aren't part of the Bible, or are contradicted by experience, are simply wrong, or don't apply to postmodern generations. This denial of New Testament tradition will inevitably lead to acceptance of "gay Christians" (covered in chapter 7).

Postmodern Egalitarianism

Because feminism and women's rights are integral pieces of the

97

postmodern puzzle, the Emergent Church also has become a voice for feminism, even though feminist views rebel against the clear values of Scripture.[177] William Bergquist's book *The Postmodern Organization* is quoted in one Emergent book as follows:

> What will be the nature of the newly emerging postmodern leader? He or she will be one who can master the unexpected, and often unwanted. He or she (and more often, it will be she) must be able to tolerate ambiguity.[178]

In *An Emergent Manifesto of Hope*, Ken and Deborah Loyd devote a section to women's rights. The authors founded The Bridge, an organization which demanded that "women receive equality in every area of endeavor."[179] They protest, "Women receive less education than men, and are paid less then men for the same work. They are poorly represented at the highest levels of power and decision making in the church, business and government."[180] Perhaps those women shouldn't even be in church, business and government leadership positions in the first place. Following a biblical pattern for women, Clement of Alexandria (195 AD) said,

> She devotes herself assiduously to prayers and supplications; avoiding frequent departures from the house, and shutting herself up as far as possible from the view of all not related to her, and deeming housekeeping of more consequence than impertinent trifling.[181]

Are men and women spiritually equal? Absolutely. Neither male

---

177 A more through treatment of this topic as it relates more generally to Evangelicalism can be found in Wayne Grudem, *Evangelical Feminism, A New Path to Liberalism* (Wheaton, IL: Crossway Books, 2006).
178 *An Emergent Manifesto of Hope*, eds. Jones and Pagitt, 186.
179 Ken Loyd and Deborah Loyd, "Our Report Card in the Year 2057," in *An Emergent Manifesto of Hope,* eds. Jones and Pagitt, 274.
180 Ibid., 273,274.
181 Clement of Alexandria, *Ante-Nicene Fathers,* volume 2, 379.

nor female has more value than the other. Both men and women are equally loved by God and may equally be accepted by God if they keep His commandments. The same early Christian writer quoted above also said:

> But if there were no difference between man and woman, both would do and suffer the same things. As then there is sameness, as far as respects the soul, she will attain to the same virtue; but as there is difference as respects the peculiar construction of the body, she is destined for child-bearing and housekeeping. "For I would have you know," says the apostle, "that the head of every man is Christ; and the head of the woman is the man: for the man is not of the woman, but the woman of the man. For neither is the woman without the man, nor the man without the woman, in the Lord."[182]

Though men and women are created equal, as far as respects the soul, God created them with unique gender-specific roles. The first woman, Eve, was created to be a helper for Adam. God said, "It is not good that the man should be alone; I will make him an help meet for him" (Genesis 2:18). The female role has not changed in the New Testament; Paul the Apostle said, "But I would have you know, that the head of every man is Christ; and the head of the woman is the man; and the head of Christ is God" (1 Corinthians 11:3).

When a man and woman get married, they become one flesh (Genesis 2:24; Matthew 19:5,6). While there is an inseparable unity between the husband and wife, it is the man who is the "head" of the wife and family. It is the responsibility of the husband to lead the home and provide for his family's spiritual and physical needs. It is the responsibility of the wife to submit to and reverence her husband. Paul wrote, "Wives, submit yourselves unto your own husbands, as unto the Lord. For the husband is the head of the wife, even as Christ is the head of the church: and he is the saviour of the body. Therefore as the church is subject unto Christ, so let the wives be to their own husbands in every

---

182 Clement of Alexandria, *Ante-Nicene Fathers,* volume 2, 420.

thing" (Ephesians 5:22-24).

Today it is especially needful to dispel the modern myth that the Bible teaches a degrading view of women. Scripture bestows much honor to virtuous women when it says to treat "elder women as mothers; the younger as sisters, with all purity," and "Honor widows that are widows indeed" (1 Timothy 5:2,3). The Apostle Peter also exhorts husbands to honor their wives (1 Peter 3:1). Husbands are exhorted to love their wives just as Jesus loved the church: "Husbands, love your wives, even as Christ also loved the church, and gave himself for it" (Ephesians 5:25); "Likewise, ye husbands, dwell with them according to knowledge, giving honour unto the wife, as unto the weaker vessel, and as being heirs together of the grace of life; that your prayers be not hindered" (1 Peter 3:7).

Thus, godly women have a vitally important and wonderful role in strengthening their families, the church, and the world when they serve in their God-ordained functions. Paul writes, "I will therefore that the younger women marry, bear children, guide the house, give none occasion to the adversary to speak reproachfully" (1 Timothy 5:14).

The pastoral epistles speak well of a woman who is "well reported of for good works; if she have brought up children, if she have lodged strangers, if she have washed the saints' feet, if she have relieved the afflicted, if she have diligently followed every good work" (1 Timothy 5:10). We read in the book of Acts about Tabitha who was "full of good works and alms deeds which she did" (Acts 9:36). The Bible says, "Favour is deceitful, and beauty is vain: but a woman that feareth the LORD, she shall be praised" (Proverbs 31:30). The Bible is far from teaching that women are inferior to men in any way. Nevertheless, God has created men and women to work together having distinct gender roles.

Emergents are quick to quote the following passage: "There is neither Jew nor Greek, there is neither bond nor free, there is neither male nor female: for ye are all one in Christ Jesus" (Galatians 3:28). For example, Peter Rollins translates what he believes in the "spirit of the text" as follows:

The apostle Paul once famously remarked that in Christ Jesus there is neither Jew nor Greek, slave nor free, male nor female. He does not say that there are both Jews and Greeks, both slaves and free, both men and woman. Rather this new identity with Christ involves the laying down of such political, biological and cultural identities. This is not an expression of 'both/and' but rather 'neither/nor'. . . And what if Paul didn't just mean these three categories, as if all the others remained intact? What if he was implying that there is neither black nor white in Christ, neither rich nor poor, neither powerful nor powerless? What if we could go even further and say that the space Paul wrote of was one in which there would be neither republican nor democrat, liberal nor conservative, orthodox nor heretic? Indeed, in the spirit of the text, what if we could offer an interpretive translation of Paul's words that would read,

You are all children of God through faith in Christ Jesus, for all of you who were baptized into Christ have clothed yourselves with Christ. There is neither high church nor low church, Fox nor CNN, citizen nor alien, capitalist nor communist, gay nor straight, beautiful nor ugly, East nor West, theist nor atheist, Israel nor Palestine, hawk nor dove, American nor Iraqi, married nor divorced, uptown nor downtown, terrorist nor freedom fighter, paedophile nor loving parent, priest nor prophet, fame nor obscurity, Christian nor non-Christian, for all are made one in Christ Jesus.[183]

Rollins' "interpretive translation" in biblically unwarranted and ridiculous. Galatians 3:28 *does* affirm the equal spiritual value and dignity of Christian women, but it does not tell us that women could govern or teach in the church assembly as feminists insist. Though Paul says there is neither Jew nor Greek, there remained distinctions in their

---

183 Peter Rollins, "Beyond the Colour of Each Other's Eyes," *PeterRollins.net*, January 1, 2009, http://peterrollins.net/2009/01/beyond-the-colour-of-each-others-eyes/

roles.[184] Though Paul says there is neither bond nor free, still by giving separate commands to the bond and free, he makes a distinction.[185] Likewise, Paul says there is neither male nor female, yet elsewhere he gives gender-specific commands respective to their unique roles as male and female.

Apart from specific governing and teaching roles restricted to men in the church, the Bible encourages certain ministries for mature and godly women. Women are not even denied the spiritual gift of teaching when in the proper context of teaching other women and their children: "The aged women likewise, that they be in behavior as becometh holiness, not false accusers, not given to much wine, teachers of good things; That they may teach the young women to be sober, to love their husbands, to love their children, To be discreet, chaste, keepers at home, good, obedient to their own husbands, that the word of God be not blasphemed" (Titus 2:3-5). We know that Timothy's mother Eunice and grandmother Lois passed on their faith in God to Timothy and instructed him in his youth (2 Timothy 1:5). Because of these very influential roles of Timothy's mother and grandmother, he knew the Holy Scriptures from his childhood (2 Timothy 3:15).

But the governing authorities over the entire church assembly are reserved for men (1 Timothy 3:2,12; Titus 1:6). When the Emergent feminists talk about equality, however, they mean to say that there are no unique leadership roles for men in church or in marriage. It is worthy of

---

184 Paul clearly put a unique difference between Jews and Gentiles when he wrote, "I say then, Have they stumbled that they should fall? God forbid: but rather through their fall salvation is come unto the Gentiles, for to provoke them to jealousy. Now if the fall of them be the riches of the world, and the diminishing of them the riches of the Gentiles; how much more their fulness?" (Romans 11:11,12).

185 Ephesians 6:5-9 addresses both *bond* and *free* along with their different obligations in relation to each other: "Servants, be obedient to them that are your masters according to the flesh, with fear and trembling, in singleness of your heart, as unto Christ; Not with eyeservice, as menpleasers; but as the servants of Christ, doing the will of God from the heart; With good will doing service, as to the Lord, and not to men: Knowing that whatsoever good thing any man doeth, the same shall he receive of the Lord, whether he be bond or free. And, ye masters, do the same things unto them, forbearing threatening: knowing that your Master also is in heaven; neither is there respect of persons with him."

note that without virtuous women there would be no qualified elders according to 1 Timothy 3:11 which says deacons' wives must be "grave, not slanderers, sober, faithful in all things."

Nadia Bolz-Weber is one influential woman who often teaches at Emergent Church events. She is the pastor and founder of the Denver-based church, the House for All Sinners and Saints. Her spiritual memoir is *Pastrix: The Cranky, Beautiful Faith of a Sinner and Saint*. She admits that she is a lousy candidate for a pastor. In addition to being a woman, she says, "I swear like a truck driver. I'm covered in tattoos, and I'm kind of selfish. Nothing about me says 'Lutheran pastor.'"[186] By her own admission, she would disqualify her own husband from being a pastor, let alone herself.

Stan Grenz questions which texts carry hermeneutical priority, "the egalitarian principle in Galatians 3:28," or "those passages which seem to place limitations on the service of women" such as 1 Corinthians 11:3-16, 14:34-35 and 1 Timothy 2:11-15.[187] In order to ask this question, Grenz must assume that Galatians 3:28 and those passages which place limitations on the ministries of women are contradictory so that one or the other must be given priority over the other. However, this is an invalid assumption. When we consider that "all scripture is given inspiration of God," we must assume that these texts are complimentary and not contradictory. The most reasonable way to reconcile these passages is to admit that Galatians 3:28 is not intended to address gender *roles*, but gender *equality*. Women have an equality with men in nature and salvation, but their roles in the church, in the home, and in society differ.

While the New Testament affirms the authority of husbands over their wives, fathers and mothers over their children, and male ministers over the congregation, *this order does not mean children are inferior to adults or that women are inferior to men.* In fact, women and children have a greater intrinsic value than men. This is the reason men will risk their lives to save women and children. Children have the most intrinsic value in a family, but they have no authority. The feminists view

---

186 Nadia Bolz-Weber quoted in Elliott Nesch, dir. *The Real Roots of the Emergent Church,* Holy Bible Prophecy, 2014.
187 Stanley Grenz. *Women in the Church: A Biblical Theology of Women in Ministry* (Downers Grove, IL: InterVarsity Press, 1995) 106, 107.

authority as a privilege rather than a *responsibility.*

God has ordained that men have greater authority and responsibility in leadership than women and children, but this status does not mean they are spiritually superior to them. On the contrary, while God commands subjection to male ministers, fathers, and parents, all people alike may be accepted by God if they fear Him and keep His commandments (See Acts 10:34,35). The early Christian Lactantius (250-325 AD) helps us understand the context of "neither male nor female" in Galatians 3:28:

> In God's sight, no one is a slave; no one is a master. Since we all have the same Father, we are all equally His children. No one is poor in God's sight except the one lacking in justice. No one is rich except the one with an abundance of virtues. . . . The reason why neither the Romans nor the Greeks could possess justice was that they had so many class distinctions. The rich and the poor. The powerful and the lowly. The highest authority of kings, and the common individual. . . . However, someone may say, "Isn't it true that among Christians some are poor and others are rich? Some are masters and others are servants? Isn't there some distinction between persons?" But there is none. In fact, the very reason we call each other brothers is that we believe we are all equal. . . . Although the physical circumstances of Christian lives may differ, we view no persons as servants. Instead, we speak of them—and treat them—as brothers in spirit and as fellow-servants of Christ.[188]

While Emergents and feminists may claim that the church's position on women was out of contempt for women or based on cultural norms, the writings of the early Christians tell us otherwise. We must assume the credibility of the biblical writers and understand that there are very natural and reasonable ways to reconcile the spiritual equality of those in Christ (Galatians 3:28) with obedience to the clear gender-

---

188 Lanctantius, *ANF,* 7.150, 151 in Bercot, *A Dictionary of Early Christian Beliefs,* 236.

specific commands of the New Testament, even if they go against the grain of our culture. So long as we allow culture to trump the Bible, women will be in authoritative roles which the Christian tradition prohibits. For instance, Emergent author and "pastor" Nadia Bolz-Weber says, "Any authority I have in my church actually comes from the people who are saying, 'We're going to allow you to hold an office for us.'" She continues, "The only reason I represent that office is because people have allowed me to. . . . As soon as they don't, I won't have it anymore."[189] This is a question of authority. She may be allowed by her people to hold an office of church authority but she is forbidden by the Word of God.

Silencing Recent Biblical Scholarship

There is reasonable debate within responsible Christian interpretation as to whether the New Testament gender-specific commands concerning women merely restrict them from teaching or also restrict them from speaking in the church. I believe Scripture supports the latter position. Nevertheless, Emergence has totally embraced the feminist agenda (sometimes with the exception of the liberal view of abortion). In a chapter entitled "Women in Ministry," in *Adventures in Missing the Point*, Tony Campolo makes his case for "Christian" feminism. He begins with 1 Timothy 2:11-12 which states: "Let the woman learn in silence with all subjection. But I suffer not a woman to teach, nor to usurp authority over the man, but to be in silence." Campolo accredits his feminist defense to recent evangelical scholarship. He explains:

> Women in the early church were abusing their newfound Christian freedom. The realization that in Christ there was neither male nor female (Galatians 3:28) and that before God women stood as equals with men—these new truths carried them into uncharitable and even shocking excesses. Even some evangelical scholars contend that that these women, emancipated by their new status in Christ, were standing up in church

---

[189] "Voices of the Emerging Church: The Wild Goose Festival 2011," vimeo video, posted by "OdysseyNetworks," http://vimeo.com/31155766.

meetings and lecturing their husbands about their behavior.[190]

He also says that this same supposed female emancipation in Christ is what Paul had in mind in 1 Corinthians 14:35: "And if they will learn any thing, let them ask their husbands at home: for it is a shame for women to speak in the church." Campolo essentially dismisses all verses that create a distinction in female roles because of recent scholarship which concludes that women were abusing their liberty in Christ. In other words, he has chosen to take scholars' words over the Bible's instruction when the Bible makes no indication that disruptive women were the cause of these commands. If this were the case, it would seem more likely that Paul would have exhorted the women how to act in an orderly way and forbid disorderly speech, but instead he forbids all speech from women. Paul himself does not indicate that disorderly women are the cause of this command, but God's Law. He says, "Let your women keep silence in the churches: for it is not permitted unto them to speak; but they are commanded to be under obedience, as also saith the law" (1 Corinthians 14:34). "The Law" is probably a reference to Genesis 3:16, specifically when God says to Eve, "Thy desire shall be to thy husband, and he shall rule over thee." Part of the curse is a woman's desire to rule over her husband. Paul's reasoning for women to keep silence in the churches has to do with women being submissive to their husband as God told Eve that Adam would rule over her. But Paul says nothing about disruptive women abusing their liberty. He is appealing to God's moral principles of subjection and order, not disorderly women. Again, Paul points to the Genesis creation account in 1 Timothy 2 when he says his reasoning for women not to teach men is that "Adam was formed first, then Eve" (1 Timothy 2:13). Paul finds something in females speakers or teachers in Church that would violate divine family order.

Not only is 1 Corinthians itself lacking any contextual evidence in support of this claim of unruly women being the cause for Paul's teachings, but there are also no historical facts to support it either. In the immediate context of judging prophecies (1 Corinthians 14:27-31), Paul

---

190 Campolo and McLaren, *Adventures in Missing the Point,* 145.

is making these commands concerning female conduct and concludes, "And if they will learn any thing, let them ask their husbands at home: for it is a shame for women to speak in the church" (1 Corinthians 14:35) which is is also consistent with 1 Timothy 2:12.

Campolo agrees with female emancipation theory wholeheartedly by saying that "the subservience of women created by the sin of the first couple (Genesis 3:16) was abolished at the crucifixion."[191] In Genesis 3:16, God told Eve, "I will greatly multiply thy sorrow and thy conception; in sorrow thou shalt bring forth children; and thy desire shall be to thy husband, and he shall rule over thee." But Eve's subservience to her husband was a part of God's order for male headship. Paul even quotes from Genesis 2 in order to establish male headship in the church. Even *after* the crucifixion, Paul says, "Let the woman learn in silence with all subjection. But I suffer not a woman to teach, nor to usurp authority over the man, but to be in silence. *For Adam was first formed, then Eve. And Adam was not deceived, but the woman being deceived was in the transgression.* Notwithstanding she shall be saved in childbearing, if they continue in faith and charity and holiness with sobriety" (1 Timothy 2:11-15). Paul not only appeals to the woman being deceived but also Adam being formed first, so that women are to be in subjection. If the Bible is in fact the Word of God, these are not only Paul's interpretations of the Genesis creation account, but they are also the Holy Spirit's interpretations and revelations of His own word.

Postmodern Emergents consider a woman's subjection as humiliating and politically incorrect. But the Bible speaks of a woman's subjection as a virtuous. Postmodern feminists cringe at the thought of Sarah calling her husband Abraham "lord," but the Bible speaks very highly of women after this manner. The Apostle Peter says, "Likewise, ye wives, be in subjection to your own husbands; that, if any obey not the word, they also may without the word be won by the conversation of the wives; While they behold your chaste conversation coupled with fear. . . . Even as Sara obeyed Abraham, calling him lord: whose daughters ye are, as long as ye do well, and are not afraid with any amazement" (1 Peter 3:1,2-6). A woman's submission to her husband is as important as her submission to the Lord. They are exhorted, "Wives, submit yourselves

---

191   Ibid., 148.

unto your own husbands, *as unto the Lord*" (Ephesians 5:22). Paul did not say, "Submit to your husband as unto the devil," that is, a woman should not submit to wickedness. Clement of Alexandria (195 AD) said,

> The wise woman, then, will first choose to persuade her husband to be her associate in what is conducive to happiness. And should that be found impracticable, let her by herself earnestly aim at virtue, gaining her husband's consent in everything, so as never to do anything against his will, with exception of what is reckoned as contributing to virtue and salvation.[192]

It is a sobering danger to favor recent scholarship over the Word of God when Paul says, "Let him acknowledge that the things that I write unto you *are the commandments of the Lord*" (1 Corinthians 14:37). Are we to take the opinion of recent scholarship over the Apostle Paul who said, "*I do not permit* a woman to teach" (1 Timothy 2:12, NKJV)? If Paul the Apostle followed this general principle in planting churches, then who are we to change it? Paul knew more about following Jesus than us because he was sent by Him as an apostle, so we ought to trust His judgment.

Unable to Resist the Culture of Our Day

Another way Emergents argue for feminism is by making all those applicable verses irrelevant by blaming patriarchal culture. While Campolo believes that the Old Testament is patriarchal, he does not believe the New Testament to be patriarchal. He writes of theologians who, "from a careful study of the Scriptures," concluded that "the apostle meant to prohibit women from preaching only in times and places where female leadership would scandalize the church in the eyes of society."[193] When portions of the Bible are dismissed as culturally irrelevant, how can we know which biblical teachings are to be obeyed today? All of Scripture becomes up for grabs and all of its authority is undermined by the culture.

---

192 Clement of Alexandria, *Ante-Nicene Fathers*, volume 2, 432.
193 Campolo, *Adventures in Missing the Point,* 146.

Brian McLaren uses the same argument by asking that if Paul were in our culture, would the Apostle "affirm women in leadership rather than restrict them?"[194] McLaren argues:

> If you want to read 1 Corinthians chapters 11-14 looking simply for propositions about the role of women in the church, you'll find them. The case is open and shut, with the result that you'll require women to be silent in church. But if you ask the more sophisticated question, what is God doing missionally in this passage? the outcome is less clear, but much more interesting . . . A missional reading of this passage reveals that St. Paul is seeking to live out the gospel in the framework of Corinthian culture—and this requires the voluntary relinquishing of certain freedoms in order to avoid cultural offense for the sake of the gospel. . . . we might decide that requiring women to be silent in church would be exactly the wrong thing to do in a culture like ours.[195]

However, when we study the Roman culture in which Paul was writing to the church, we find that it was actually much like our own culture. In reality, Paul's commands to the church regarding women were radically counter-cultural. So the apostles were not simply reinforcing the attitudes of their time concerning women, as Emergents argue, but were going against the roles of women in religion and society. While women couldn't hold political office or serve in the military in Roman society, women were just as engaged in business as men,[196] they played a crucial role in the official religion of Rome,[197] and they took great care for their outer appearance and adornment.[198] Therefore, the apostles' commands to the Gentile churches were just as radically counter-cultural then as they are today.

---

194 Ibid., 151.
195 Ibid., 83, 84.
196 See Gaston Boissier, *Cicero and His Friends: A Study of Roman Society in the Time of Caesar,* trans. Adnah David Jones (London: A.D. Innes, 1897), 96.
197 See Marccus Minucius Felix, *Octavius,* chapter 24.
198 See Janine Assa, *The Great Roman Ladies* (New York, 1960), 65, 67.

In spite of these Roman cultural norms, the early Christian Clement of Rome (96 AD) said,

> Let [women] show forth the sincere disposition of meekness; let them make manifest the command which they have of their tongue, by their silence; let them display their love, not by preferring one to another, but by showing equal affection to all that piously fear God.[199]

But this does not mean that Clement of Rome had a degrading view of women. He also said:

> Many women, also, being strengthened by the grace of God, have performed numerous manly exploits. The blessed Judith, when her city was besieged, asked the elders for permission to go forth into the camp of the strangers, . . . and the Lord delivered Holofernes into the hands of a woman. Esther also, being perfect in faith, exposed herself to no less danger, in order to deliver the twelve tribes of Israel from impending destruction.[200]

Just as the early church resisted Roman culture and its views on women, the church today has the same power and grace to resist postmodern culture and obey Christ. For example, early Christian Tertullian (198 AD) wrote, "It is not permitted to a woman to speak in the church, nor to teach, baptize, offer, or to claim to herself a lot in any manly function, not to mention the priestly office."[201] Yet the female practices of Tertullian's culture were just the opposite:

> I must not omit an account of the conduct also of the heretics – how frivolous it is, how worldly, how merely human, without seriousness, without authority, without

199 Clement of Rome, *Ante-Nicene Fathers,* volume 1, 11.
200 Clement of Rome, *Ante-Nicene Fathers,* volume 1, 20.
201 Tertullian, *ANF*, 4.33 in Bercot, *A Dictionary of Early Christian Beliefs,* 694.

discipline, as suits their creed. . . . The very women of these heretics, how wanton they are! For they are bold enough to teach, to dispute, to enact exorcisms, to undertake cures – it may be even to baptize.[202]

Thus, concerning gender roles, the early Christians were faced with the same cultural challenges as we are. But they maintained a radical Christian counter-culture based upon the Bible. It was the heretics who promoted and allowed female teachers.

Was the early church following *Jewish* culture even though it didn't follow Roman culture? The vast majority of believers in the churches to which Paul was writing were Gentiles. If Paul were following Brian McLaren's "missional" reasonings, he wouldn't have commanded anything counter-cultural whether it was Jewish or not. But we know that Paul, for the most part, wasn't encouraging Jewish culture upon these Gentile Christians because they didn't keep Sabbath, practice circumcision, follow Jewish dietary restrictions, observe Jewish feasts, or follow other Jewish customs.[203] In fact, much of what Paul commanded went against the existing Jewish and Roman cultures. These were not existing Jewish or Roman customs, but Paul said these were the "ordinances" that *he* delivered to them as an apostle of Christ.

Again, Paul has made these commands not because he found himself within a patriarchal culture. Instead, he instructed women in this manner because it is taught in God's creation (1 Timothy 2:12-15) and God's Law (1 Corinthians 14:34). A postmodern Paul would say the same because time and place are irrelevant to God's principle of submission and authority. McLaren is very bold when he suggests that there is a "better way" to treat our sisters in Christ than what the Scriptures declare. This "better way" would include female pastors, female elders, and female teachers according to McLaren.[204] But aren't the Scriptures the best way?

---

202 Tertullian, *Ante-Nicene Fathers,* volume 3, 263.
203 Cf. Acts 15:1-20; Romans 14:1-5; Colossians 2:16,17; Galatians 2:3; 4:9-11. 1 Corinthians 11:2-16 which commanded the veiling for women may have already existed in Jewish culture (Numbers 5:18). See also David Bercot, *Will the Real Heretics Please Stand Up,* 3rd ed. (Amberson, PA, 1989), 36-38.
204 Campolo and McLaren, *Adventures in Missing the Point,* 152.

New Christians, like the ancient heretics, go to great lengths in their quest to exalt women as leaders and teachers over men. Campolo cites Philippians 4:2-3 and says "Paul acknowledged the women Euodias and Syntyche as leaders and cofounders of that church."[205] Euodias and Syntyche are not described as leaders or cofounders of the church, but Paul merely exhorts them to "be of the same mind in the Lord" (Philippians 4:2). Campolo makes mention of the four daughters of Philip who, he says, became "preachers" (Acts 21:9).[206] Again, Campolo takes advantage of our modern-day conception of a "preacher" as a man that preaches or teaches the congregation in church gatherings. The four daughters of Philip were not preachers, but the historian Luke records that they were "virgins, which did prophesy" (Acts 21:9). Nevertheless, when Paul and Luke stayed in Philip's house in the company of his four daughter prophetesses, it is interesting that God sent a man by the name of Agabus to deliver a prophesy to Paul rather than prophesying through Philip's daughters (Acts 21:10-12).

In Romans 16:7, Campolo says that Junias "whom he recognizes as an apostle" is actually a mistranslation of the feminine name Junia which is also translated Julia.[207] He is correct about the name Junia (as it is translated in the KJV) being a woman, but Paul did not recognize her as an apostle as Campolo says. Paul says that she was "*of note among the apostles*" (Romans 16:7). This is a huge difference! She was just a Christian woman at Rome mentioned by Paul as one of his kinsfolk and fellow prisoners who was in Christ before him. She did not have any leadership role or anything of the sort as Campolo would have us to believe.

Emasculating the Bible

The logical conclusion for Emergents on this issue is that women would inevitably rule over and lead men, contrary to God's order. A leadership trainer for postmodern female evangelicals, Sally Morgenthaler, writes of men looking to women "as their own leaders,

---

205 Campolo, *Adventures in Missing the Point,* 148.
206 Ibid.
207 Ibid., 149.

mentors, and guides."[208] She also says:

> Yet what happens when women begin to release their voices? They begin to understand just how well they are wired to lead in the new "flattened" landscape. . . Female Christ-followers who possess true leadership skills do not need to lead because it is politically correct. Neither do they need to lead to assuage what is most often a millimeter-thin veneer of male guilt. Women with leadership abilities need to lead because, more often than not, they get this new world and they get it really well.[209]

The fact that the Emergent Church is allowing women to rule over them is another evidence of their drift into liberalism. Rather than submitting to the lordship of Jesus and His word, they have submitted to women which is a sure sign of rebellion from God's natural order. The prophet Isaiah mentions that women ruling over a people is a characteristic of God's judgment. In the same way, women ruling over the church in leadership and teaching roles that God has reserved for men is a sign of error: "As for my people, children are their oppressors, and women rule over them. O my people, they which lead thee cause thee to err, and destroy the way of thy paths" (Isaiah 3:12).

One result of this feminist undermining of biblical authority is the dislike of anything uniquely masculine. For example, this would include calling God a "she" rather than "He." Doug Pagitt refers to the Bible as "her."[210] On Twitter, Tony Jones calls the Holy Spirit a "she" while quoting from a U2 song. Jones writes, "Singing 'She Moves' about the Holy Spirit at Solomon's Porch."[211] The lead U2 singer and Emergent pop icon Bono also says, "I've always believed that the spirit is a feminine thing."[212] But nowhere is the Holy Spirit called "she" in the

---

208 Sally Morgenthaler, "Leadership in a Flattened World," in *An Emergent Manifesto of Hope,* eds. Jones and Pagitt, 188.

209 Ibid., 187.

210 Pagitt, *Preaching Re-imagined*, 44.

211 Tony Jones, Twitter post, October 4, 2009, 3:30pm, http://twitter.com/jonestony/status/4613292313.

212 Christian Scharen *One Step Closer: Why U2 Matters to Those Seeking God*

Bible. In fact, repeatedly Jesus referred to the Holy Spirit as masculine. Jesus said, "Howbeit when *he*, the Spirit of truth, is come, *he* will guide you into all truth: for *he* shall not speak of *himself*; but whatsoever *he* shall hear, that shall *he* speak: and *he* will shew you things to come. *He* shall glorify me: for *he* shall receive of mine, and shall shew it unto you" (John 16:13,14).

The book *Christianity After Religion: The End of Church and the Birth of a New Spiritual Awakening* is hailed by Emergents like Rob Bell, Richard Rohr, Phyllis Tickle and Shane Claiborne. The author Diana Butler Bass says, "We experienced Jesus as our friend and daringly prayed to God who was our Mother."[213] Likewise, Tony Jones says, *"God changes. Yes She does."*[214] Though the Bible contains feminine metaphors to describe God's activity, it never uses feminine nouns to describe God Himself. God will always be our Father. However, this feminist spirit refuses to submit to male authority, specifically the authority of our Father in heaven.

Nadia Bolz-Weber opposes the exclusive male pronouns for God such as praying to "Father God." She said, "I have struggled with what that God looks like. I was told that God was a man, for instance." She then repeated a quote from Mary Daly: "If God is male, then the male is God." She continued, "Whenever you attribute a human characteristic to God that some people have and some people don't, it becomes problematic."[215] Her criticism goes directly against Jesus because Jesus never spoke of God in female terms. The Lord spoke of God as Father and uses male pronouns such as he, his, him, and himself to speak of the Father: "And the *Father himself*, which hath sent me, hath borne witness of me. Ye have neither heard *his* voice at any time, nor seen *his* shape" (John 5:37); And *he* that sent me is with me: the *Father* hath not left me alone; for I do always those things that please *him*" (John 8:29); "If ye

---

(Grand Rapids, MI: Brazos Press), 52.
213 Diana Butler Bass. *Christianity After Religion: The End of Church and the Birth of a New Spiritual Awakening* (New York, NY: Harper Collins, 2012), 218.
214 Tony Jones, "Doctrine DOES Change," Theoblogy, October 20, 2014, http://www.patheos.com/blogs/tonyjones/2014/10/20/doctrine-does-change/#more-10203
215 Nadia Bolz-Weber quoted in Elliott Nesch, dir. *The Real Roots of the Emergent Church,* Holy Bible Prophecy, 2014.

keep my commandments, ye shall abide in my love; even as I have kept my *Father's* commandments, and abide in *his* love" (John 15:10).

Modesty or Manly?

A final result of Emergent feminism is the approval of homosexuality. Feminism is a misnomer for this movement because it actually seeks to turn women into men by erasing the distinctions between God's unique and proper roles for men and women in the family and in the church. This uncharitably emasculates God's men by subjecting them to female authorities which were never meant to have that responsibility. Likewise, women embrace the appearances of men in their manners and dress when they assume positions of authority which God has reserved for men.

Incidentally, Emergent female pastor Nadia Bolz-Weber appears in public with cropped and moussed hair, hipster glasses, skin-tight jeans, a tight black tank top, and colorful tattoos exposed on her arms and chest. Not only is her appearance a violation of biblical modesty, but also very manly for a woman. She should be ashamed not only for her manliness, but also her immodesty.

The apostles Peter and Paul both exhorted Christian women to be modestly clothed: "In like manner also, that women adorn themselves in modest apparel, with shamefacedness and sobriety; not with broided hair, or gold, or pearls, or costly array; But (which becometh women professing godliness) with good works" (1 Timothy 2:9,10); "Whose adorning let it not be that outward adorning of plaiting the hair, and of wearing of gold, or of putting on of apparel; But let it be the hidden man of the heart, in that which is not corruptible, even the ornament of a meek and quiet spirit, which is in the sight of God of great price" (1 Peter 3:3,4).

Christian women should take modesty very seriously. Does your apparel provoke others to lust? In the Sermon on the Mount Jesus taught, "Whosoever looketh on a woman to lust after her hath committed adultery with her already in his heart" (Matthew 5:28). While this is primarily a challenge for each of us individually to control our thoughts, we must also recognize the responsibility we have not to put a temptation before others. A woman dressing in tight fitting or low cut attire causes weak men to stumble. Of course we can't fully control if others choose to lust but we can avoid unnecessarily presenting temptation to them. You cannot control if others look upon you with lust, but you can control the way you dress.

Men and women differ profoundly, in far more ways than are usually observable. When the Scriptures speak of adornment, modesty, vanity and enticement, they refer to women (1 Timothy 2:9,10; 1 Peter 3:3,4). When they speak of adultery through visual lust, they refer to men (Matthew 5:28). In a natural, carnal state, women are inclined to display themselves, men to leer at them: women to entice, men to pursue. These principles can also be observed through the workings of human society with regard to advertising, commerce, art, media, and fashion.

Every aspect of a woman attracts a man: her voice, her relative weakness, her hair, her stride, texture of skin, dependence, posture and most obviously her anatomy. Most of these attractions are easily governed and kept in check by a godly man, ruling his own spirit well. If a man of God is in the presence of a woman who is dressed in a manner that obscures the dimension and detail of her physical form, it is a reasonable expectation that he can freely interact with her in all purity of thought and attention, not withstanding the feminine pleasantness of her presence. However, if in the same circumstance of Christians interaction, she is dressed in a manner that displays and emphasizes the particular nature of her physical features, the Christian man becomes horrified and doomed by the inescapable sight.

Without the component of charity, modesty in clothing can become an ill-defined affectation of religious tradition and arbitrary judgment, or on the other hand, a careless conformity to worldly fashion, without regard or awareness of its effect. However, with simple and unalloyed charity as her guide and goal, biblical modesty suddenly becomes consistent, rational, simple, and practical for a godly Christian woman. Jesus said, "Thou shalt love thy neighbour as thyself" (Matthew 22:39); "All things whatsoever ye would that men should do to you, do ye even so to them: for this is the law and the prophets" (Matthew 7:12). So a godly Christian woman should dress and behave exactly as they would want themselves to, if they were a Christian man seeking after righteousness.

Dressing modestly is no more complicated or demanding than simply being charitable, and dressing the way you would want you to, if you were a godly man trying to be pure in heart. There are a few principles to guide us in charitable and biblical modesty.

First of all, God will never judge a woman for being *too modest.* If a Christian sister can be *more modest,* then she is probably not abiding in the biblical ideal of modesty. For example, clothing that covers the body is *more modest* than being uncovered and exposed. Obviously, longer sleeves are more modest than short sleeves and longer skirts are more modest than short skirts.

Secondly, there is immodest clothing that emphasizes the particular nature of a woman's shape and physical features. In other words, a woman may be completely covered, yet she is still immodest because her clothing is tight and form-fitting. Such clothing does not conceal her form. Even though she is covered, there is nothing left to the imagination about her physical features. Loose and relaxed clothing is *more modest* than tight and form-fitting apparel. Clothing is meant to conceal the body, not reveal the body. Clement of Alexandria (195 AD) wrote,

> For these superfluous and diaphanous materials are the proof of a weak mind, covering as they do the shame of the body with a slender veil. For luxurious clothing, which cannot conceal the shape of the body, is no more a covering. For such clothing, falling close to the body, takes its form more easily, and adhering as it were to the flesh, receives its shape, and marks out the woman's figure, so that the whole make of the body is visible to spectators, though not seeing the body itself.[216]

Thirdly, modest clothing is plain and simple. A woman who is totally covered with loose clothing may still be immodest because her clothing is luxurious, elaborate, decorative, or attractive. Jesus said, "Behold, they which are gorgeously apparelled, and live delicately, are in kings' courts" (Luke 7:25). Gorgeous and decorative clothing or jewelry

---

216 Clement of Alexandria, *Ante-Nicene Fathers,* volume 2, 265.

draws attention rather than deters the attention of others. Wearing costly apparel is also uncharitable to the poor, the widows and the orphans who are without basic clothing. Therefore, unadorned is *more modest* than adorned. Cyprian (250 AD) wrote,

> The characteristics of ornaments, and of garments, and the allurements of beauty, are not fitting for any but prostitutes and immodest women; and the dress of none is more precious than of those whose modesty is lowly. Thus in the Holy Scriptures, by which the Lord wished us to be both instructed and admonished, the harlot city is described more beautifully arrayed and adorned, and with her ornaments; and the rather on account of those very ornaments about to perish. "And there came," it is said, "one of the seven angels, which had the seven phials [vials], and talked with me, saying, Come hither, I will show you the judgment of the great whore, that sits upon many waters, with whom the kings of the earth have committed fornication. And he carried me away in spirit; and I saw a woman sit upon a beast, and that woman was arrayed in a purple and scarlet mantle, and was adorned with gold, and precious stones, and pearls, having a golden cup in her hand, full of curses, and filthiness, and fornication of the whole earth." Let chaste and modest virgins avoid the dress of the unchaste, the manners of the immodest, the ensigns of brothels, the ornaments of harlots.[217]

Let a holy woman, if naturally beautiful, give none occasion for carnal appetite. Paul said, "For, brethren, ye have been called unto liberty; only use not liberty for an occasion to the flesh, but by love serve one another" (Galatians 5:13). Certainly, if even she be so, she ought not to set off (her beauty), but even to obscure it. Cyprian (250 AD) said,

> For the rest, if you dress your hair sumptuously, and

---

217 Cyprian, *Ante-Nicene Fathers,* volume 5, 433.

walk so as to draw attention in public, and attract the eyes of youth upon you, and draw the sighs of young men after you, nourish the lust of concupiscence, and inflame the fuel of sighs, so that, although you yourself perish not, yet you cause others to perish, and offer yourself, as it were, a sword or poison to the spectators; you cannot be excused on the pretense that you are chaste and modest in mind. Your shameful dress and immodest ornament accuse you; nor can you be counted now among Christ's maidens and virgins, since you live in such a manner as to make yourselves objects of desire.[218]

The early Christians disdained the use of cosmetics because of their desire to be modest.[219] How much more should the Emergent

---

218 Cyprian, *Ante-Nicene Fathers,* volume 5, 432.

219 "Unawares the poor wretches destroy their own beauty, by the introduction of what is spurious. At the dawn of day, mangling, racking, and plastering themselves over with certain compositions, they chill the skin, furrow the flesh with poisons, and with curiously prepared washes, thus blighting their own beauty. Wherefore they are seen to be yellow from the use of cosmetics, and susceptible to disease, their flesh, which has been shaded with poisons, being now in a melting state. So they dishonor the Creator of men, as if the beauty given by Him were nothing worth. As you might expect, they become lazy in housekeeping, sitting like painted things to be looked at, not as if made for domestic economy." Clement of Alexandria, *Ante-Nicene Fathers* volume 2, 272; "But why are we a (source of) danger to our neighbor? Why do we import concupiscence into our neighbor? ...Are we to paint ourselves out that our neighbors may perish? Where, then, is (the command), "You shall love your neighbor as yourself"? Tertullian, *Ante-Nicene Fathers* volume 4, 19; "But are sincerity and truth preserved, when what is sincere is polluted by adulterous colors, and what is true is changed into a lie by the deceitful dyes of medicaments? Your Lord says, 'You canst not make one hair white or black;' and you, in order to overcome the word of your Lord, will be more mighty than He, and stain your hair with a daring endeavor and with profane contempt. With evil presage of the future, you make a beginning to yourself already of flame-colored hair; and sin (oh, wickedness!) with your head – that is, with the nobler part of your body! And although it is written of the Lord, 'His head and His hair were

Church be ashamed of tattoos? But the Emergent Church is unabashed about their "Christian" tattoos. Chris Seay, a pastor at the Ecclesia Church in Houston, Texas, "called on members to get permanent tattoos that would depict designs symbolizing the crucifixion and death of Jesus." The tattoos by church members were collectively part of an art exhibit for Lent, Stations on Skin. Leviticus 19:28, "Ye shall not make any cuttings in your flesh for the dead, nor print or tattoo any marks upon you: I am the Lord," is explained away by context. [220] Nadia Bolz-Weber waves a gift certificate for a free tattoo and says from the pulpit, "You ladies over 70 dig deep, because you know you want it!"[221]

I'm not trying to attack Nadia Bolz-Weber as an individual, but she is one of the most well-known female leaders in the Emergent Church. Her public appearance represents the sentiments of the movement as a whole. Modesty, shamefacedness, sobriety, meekness and quietness is hardly a description of Bolz-Weber. She is immodest, unashamed, assertive, loudmouthed and foulmouthed. One reporter for *The Washington Post* had the impression that Nadia was trying to show off her body. She observed,

> Her 6-foot-1 frame is plastered with tattoos, her arms are sculpted by competitive weightlifting and, to show it all off, this pastor is wearing a tight tank top and jeans. . . .
> In her body and her theology, Bolz-Weber represents a new, muscular form of liberal Christianity, one that merges the passion and life-changing fervor of evangelicalism with the commitment to inclusiveness

---

white like wool or snow,' you curse that whiteness and hate that hoariness which is like to the Lord's head." Cyprian, *Ante-Nicene Fathers* volume 5, 434.

220 Michael Gryboski, "Emergent Church Members Get Tattoos of Jesus' Death for Lent," *Christian Post,* February 24, 2012, http://www.christianpost.com/news/emergent-church-members-get-tattoos-of-jesus-death-for-lent-70258/

221 Michelle Boorstein, "Bolz-Weber's Liberal, Foulmouthed Articulation of Christianity Speaks to Fed-up Believers," *The Washington Post,* November 3, 2013, http://www.washingtonpost.com/local/bolz-webers-liberal-foulmouthed-articulation-of-christianity-speaks-to-fed-up-believers/2013/11/03/7139dc24-3cd3-11e3-a94f-b58017bfee6c_story.html

and social justice of mainline Protestantism. She's a tatted-up, foul-mouthed champion to people sick of being belittled as not Christian enough for the right or too Jesus-y for the left. . . . Bolz-Weber springs onstage to do a reading from her book, but first she addresses the language that's about to be unleashed on the pulpit: "I don't think church leaders should pretend to be something they're not."[222]

The confusion of God's gender roles inevitably contributes to the homosexual agenda. Romans 1:26,27 states, "For this cause God gave them up unto vile affections: for even their women did change the natural use into that which is against nature: And likewise also the men, leaving *the natural use of the woman*, burned in their lust one toward another; men with men working that which is unseemly, and receiving in themselves that recompense of their error which was meet." The "natural use" of women seems to be referring to a woman's "natural use" as a mother and keeper of the home. When women change their "natural use" of being mothers and keepers at home to that which is against nature, they take on the duties and appearances of men like Bolz-Weber. As a result of feminism, unregenerate men also leave the natural use of the women and burn in their lusts in homosexuality.

Women's Prayer Veils

Ironically, Tony Jones takes advantage of the fact that most churches today do not follow Paul's instructions about women wearing head coverings (which admittedly goes against the grain of modern culture). From this observation, he also dismisses the Scriptural prohibitions of homosexuality based on cultural relativism and non-literal biblical interpretation. Connecting feminism with homosexuality, Jones writes:

---

222 Michelle Boorstein, "Bolz-Weber's Liberal, Foulmouthed Articulation of Christianity Speaks to Fed-up Believers," *The Washington Post,* November 3, 2013, http://www.washingtonpost.com/local/bolz-webers-liberal-foulmouthed-articulation-of-christianity-speaks-to-fed-up-believers/2013/11/03/7139dc24-3cd3-11e3-a94f-b58017bfee6c_story.html

For years, I've had a common retort to those who oppose gay marriage on biblical grounds: Do you make women wear head coverings in church? That's because prohibitions of homosexuality and head coverings have about the same amount of biblical attestation. When I ask that question, my interlocutors most often pivot to arguments from natural law. That's because no one — NO ONE — is really a biblical literalist. We all live on the slippery, relativistic slope of biblical interpretation.[223]

I do not excuse those evangelical churches who are neglectful of veiling female members of their congregations. Even though a woman's head covering is religiously and politically incorrect, Paul said, "If any man think himself to be a prophet, or spiritual, let him acknowledge that the things that I write unto you *are the commandments of the Lord*" (1 Corinthians 14:37). It is a commandment of the Lord for women to veil their heads: "Every woman that prayeth or prophesieth with her head uncovered dishonoureth her head: for that is even all one as if she were shaven. For if the woman be not covered, let her also be shorn: but if it be a shame for a woman to be shorn or shaven, let her be covered" (1 Corinthians 11:5,6). If more professing Christian women obeyed the Lord's commandments on veiling their heads, then Jones would have no argument. The Bible says that women who don't veil their heads dishonor their husbands (1 Corinthians 11:4-5).

The refusal of professing Christian women to veil their heads is evidence that feminism has already crept into the Church. These evangelical women who disregard the veil are guilty of the same cultural compromise of which Emergents have been accused. Paul the Apostle said nothing about cultural reasons behind this commandment for a woman to be veiled. This was the reason: "For this cause ought the woman to have power on her head *because of the angels*" (1 Corinthians 11:10). It is because of the angels and headship that Christian women are instructed to wear head coverings, not culture. The primitive Christian

223 Tony Jones, "Fresh Website, Stale Theology," *Theoblogy,* July 19, 2013, http://www.patheos.com/blogs/tonyjones/2013/07/19/fresh-website-stale-theology/

Tertullian (198 AD) noted that the head covering had nothing to do with culture:

> Throughout Greece, and certain of its barbaric provinces, the majority of Churches keep their virgins covered. There are places, too, beneath this (African) sky, where this practice obtains; lest any ascribe the custom to Greek or barbarian Gentilehood. But I have proposed (as models) those Churches which were founded by apostles or apostolic men.[224]

As one of Tony Jones' interlocutors, I must point out that not only is homosexuality a violation of natural law, but Paul also appealed to natural law as justification for a woman's veil: "For as the woman is of the man, even so is the man also by the woman; but all things of God. Judge in yourselves: is it comely that a woman pray unto God uncovered? *Doth not even nature itself teach you*, that, if a man have long hair, it is a shame unto him? But if a woman have long hair, it is a glory to her: for her hair is given her for a covering" (1 Corinthians 11:12-15). The biblical cases *for* a woman's head covering and *against* homosexuality are both defended by natural law. The primitive Christian Tertullian (198 AD) made the same point:

> Demanding then a law of God, you have that common one prevailing all over the world, engraved on the natural tables to which the apostle too is wont to appeal, as when in respect of the woman's veil he says, "Does not even Nature teach you?" - as when to the Romans, affirming that the heathen do by nature those things which the law requires, he suggests both natural law and a law-revealing nature.[225]

A radical Christian counter-culture cannot be compromised by postmodernism. A sure way to resist the tide of postmodern feminism within the Church is the practice of veiling females. Regardless of the

---

224 Tertullian, *Ante-Nicene Fathers,* volume 4, 28.
225 Tertullian, *ANF*, volume 3, 96.

amount of biblical attestation for any given subject, Christians must read the Scriptures seriously and literally. The head covering is mentioned in one chapter of the New Testament (1 Corinthians 11), nevertheless it is a clear apostolic teaching. Head coverings should be encouraged and homosexual marriage should be forbidden because the Scriptures teach both, regardless of how often they are taught.

Tony Campolo cited 1 Corinthians 11:5 to suggest that "Paul acknowledged women as legitimate preachers when he advised them how to dress when they prophesy—which means preach."[226] What Camplolo failed to mention in his argument here is that the actual dress Paul advised the women to wear when praying or prophesying was the veil over their head which served as a symbol of her submission to her husband (1 Corinthians 11:3-17). Secondly, prophesying and preaching are not the same, especially in the way we understand preaching today. To prophesy is to speak forth by divine inspirations or revelations or to predict or to prophesy future events. These instructions must be viewed as complimentary (not contradictory) to other commands concerning women in the church. Paul's instructions for women praying and prophesying was a general exhortation, not to contradict his later commands in 1 Corinthians 14:34: "Let your women keep silence in the churches: for it is not permitted unto them to speak." 1 Corinthians 11:18 is Paul's transition from general instructions for women praying and prophesying to the order of church meetings: "For first of all, when ye come together in the church . . ." In other words, the instructions concerning women praying and prophesying with prayer veils over their heads (in less-formal circumstances) preceded Paul's commands about women being silent "when ye come together *in the church*."

---

226 Ibid., 148.

7

Queermergent

"Have ye not read, that he which made them at the beginning made them male and female, And said, For this cause shall a man leave father and mother, and shall cleave to his wife: and they twain shall be one flesh?"
– Jesus (Matthew 19:4,5)

While there are numerous examples within the Emergent trend of downplaying sin, let us focus on the particular view of their leadership concerning homosexuality, a controversial sin that will prove to be a dividing line in our time and culture for those who seek and stand for the truth in Jesus Christ.

An eclectic movement, the Emerging Church embraces a variety of positions on homosexuality within the Emerging Church. For instance, Peter Rollins and others will talk about the need to love homosexuals but remain gray on issues like homosexual marriage[227] Emergents like Rob Bell and Brian McLaren have been loving and supportive of homosexuals, but only recently "came out of the closet" with regard to their true stance on the issue.[228] Tony Jones believes homosexuals should

---

227 See Peter Rollins, "I do not bring peace but a sword," Peter Rollins, October 29, 2011, http://peterrollins.net/?p=1357.
228 In a Q&A session following "Still Painting," a live stream event July 24, 2012 from The Viper Room in West Hollywood, CA, Bell said, "Some people are gay. And you're our brothers. And you're our sisters. And we love you. . . . At

be given the same rights as heterosexuals including marriage, membership and leadership in the church. Shane Claiborne[229] will love and support homosexuals, but won't marry them.[230] As a whole, the Emergent Church movement has proven to be compromising on this issue.

As I stated earlier, some of the leaders' positions on homosexuality has "emerged" over the years. For instance, Brian McLaren in years past has been unclear about the issue. But as time

---

an early age, I was like, 'Some people are gay. And God loves them just like God loves me. And they're passionate disciples of Jesus just like I'm trying to be.'" http://www.submergingchurch.com/wp-content/uploads/2012/08/Bell.mov. In a video entitled "Interview Why Rob Bell Supports Gay Marriage," Bell states, "What we're seeing right now in this day is, I believe, God pulling us ahead into greater and greater affirmation and acceptance of our gay brothers and sisters, and pastors, and friends, and neighbors, and co-workers." YouTube video, posted by "OdysseyNetworks," March 20, 2013, http://www.youtube.com/watch?feature=endscreen&v=-q0iDaW6BnE&NR=1.

229 Shane Claiborne, founder of the Simple Way Community in Philadelphia and author of *The Irresistible Revolution* and *Jesus for President*, has also been found in the Emergent circle. Claiborne says he agrees with critics of the Emerging church but has been "merely guilty by association, and an association with something [he] could not even identify, much less align with." Claiborne made this defense because he has been labeled Emergent by his associations. He says, "I find the 'emerging church' language, at least the Emergent™ brand, utterly unhelpful." Claiborne adds, "While there are many voices who self-identify as 'emerging church' or 'emergent' whom I consider close friends and refreshing voices in the church, there are also folks who identify as such whose beliefs and practices, or lack thereof, I find very problematic." See Shane Claiborne. "The Emerging Church Brand: The Good, the Bad, and the Messy," *The Simple Way,* Aprkl 13, 2010, available: http://www.thesimpleway.org/index.php/resources/content/the-emerging-church-brand-the-good-the-bad-and-the-messy/. However, the Emergent folks with the most problematic beliefs and practices such as Brian McLaren, Rob Bell, Tony Campolo and others are those whom Claiborne has directly associated himself.

230 Claiborne says, "Personally, I would not be able to [marry a same-gendered couple] if I were a pastor, but I also don't have any shame in saying, 'I've got a pastor friend who would love to marry you.'" Jamie L. Manson, "Tainted Love: The Cost of Sojourners' Refusal to Take Sides on LGBT Issues," Religion Dispatches Magazine, May 14, 2011, available:

progressed, he has come more and more out of the closet. In 2005, when asked what he thought about gay marriage, McLaren replied, "You know what, the thing that breaks my heart is that there's no way I can answer it without hurting someone on either side."[231] McLaren also writes,

> Frankly, many of us don't know what we should think about homosexuality. We've heard all sides but no position has yet won our confidence so that we can say 'it seems good to the Holy Spirit and us.' That alienates us from both the liberals and conservatives who seem to know exactly what we should think. Even if we are convinced that all homosexual behavior is always sinful, we still want to treat gay and lesbian people with more dignity, gentleness, and respect than our colleagues do. If we think that there may actually be a legitimate context for some homosexual relationships, we know that the biblical arguments are nuanced and multilayered, and the pastoral ramifications are staggeringly complex. We aren't sure if or where lines are to be drawn, nor do we know how to enforce with fairness whatever lines are drawn.

> Perhaps we need a five-year moratorium on making pronouncements. In the meantime, we'll practice prayerful Christian dialogue, listening respectfully, disagreeing agreeably. When decisions need to be made, they'll be admittedly provisional. We'll keep our ears attuned to scholars in biblical studies, theology, ethics, psychology, genetics, sociology, and related fields. Then in five years, if we have clarity, we'll speak; if not, we'll set another five years for ongoing reflection. After all, many important issues in church history took centuries to figure out. Maybe this moratorium would help us

http://www.religiondispatches.org/archive/sexandgender/4605/tainted_love%3A_the_cost_of_sojourners'_refusal_to_take_sides_on_lgbt_issues/.
231 "The 25 Most Influential Evangelicals in America," Time, February 7, 2005, http://www.time.com/time/covers/1101050207/photoessay/17.html.

resist the "winds of doctrine" blowing furiously from the
left and right, so we can patiently wait for the wind of
the Spirit to set our course.[232]

By suggesting that gay marriage could be a possible worldview,
Emergents abandon the biblical worldview and cater to today's pagan
culture. Yes, homosexuals should be treated with more dignity,
gentleness and respect, but homosexual behavior is always sinful. There
is no need to have a conversation about this. If McLaren isn't sure where
the lines are to be drawn, he should consult the Scriptures. What we
"should think" about homosexuality is what God thinks:

- "Thou shalt not lie with mankind, as with womankind: it
  is abomination" (Leviticus 18:22).

- "If a man also lie with mankind, as he lieth with a
  woman, both of them have committed an abomination:
  they shall surely be put to death; their blood shall be
  upon them" (Leviticus 20:13).

- "There shall be no whore of the daughters of Israel, nor a
  sodomite of the sons of Israel" (Deuteronomy 23:17).

- "For this cause God gave them up unto vile affections:
  for even their women did change the natural use into that
  which is against nature: And likewise also the men,
  leaving the natural use of the woman, burned in their lust
  one toward another; men with men working that which is
  unseemly, and receiving in themselves that recompence
  of their error which was meet" (Romans 1:26-27).

- "Know ye not that the unrighteous shall not inherit the

---

232 "Brian McLaren on the Homosexual Question 4: McLaren's Response,"
Out of Ur, January 30, 2006, available:
http://blog.christianitytoday.com/outofur/archives/2006/01/brian_mclaren_3.htm
l.

kingdom of God? Be not deceived: neither fornicators, nor idolaters, nor adulterers, nor effeminate, nor abusers of themselves with mankind, Nor thieves, nor covetous, nor drunkards, nor revilers, nor extortioners, shall inherit the kingdom of God" (1 Corinthians 6:9,10).

- "But we know that the law is good, if a man use it lawfully; Knowing this, that the law is not made for a righteous man, but for the lawless and disobedient, for the ungodly and for sinners, for unholy and profane, for murderers of fathers and murderers of mothers, for manslayers, For whoremongers, for them that defile themselves with mankind, for menstealers, for liars, for perjured persons, and if there be any other thing that is contrary to sound doctrine; According to the glorious gospel of the blessed God, which was committed to my trust." (1 Timothy 1:8-11)

When Emergents like McLaren consider homosexuality as a possible valid lifestyle, they promote acceptance of it. Sure enough, over five years after McLaren exhorted the church to take a five-year moratorium, McLaren sided with the homosexual agenda. In 2012, McLaren led the commitment ceremony for the homosexual union of his own son with another man. The *New York Times* reported that "Trevor Douglas McLaren and Owen Patrick Ryan were married," and Brian McLaren "led a commitment ceremony with traditional Christian elements before family and friends."[233]

Tony Jones introduced Adele Sakler by saying, "Adele Sakler, whom I've known for a few years, has started yet another 'hyphenated' group within the emergent network-of-networks. She's calling it 'Queermergent,' and, as you might guess, it's focused on GLBTQ issues."[234] GLBTQ stands for gay, lesbian, bisexual, transgender and

---

233 "Trevor McLaren and Owen Ryan." New York Times, September 23, 2012, http://www.nytimes.com/2012/09/23/fashion/weddings/trevor-mclaren-owen-ryan-weddings.html?_r=5&.
234 Tony Jones, "Announcing Queermergent." Beliefnet. January, 2009, http://blog.beliefnet.com/tonyjones/2009/01/announcing-queermergent.html.

queer people. Sakler says attributes her beliefs and efforts to the Emergent leadership saying:

> In 1997 I moved to Los Angeles and began living a double life as a Christian and as a gay woman. I began to read Brian McLaren and found him writing things I had felt inside but was very afraid to express outwardly to anyone. In 2002 I went to Northern Ireland to do a DTS with YWAM. I met the great Peter Rollins and we developed a great friendship. His teachings and writings on postmodernism and Christianity radically shaped how I viewed my faith.[235]

How can these new Christians make such great compromise? Doug Pagitt attributes this change in Christian theology to culture and genetics:

> Issues of sexuality can be among the most complex and convoluted we need to deal with. It seems to me that the theology of our history does not deal sufficiently with these issues for our day. I do not mean this as a critique, but as an acknowledgement that our times are different. I do not mean that we are a more or less sexual culture, but one that knows more about the genetic, social and cultural issues surrounding sexuality and gender than any previous culture. Christianity will be impotent to lead a conversation on sexuality and gender if we do not boldly integrate our current understandings of humanity with our theology. This will require us to not only draw new conclusions about sexuality but will force us to consider new ways of being sexual.[236]

"I Was Born Gay"

---

235 Adele Sakler, "Why Queermergent?" Queermergent, January 15, 2009, http://queermergent.wordpress.com/2009/01/15/why-queermergent/.
236 Robert Webber, *Listening to the Beliefs of the Emerging Churches* (Grand Rapids: Zondervan. 2007), 140.

Today, many are teaching that homosexuality is genetically determined and is therefore no different than a person being born with white or black skin. Just as nobody chooses what color skin he or she will have at birth, so the Emerging Church teaches that nobody chooses to be gay, lesbian, bisexual or transgender. Thus, declaring homosexuality as no different than racial discrimination or segregation, they view it not a sin.

Dan Kimball devotes an entire chapter called "The Church is Homophobic" in his book *They Like Jesus but Not the Church.* He states:

> Quite honestly, and some people might get mad at me for saying this, I sometimes wish this [homosexuality] weren't a sin issue, because I have met gay people who are the most kind, loving, solid, and supportive people I have ever met. As I talk to them and hear their stories and get to know them, I come to understand that their sexual orientation isn't just something they can just turn off. Homosexual attraction is not something people simply choose to have, as is quite often erroneously taught from many pulpits.[237]

Again the problem of the Emerging Church is being unable to resist postmodern culture. Dan Kimball says that because homosexuality "is such a huge issue in our culture, and because all of the tension and discussion on this issue is over what the Bible says about it, we can no longer just regurgitate what we have been taught about homosexuality."[238] However, homosexuality, like feminism, is not unique to postmodern cultures, but was prevalent in Greco-Roman cultures where Christianity first flourished. For example, Aristides, a converted Greek philosopher of second century Athens, wrote one of the earliest Christian apologies. While he admits that "some polluted themselves by lying with males,"[239] he didn't allow his culture to prevent him from

237 Dan Kimball, *They Like Jesus But Not the Church* (Grand Rapids, MI: Zondervan, 2007), 138.
238 Ibid., 137.
239 Aristides, ANF, 9.269 in Bercot, A Dictionary of Early Christian Beliefs,

131

speaking against it. He said that the Greeks, "follow debased practices in intercourse with males, or with mothers, sisters, and daughters."[240] Aristides also called homosexuality a "monstrous impurity."[241] If Christians embrace the "monstrous impurity" of homosexuality as the new "Christians" of the Emerging Church are doing, then what will prevent them from also embracing incest and pederasty when society accepts these "debased practices" as acceptable also?

The early Christians were confronted with homosexuality *and* paederasty in their culture, yet they took an uncompromising stance on both. These second century Christians said:

> And any one who uses such persons, besides the godless and infamous and impure intercourse, may possibly be having intercourse with his own child, or relative, or brother. And there are some who prostitute even their own children and wives, and some are openly mutilated for the purpose of homosexuality.[242]

> The Greeks consider intercourse with a mother as unlawful, but this practice is esteemed most becoming by the Persian Magi; paederasty is condemned by the Barbarians, but by the Romans, who endeavour to collect herds of boys like grazing horses, it is honored with certain privileges.[243]

> (The pagans) do not abstain even from males, males with males committing shocking abominations, outraging all the noblest and comeliest bodies in all sorts of ways, so dishonoring the fair workmanship of God (for beauty on earth is not self-made, but sent hither by the hand and will of God), - these men, I say, revile us for the very

---

347.
240 Aristides, ANF, 9.279 in Bercot, A Dictionary of Early Christian Beliefs, 347.
241 Ibid.
242 Justin Martyr, *Ante-Nicene Fathers* volume 1, 172.
243 Tatian, *Ante-Nicene Fathers,* volume 2, 77.

things which they are conscious of themselves.[244]

Is it possible that the Emergent Church is unable to resist the culture of their day? Though Tony Campolo affirms that "same-gender eroticism [homosexual activity] is not a Christian lifestyle," he presents a powerless false Gospel message saying in a *Beliefnet* interview that

> the overwhelming proportion of the gay community that love Jesus, that go to church, that are deeply committed in spiritual things, try to change and can't change. And the Church acts as though they are just stubborn and unwilling, when in reality they can't change.[245]

Thus, if the Emergent Church is unwilling to admit that homosexuality is a moral choice, they must inevitably accept homosexual marriage. Brian McLaren does just this in exploring the possibility of gay marriage in his book *A New Kind of Christianity:* "[W]e can ask whether humans were made to fit into an absolute, unchanging institution called marriage, or whether marriage was created to help humans—perhaps including gay humans?—live wisely and well in this world."[246]

In generations past, not only was homosexuality commonly recognized as perversion within and without the Church, but terms like "gay Christian" or "queermergent" were inconceivable. But now, it is politically incorrect to condemn homosexuality because it is likened to discriminating against a person that had no choice in the matter. In this regard, those who do not support gay marriage are equated with racists who have no concern for equal rights and justice. These politically incorrect and conservative Christians are seen as denying homosexuals the fundamental human right to love. In fact, Emergent icon Bono stated, "My bottom line on any sexuality is that love is the most important thing.

---

244 Athenagoras, *Ante-Nicene Fathers,* volume 2, 147.
245 Laura Sheahan. "'Evangelical Christianity Has Been Hijacked': An Interview with Tony Campolo," Beliefnet, July, 2004, http://www.beliefnet.com/story/150/story_15052_1.html.
246 Brian McLaren, *A New Kind of Christianity* (New York, NY: HarperCollins Publishers, 2010), 176.

That love is it. Any way people want to love each other is OK by me. That's different from abuse, be it homosexual or heterosexual."[247]

According to the Emergent Church, if a person is born gay, then it is dehumanizing and alienating to exclude homosexuals from the Church. In an article called "How I Went from There to Here: Same Sex Marriage Blogalogue", Tony Jones wrote:

> And yet, all the time I could feel myself drifting toward acceptance that gay persons are fully human persons and should be afforded all of the cultural and ecclesial benefits that I am. ("Aha!" my critics will laugh derisively, "I knew he and his ilk were on a continuous leftward slide!")
>
> In any case, I now believe that GLBTQ [gay, lesbian, bisexual, transgender, and queer people] can live lives in accord with biblical Christianity (at least as much as any of us can!) and that their monogamy can and should be sanctioned and blessed by church and state.[248]

The Emergent voice is a far cry from the biblical truth. Thankfully, the first comment that was posted on Tony Jones' "Same Sex Marriage Blogalogue" was from a man who prior to becoming a Christian lived a homosexual lifestyle of which he repented. This man John Boyer shares his incredible testimony that demonstrates how mistaken Tony Jones is. John responded:

> I met the Lord Jesus Christ [four] years ago as a 30 [year] old gay man. For the first time in my life I felt Loved and Forgiven, He came into my heart and washed all my pain away. I ran hard and fast after this Jesus and

---

247 Adam Block. "Bono Bites Back," Mother Jones, May 1, 1989, http://www.motherjones.com/media/1989/05/bono-bites-back.
248 Tony Jones. "How I Went from There to Here: Same Sex Marriage Blogalogue," Beliefnet. November 19, 2008, http://blog.beliefnet.com/tonyjones/2008/11/same-sex-marriage-blogalogue-h.html.

He very quickly told me He did not want me to be gay or indulge in that lifestyle any longer. He told me "this is not who I created you to be." I had been gay my whole life, as far back as my memory goes I was attracted to the same-sex. I thought I was born like that. He showed me through His own eyes how disgusting these acts were, these things I did with my body as a gay man with other men. He let me know how much it grieved His Heart. From that day on I turned away from being gay, no longer wanting to hurt my God like that ever again. He showed me love like I never imagined was even possible to experience while alive here in this body! Our Lord Jesus Christ loves each and everyone of us, died for each and everyone of us, but is calling each and everyone of us out of darkness into His Marvelous Light. . . . I never thought I would be saying these things but I have found the truth and the truth has set me free from a life of sexual slavery. I pray that you will ask the Lord Jesus Christ to reveal to you the truth. Ask Him to make Himself real to you and convict you of your sin. You are deceived if you think He is ok with you living this way.[249]

Praise God for John's testimony of turning from his homosexual slavery by the powerful grace of God in Jesus Christ. The Bible speaks of those who have been washed and sanctified from their sinful lifestyles and entered into the Body of Jesus Christ: "And such were some of you: but ye are washed, but ye are sanctified, but ye are justified in the name of the Lord Jesus, and by the Spirit of our God" (1 Corinthians 6:11). Unfortunately, the moderator of the Emergent blog removed John's response to Tony Jones just days after I read it. Could it be that John's testimony was removed from the blog because he admittedly thought he was born gay but found God's grace to become a new creature in Christ?

---

249 John Boyer, January 21, 2009, comment on Tony Jones, "How I Went from There to Here: Same Sex Marriage Blogalogue," Beliefnet, November 19, 2008, http://blog.beliefnet.com/tonyjones/2008/11/same-sex-marriage-blogalogue-h.html.

John's personal testimony destroys the entire Emergent argument that people are born gay.

Even if homosexuality was genetically determined, it is no more morally acceptable than the sexual sins of lust, fornication or adultery. The Apostle Paul says, "all have sinned," (Romans 5:12) and describes how all humanity in Adam has inherited a sinful nature (Romans 5:12-21). Thus, people are going to have propensities toward sexual sin, whether it be heterosexual or homosexual, but God can give us a new nature in Jesus Christ.

But aside from the Bible's clear testimony that homosexuality is a moral choice, there is no scientific evidence in support of homosexuality being caused by genetics. The pro-gay American Psychiatric Association readily admits that "no one knows" what causes homosexuality. They say that there is currently a "renewed interest in searching for biological etiologies for homosexuality," but they conclude that to date, "there are no replicated scientific studies supporting any specific biological etiology for homosexuality."[250] Furthermore, in his summary of 20 years of scientific research into homosexuality covering more than 10,000 scientific papers and publications from all sides of the debate, Dr. NE Whitehead concludes:

> Geneticists, anthropologists, developmental psychologists, sociologists, endocrinologists, neuroscientists, medical researchers into gender, and twin study researchers are in broad agreement about the role of genetics in homosexuality. Genes don't make you do it. There is no genetic determinism, and genetic influence at most is minor. . .
>
> There is no one cause. No single genetic, hormonal, social, or environmental factor is predominant. There are

---

250 "Gay, Lesbian, and Bisexual Issues," American Psychiatric Association, May, 2000, http://www.healthyminds.org/More-Info-For/GayLesbianBisexuals.aspx. See also Robert H. Knight, "Born or Bred? Science Does Not Support the Claim That Homosexuality is Genetic," Concerned Women for America, http://www.cwfa.org/images/content/bornorbred.pdf.

similar themes, e.g. childhood gender non-conformity, sexual abuse, peer and family dynamics, sexual history, but the mix varies with individuals, making individual personal responses the single overriding factor. [251]

Despite what Hollywood, the postmodern culture or the Emergent Church may tell you, a person is not born gay.[252] While this objective scientific evidence is helpful, it is far more important for us as Christians to consider what God's word has to say about homosexuality and what a Christ-like response is toward those who are homosexual.

Jesus' View of Marriage

Tony Jones says, "Many of us who argue for the full acceptance of GLBT [gay, lesbian, bisexual, transgender] persons in the church like to say that if Jesus didn't want gays in the church, he would have said something."[253] Others suggest that Jesus nowhere openly condemns gays or lesbians or even mentions homosexuality.[254] Did Jesus ever say *anything* about homosexuality?

While Jesus did not explicitly condemn homosexuality, He approved of God's creative plan for sexual union of one man and one woman. Jesus also affirmed the command: "Honor thy father and mother" (Matthew 15:4). He is asserting that a child's parents consist of a father and a mother. This assertion rules out the possibility for homosexual union. Again, Jesus said, "A man leave father and mother, and shall cleave to his wife: and they twain shall be one flesh?"

---

251 NE Whitehead, *My Genes Made Me Do It* (USA, Whitehead Association, 2010). A summary of the book may be viewed here: http://www.mygenes.co.nz/summary.htm.
252 For a chronicle of the gay agenda in the last 40 years of American history, see Michael Brown, *A Queer Thing Happened To America: And what a long, strange trip it's been* (Concord, NC: EqualTime Books, 2011).
253 Tony Jones. "The Silence of Jesus (on Homosexuality)," The Tony Jones Blog, January 23, 2012, http://www.patheos.com/blogs/tonyjones/2012/01/23/the-silence-of-jesus-on-homosexuality/.
254 McLaren and Campolo, *Adventures in Missing the Point,* 201.

(Matthew 19:5). In this single declaration, Jesus does not leave the options for people to be brought up with homosexual parents or marry a person of the same sex.

He says more specifically: "Have ye not read, that he which made them at the beginning made them male and female" (Matthew 19:4). First of all, Jesus explains that this design was intended for procreation because God created a man and a woman. Secondly, Jesus acknowledges that parents consist of a father and a mother. Thirdly, Jesus conveys God's intent that proceeding generations would follow the same pattern of procreation with a spouse of the opposite sex. Because Jesus approves God's plan for sexual union in conjunction with the creation of the universe and nature, we can safely say that Jesus condemned homosexuality as sin because it is against God's good design revealed in nature.

Jesus' comments on God creating the man and woman, and the man leaving his father and mother to be joined to his wife was in response to a question from the Pharisees about divorce. They asked him if it was lawful for a man to divorce his wife for any cause (Matthew 19:3). Matthew tells us that when they asked this question, they tempted Jesus. Doesn't the Emergent Church tempt Jesus in a similar way? We could expect Jesus to respond to the new Christians in the same way:

> The postmodern Christians came to Jesus, tempting him, and said to him, "Is it lawful for a man to have sexual relations with another man?" Jesus answered them, "Have you not read that He who made them at the beginning 'made them male and female,' and said, 'For this reason a man shall leave his father and mother and be joined to his wife, and the two shall become one flesh.'"

Jesus' statement to the Pharisees also answers any argument for homosexuality from the Emerging Church. Silence is the worst kind of argument. Jesus never mentioned many sins. But are we to assume that just because Jesus didn't explicitly say something about a certain sin, it is then okay to practice? Emergents are making an argument from silence.

Furthermore, in Jesus' teaching on divorce, He offered one

exception clause wherein divorce was permissible: "Whosoever shall put away his wife, saving for the cause of fornication, causeth her to commit adultery: and whosoever shall marry her that is divorced committeth adultery" (Matthew 5:32). "Fornication" (*porneia* in Greek) includes any and all sexual immorality including homosexuality, incest, adultery, fornication, and intercourse with animals. Also notice that Jesus, once again, asserts that marriage never consisted of two men or two women.

I believe that a primary reason for the Emergent Church's compromised position on homosexuality is the professing church's compromise on divorce and remarriage. When divorce and remarriage is considered acceptable, the acceptance of homosexuality is next. We would not even be having this conversation about homosexuality if those who claimed the name of Christ would boldly proclaim Jesus' radical view of marriage: "Whosoever shall put away his wife, and marry another, committeth adultery against her. And if a woman shall put away her husband, and be married to another, she committeth adultery" (Mark 10:11,12); "Whosoever putteth away his wife, and marrieth another, committeth adultery: and whosoever marrieth her that is put away from her husband committeth adultery" (Luke 16:18).

The primitive church was not having this conversation about homosexuality because they upheld the Lord's radical teaching on marriage. The early Christians forbid divorce except in the case of a man separating from his wife for her sexual immorality (Matthew 5:32; 19:9). The early Christians always considered divorce and remarriage to be adultery (Matthew 5:32; 19:9; Mark 10:11,12; Luke 16:18; 1 Corinthians 7:10,11,39). Consider these quotations from four different Christians who lived in the second century:

> So that all who, by human law, are twice married, are in the eye of our Master sinners, and those who look upon a woman to lust after her. For not only he who in act commits adultery is rejected by Him, but also he who desires to commit adultery: since not only our works, but also our thoughts, are open before God.[255]

---

255 Justin Martyr, *Ante-Nicene Fathers,* volume 1, 167.

A second marriage is only a specious adultery. "For whosoever puts away his wife," says He, "and marries another, commits adultery."[256]

Now that the Scripture counsels marriage, and allows no release from the union, is expressly contained in the law, "You shall not put away your wife, except for the cause of fornication;" and it regards as fornication, the marriage of those separated while the other is alive. . . . "He that takes a woman that has been put away," it is said, "commits adultery; and if one puts away his wife, he makes her an adulteress," that is, compels her to commit adultery. And not only is he who puts her away guilty of this, but he who takes her, by giving to the woman the opportunity of sinning; for did he not take her, she would return to her husband.[257]

For in the Gospel of Matthew he says, "Whosoever shall put away his wife, saving for the cause of fornication, causes her to commit adultery." He also is deemed equally guilty of adultery, who marries a woman put away by her husband... You find Him also protecting marriage, in whatever direction you try to escape. He prohibits divorce when He will have the marriage inviolable; He permits divorce when the marriage is spotted with unfaithfulness.[258]

The Old Testament Morality on Homosexuality

We have previously demonstrated how Jesus quoted from the Old Testament (Matthew 4:4,7,10), affirmed that the Old Testament Scriptures were unbreakable (John 10:35), authoritative (Matthew 22:29), truthful (John 17:17), historically and scientifically reliable (Matthew 12:40; 19:4-6; 24:37-38). While Jesus did not perpetuate the

---

256 Athenagorus, *Ante-Nicene Fathers,* volume 2, 146.
257 Clement of Alexandria, *Ante-Nicene Fathers* volume 2, 379.
258 Tertullian, *Ante-Nicene Fathers* volume 3, 405.

Law of Moses, specifically the ceremonial and civil ordinances, He did affirm God's moral standards of living. Jesus initiated a New Covenant, distinct from the Old Covenant but both covenants came from the same Father whose morality cannot change. While there are some differences between the two, there is much similarity such as God's transcendent moral law within the Law of Moses and the Prophets.

Like other in the Emergent movement, Campolo criticizes the position of most Christians that homosexuals can be transformed into heterosexuals through prayer. He scrutinizes every one of the passages in the Bible which condemns homosexuality.[259] For instance, he argues that the Torah prohibitions of homosexuality found in Leviticus 18:22, 20:13 and Deuteronomy 23:17 are not moral standards but part of the Kosher rules for Orthodox Jews in the same category of other Kosher practices such as the prohibition of wearing mixed fabrics, and eating shellfish or pork.[260]

An honest reading of Leviticus chapters 18 and 20 would lead us to the conclusion that God's command is not merely part of Kosher rules, but God's universal moral law. These chapters declare: "Thou shalt not lie with mankind, as with womankind: *it is abomination*" (Leviticus 18:22); "If a man also lie with mankind, as he lieth with a woman, both of them have committed *an abomination*: they shall surely be put to death; their blood shall be upon them" (Leviticus 20:13). These commands are not surrounded by ceremonial or civil ordinances but other binding moral commands against incest (Leviticus 18:6-19; 20:11-20,16-17,19-21), adultery (Leviticus 18:20; 20:10), child sacrifice (Leviticus 18:21; 20:2-5) and bestiality (Leviticus 18:23; 20:15).

Likewise, Deuteronomy 23:17 couples homosexuality with the sin of prostitution saying: "There shall be no whore of the daughters of Israel, nor a sodomite of the sons of Israel." Only a morally corrupt people would find these practices acceptable. Jesus' view of marriage agrees with the morality of both the Old and New Testaments. Today, what has long been considered perversion and murder such as homosexuality and child sacrifice or abortion are now acceptable. The fruit of Emergent theology will be the acceptance of other immoral abominations such as anal sex (sodomy), incest and bestiality. The

---

259 McLaren and Campolo, *Adventures in Missing the Point*, 201.
260 Ibid.

Emergent church seems to be glorifying these animalistic behaviors and violating all taboos in the current culture. In his book *Real Marriage*, Mark Driscoll advocates cosmetic surgery, cybersex, sex toys, menstrual sex, and anal sex for married couples.[261]

Lost in Translations

Heralded on the Emergent Village Weblog, the Emergent Bible translation called *The Voice* is a prime example of how the Emergent movement is preaching a false message that is accepted by unbelievers.[262] The project was founded by speaker and pastor Chris Seay. Contributing to the translation was Brian McLaren, *Blue Like Jazz* author Donald Miller, and author Leonard Sweet among a collaborative team of 80 writers, scholars, poets and songwriters.

One way *The Voice* has effectively been marketed is by mistranslating the sin of homosexuality. In 1 Corinthians 6:9, the "abusers of themselves with mankind" (KJV) can be defined as those men who would lie with a male as with a female, sodomite, homosexual and the "effeminate" are defined as a boy kept for homosexual relations or a male prostitute. Other translations of this phrase are "men who have sex with men" (NIV) "homosexuals" (NASB), "those who participate in homosexuality" (Amplified Bible), and "sodomites" (NKJV). But *The Voice* translates this as "sexual deviancy."[263] This phrase obscures the intended meaning of this passage, especially since homosexuality is currently seen as a socially acceptable standard of behavior in our modern culture. Contemporary readers might not believe that homosexuality is a sexually deviant behavior, so they'd be left with the impression that homosexuals can inherit the kingdom of God since the

---

261 Mark Driscoll, *Real Marriage: The Truth About Sex, Friendship & Life Together* (On Mission LLC, 2012), 185-200.
262 "'The Voice,' Dubbed a 'New Bible Translation,' Bows in October." Emergent Village Weblog, June 17, 2010, http://www.emergentvillage.com/weblog/the-voice-dubbed-a-new-bible-translation-bows-in-october.
263 The Voice may be compared to other translations online, see http://www.hearthevoice.com/compare-translations; http://www.hearthevoice.com/search-bible.

translation does not explicitly name the sin of homosexuality as the original Greek suggests.

Likewise, *The Message Bible* translation by Eugene Peterson deletes the politically incorrect words like "effeminate" and "homosexual." *The Message* states, "Those who use and abuse each other, use and abuse sex, use and abuse the earth and everything in it, don't qualify as citizens in God's kingdom. A number of you know from experience what I'm talking about, for not so long ago you were on that list. Since then, you've been cleaned up and given a fresh start by Jesus, our Master, our Messiah, and by our God present in us, the Spirit."[264] What kind of message is this? Obviously to a Christian, those who "use and abuse sex" would include homosexuals, but to an unbeliever this vague phrase could mean something completely different. To unregenerated unbelievers, this justifies fornication and even homosexual behavior in their minds as long as it is accompanied with commitment.

In fact, in 1 Corinthians 6:18-20, *The Message* deletes the phrase "Flee fornication" (KJV) and says instead, "There's more to sex than mere skin on skin," and "we must not pursue the kind of sex that avoids commitment and intimacy."[265] Again, to an unbeliever, this "kind of sex" could refer to sex outside of marriage and even homosexuality, as long as there is intimacy and commitment. This is an abomination! *The Message* is turning the grace of our God into lasciviousness, and denying the only Lord God, and our Lord Jesus Christ, and is thus ordained to condemnation (Jude 1:4). By the way, *The Message* is Emergence icon Bono's favorite Bible version.[266]

It seems that there is a homosexual agenda when we compare these ambiguous translations of the Bible to word for word translations supported by early Christian interpretations of these passages. These new

---

264 Eugene Peterson, *The Message Remix* (Colorado Springs, CO: NavPress Publishing Group, 2003), 1,674.
265 Ibid.
266 One online article reports, "Bono takes a knee and recites a few lines from Eugene Peterson's paraphrase of Psalm 116 (the version of the Good Book promoted by Bono and known as The Message): "What can I give back to God for the blessings he's poured out on me? I'll lift high the cup of salvation as a toast to our Father." See "Tebow, Bono & Jesus." Interference, January 10, 2012. available: http://www.u2interference.com/15343-tebow-bono-jesus/.

supposed translations might as well delete all the passages that address the sin of homosexuality. Actually, the *Queen James Bible* does just that! It sounds horrendous and absurd, but that's no twisted joke. The website states, "You can't choose your sexuality, but you can choose Jesus."[267] Complete with a rainbow-colored cross on the front cover, the *Queen James Bible* "edited those eight verses in a way that makes homophobic interpretations impossible" (those verses included Genesis 19:5, Leviticus 18:22; 20:13, Romans 1:26-27, 1 Corinthians 6:9-10, 1 Timothy 1:10 and Jude 1:7). The "editors" have the audacity and arrogance to claim, "The Bible says nothing about homosexuality. However, there might be no other argument in contemporary faith as heated as what the Bible is interpreted to say about homosexuality."[268]

If the issue is one of *interpretation,* why not let the early Christians help us interpret these passages? Certainly the early Christians had a great advantage over the new Emergence Christians because they fluently spoke ancient Greek and shared the same cultural setting as the Apostle Paul. For instance, Clement of Rome (96 AD) was a first century bishop of the church at Rome, and he may well have been a companion of both apostles Paul and Peter (Philippians 4:3). He wrote, "It is well that they should be cut off from the lusts of the world, since 'every lust wars against the spirit' and 'neither fornicators, nor homosexuals . . . will inherit the kingdom of God.'"[269]

Pauline Letters

Paul states in his letter to the Romans: "For this cause God gave them up unto vile affections: for even their women did change the natural use into that which is against nature: And likewise also the men, leaving the natural use of the woman, burned in their lust one toward another; men with men working that which is unseemly, and receiving in themselves that recompense of their error which was meet. And even as they did not like to retain God in their knowledge, God gave them over to a reprobate mind, to do those things which are not convenient; Being

---

267 *Queen James Bible*, http://queenjamesbible.com/.
268 *Queen James Bible,* http://queenjamesbible.com/gay-bible/.
269 Clement of Rome, *ANF*, 1.34 in Bercot, *A Dictionary of Early Christian Beliefs*, 347.

filled with all unrighteousness, fornication, wickedness, covetousness, maliciousness; full of envy, murder, debate, deceit, malignity; whisperers, Backbiters, haters of God, despiteful, proud, boasters, inventors of evil things, disobedient to parents, Without understanding, covenant breakers, without natural affection, implacable, unmerciful: Who knowing the judgment of God, that they which commit such things are worthy of death, not only do the same, but have pleasure in them that do them" (Romans 1:26-32).

Thus, homosexuality is a grievous sin which is part of the judgment of God upon a society that has rejected Him. The early Christian Athenagoras (175 AD) repeated the general message of Romans 1: "They do not abstain even from males, males with males committing shocking abominations, outraging all the noblest and comeliest bodies in all sorts of ways."[270] How much more will this sin be evidence of the judgment of God when it is committed under the banner of Christ? The term "gay Christian" is becoming more and more common because of the "queermergent" theology.

Campolo offers the argument that "Paul does not condemn those born with homosexual orientations, but rather heterosexuals who . . . become debased and decadent."[271] Advocates of the term "sexual orientation" claim that it is fixed at a person's birth. But the term is hypocritically selective in its application to homosexuality only and to pedophilia or other sexual sin. If we allow God's word to correct sinful feelings, motives, thoughts, and orientations at the root of sinful behavior, then our lives will be pleasing to God. Jesus identified evil thoughts and motives which defile a person (Mark 7:15,20-23). Thus, even a person's "sexual orientations" can be sinful.

Campolo's argument does not account for the condemnation of homosexuality throughout the Bible and the moral declaration of such behavior as unseemly, not convenient, unrighteous and wicked. He further dismisses the Pauline letters arguing that the Greek word *arsenokoitai* found in 1 Corinthians 6:9 and 1 Timothy 1:10, translated "homosexual" has an ambiguous meaning, that Paul was "condemning

---

270 *Aathenagoras, NF,* 2.143 in Bercot, *A Dictionary of Early Christian Beliefs,* 347.
271 McLaren and Campolo, *Adventures in Missing the Point,* 206,207.

not homosexuality per se, but pederasty."[272] The Strong's Concordance is probably the most often used and trusted Greek and Hebrew concordance for the Bible. It defines this word as "one who lies with a male as with a female, sodomite, homosexual." The word is only ambiguous to those who refuse to acknowledge the clear meaning of the Bible.

Likewise, McLaren bypassed the Pauline letters by criticizing a conservative Christian spokesperson for putting the teachings of Paul on the same authoritative ground as the teachings of Jesus in regard to the gay marriage debate by saying his "willingness to grant Jesus no more authority than Paul renders me speechless."[273] McLaren's comment renders *me* speechless. No doubt Jesus has all authority in heaven and earth (Matthew 28:18), an authority that Paul did not have in himself, but when it comes to the authority of the Scriptures as McLaren is talking about in relation to the gay marriage issue, Paul's words are equally as authoritative as Christ's and "given by inspiration of God" (2 Timothy 3:16). The Bible does not teach that some Scriptures are more God-breathed or more authoritative or more inspired than other Scriptures. *All scripture* is given by inspiration of God! God breathed out the words that the apostles penned in their epistles. Peter esteemed Paul's letters to the churches equivalent to the Old Testament Scriptures (2 Peter 3:15,16). Peter clearly believed Paul's epistles to be the inspired Word of God. But "queermergent" theologians may be described as those "unlearned and unstable" men who distort the meaning and interpretation to suit their own interests or views.

While McLaren argues that the writings of Paul are not as authoritative as the words of Jesus, the New Testament conveys otherwise according to Jesus Himself. Jesus said, "I have yet many things to say unto you, but ye cannot bear them now. Howbeit when he, the Spirit of truth, is come, he will guide you into all truth: for he shall not speak of himself; but whatsoever he shall hear, that shall he speak: and he will shew you things to come. He shall glorify me: for he shall receive of mine, and shall shew it unto you. All things that the Father hath are mine: therefore said I, that he shall take of mine, and shall shew it unto you" (John 16:12-15). Since the apostles would be guided by the Holy Spirit, they were preaching, writing, and teaching by the authority of

272 Ibid., 205.
273 Ibid., 274.

Christ. Confirming the Holy Spirit's guidance, Paul says, "If any man think himself to be a prophet, or spiritual, let him acknowledge that *the things that I write unto you are the commandments of the Lord*" (1 Corinthians 14:37). Apparently, the Emergent church movement is not "spiritual." Sadly, they are twisting the Scriptures to their own destruction (2 Peter 3:15,16). Moreover, the Lord spoke to Paul in a vision by night: "Be not afraid, but speak, and hold not thy peace: For I am with thee" (Acts 1:9,10). Paul did not receive the Gospel by any man, nor was he taught it, but by the revelation of Jesus Christ (Galatians 1:12).

In the Name of Love

Emerging Church leaders offer a wise precaution about demonizing homosexuals. But narrow is the way, which leadeth unto life, and few there be that find it (Matthew 17:14). A Christian on the narrow path can stray to the right or to the left. On either side is a pitfall if we fail to emphasize truth and love simultaneously. For example, Westboro Baptist church falls into one pit with its rude, unkind, and proud picketing with signs that display provoking messages such as "God Hates Fags." This behavior is unseemly and unloving. Equally wrong are the Emergents who fall into the other pit by not aligning themselves with the truth. This is not to say that Emergents don't demonstrate compassion and love for homosexuals. But love without truth is a liar and truth without love is a killer. Thus we are exhorted to *speak the truth in love* (Ephesians 4:15).

Shane Claiborne essentially says that we just need to love. But this stance appears to be at the expense of the truth when he says,

> Well, Billy Graham said really well once that it's God's job to judge, the Spirit's job to convict and my job to love. And if we get those right, this issue looks very different to us. If we don't simply talk about the gay issue but we are living in relationship to people who are working out their sexuality and struggling with it, the question changes. I had all these ideas about homosexuality and civil union and gay when I was in

147

high school, and then I met a kid who was attracted to other men and he told me that he felt God had made a mistake when He made him and that he wanted to kill himself. If that brother can't find a home in the Church, then I wonder who have we become.[274]

That sounds good at first. Christians are not to judge those in the world, but we are exhorted to judge those within the church (1 Corinthians 5:12). One of the most often cited and favorite Bible passages is "Judge not" (Matthew 7:1). "You're judging me," they say in response to the Gospel proclamation of the Lordship of Jesus Christ. However, that is actually taking that verse totally out of context. Jesus is really encouraging us *to* judge, but to *first* judge ourselves. Notice what He says afterwards: "Judge not, that ye be not judged. For with what judgment ye judge, ye shall be judged: and with what measure ye mete, it shall be measured to you again. And why beholdest thou the mote that is in thy brother's eye, but considerest not the beam that is in thine own eye? Or how wilt thou say to thy brother, Let me pull out the mote out of thine eye; and, behold, a beam is in thine own eye? Thou hypocrite, first cast out the beam out of thine own eye; and then shalt thou see clearly to cast out the mote out of thy brother's eye" (Matthew 7:1-5). That means that people like ex-homosexuals (those who have removed the beam from their eye by God's grace through faith in Christ, those who have repented of their sin and turned to Christ for forgiveness) can now see clearly to judge another sinner in need of the Gospel.

Shane Claiborne speaks of this homosexual "brother" finding a home in the church whereas Paul tells us to break fellowship with those who would call themselves a brother and be given to such immorality: "But now I have written unto you not to keep company, if any man that is called a brother be a fornicator, or covetous, or an idolater, or a railer, or a drunkard, or an extortioner; with such an one no not to eat. For what have I to do to judge them also that are without? do not ye judge them that are within?" (1 Corinthians 5:11,12). Yes, Jesus ate with tax collectors and sinners, but they were not called brothers; they were

---

274 "7 Burning Issues: Gay Rights," *Relevant Magazine,* May/June 2008, http://www.relevantmagazine.com/god/church/features/1457-7-burning-issues-gay-rights.

worldly sinners. *These are the type of immoral people that we can and should eat with for the sake of preaching the Gospel.* Thus Paul said, "I wrote unto you in an epistle not to company with fornicators: *Yet not altogether with the fornicators of this world,* or with the covetous, or extortioners, or with idolaters; *for then must ye needs go out of the world*" (1 Corinthians 5:9,10). Therefore, we would be known as friends of sinners (Luke 7:34).

Paul was confronted with a congregation in which there was a man practicing immorality, "such fornication as is not so much as named among the Gentiles, that one should have his father's wife" (1 Corinthians 5:1). In his instruction to the church, Paul says to "deliver such an one unto Satan for the destruction of the flesh" (1 Corinthians 5:5). This command was not culturally sensitive or seeker-friendly. Paul didn't say this because he hated fornicators or because he didn't want that man to find a home in the church. Paul said this because he loved this man. He said later in the second letter to the Corinthians: "out of much affliction and anguish of heart I wrote unto you with many tears; not that ye should be grieved, but that ye might know *the love* which I have more abundantly unto you. . . Sufficient to such a man is this punishment, which was inflicted of many. So that contrariwise ye ought rather to forgive him, and comfort him, lest perhaps such a one should be swallowed up with overmuch sorrow. Wherefore I beseech you that ye would confirm *your love* toward him." (2 Corinthians 2:4,6-8).

In love, Paul commanded that a person who is living in such grievous sin like homosexuality should be cast out of the church. Why? That the spirit may be saved in the day of the Lord Jesus (1 Corinthians 5:5). The discipline is loving, corrective and restorative. Put him out of the church unto Satan that he would become disgraced and ashamed over his lifestyle. Ideally, the poor soul would turn form his sin and be restored. But Emergence Christianity pats the sinner on the back in the name of love.

Like other Emergents, Claiborne is loving his homosexual friend to an extent that outweighs the love we should have toward God and His commandments. Jesus was asked by a certain lawyer, "Master, which is the great commandment in the law?" Jesus responded, "Thou shalt love the Lord thy God with all thy heart, and with all thy soul, and with all thy mind. This is the first and great commandment. And the second is like

149

unto it, Thou shalt love thy neighbor as thyself" (Matthew 22:36-39). Our love for God should be elevated over the love we have for our neighbor. And this is the love of God, that we keep his commandments (1 John 5:3). When the love for our friends and neighbors outweighs the love we have toward God and truth, then we are giving prime importance to people rather than to God. This is humanism. Our loving and forthright response should be to confront homosexuality with the truth of God's word.

8

A Place Called Hell

"And I say unto you my friends, Be not afraid of them that kill the body, and after that have no more that they can do. But I will forewarn you whom ye shall fear: Fear him, which after he hath killed hath power to cast into hell; yea, I say unto you, Fear him"
— Jesus (Luke 12:4,5)

Heaven and Hell, Here and Now

Because of the Emergents' low view of sin, they have adopted a warped understanding of how exceedingly sinful sin truly is, and how sin is an offense to the holiness of God. Thus, they have also redefined the doctrine of hell and the justice of God's wrath against sin. Although many of the Emergents will not admit to being universalists, they are generally anti-condemnation and speak against the traditional understanding of hell as God's judgment for those who reject the truth.

Rob Bell asks, "When people use the word hell, what do they mean?" and answers, "They mean a place, an event, a situation absent of how God desires things to be. Famine, debt, oppression, loneliness, despair, death, slaughter—they are all hell on earth."[275] Though there are desperate and miserable circumstances in this life which people may call

---

275 Bell, *Velvet Elvis,* 148.

"hell on earth," people generally think of a place of future punishment after the Day of Judgment when the word hell is used within the Bible. But Bell goes on to describe heaven and hell as here and now on earth rather than future realities:

> For Jesus, heaven and hell were present realities. Ways of living we can enter into here and now. He talked very little of the life beyond this one because he understood that the life beyond this one is a continuation of the kinds of choices we make here and now.
>
> For Jesus, the question wasn't how do I get into heaven? but how do I bring heaven here? . . .
>
> The goal isn't escaping this world but making this world the kind of place God can come to. And God is remaking us into the kind of people who can do this kind of work.[276]

Bell has the right idea of bringing God's will in heaven to earth as Jesus taught us to pray, "Thy kingdom come, Thy will be done, as in heaven, so in earth" (Luke 11:2). But heaven and hell are chiefly future, eternal, and spiritual realities. Perhaps Bell is integrating the concept of heaven with the "kingdom of heaven" or the "kingdom of God," when those terms are biblically distinct from simply *heaven*.[277] Indeed, the

---

276 Ibid., 147,150.

277 "Kingdom of heaven" is only found in the Gospel of Matthew who uses this term to cater to Jewish sensitivities of overusing the word "God." The pious Jews avoided the revealed name of Yahweh and Elohim (God) by substituting *Adonai* (Lord), *ha-shem* (the Name) or *mayim* (heaven). This is found in the expression "kingdom of heaven" where Matthew substitutes "heaven" for "God." The prodigal son said, "I have sinned against heaven" (Luke 15:18) replacing "heaven" with "God." Matthew uses these terms "kingdom of heaven" and "kingdom of God" interchangeably within his own gospel saying, "Verily I say unto you, That a rich man shall hardly enter into the kingdom of heaven. And again I say unto you, It is easier for a camel to go through the eye of a needle, than for a rich man to enter into the kingdom of God" (Matthew 19:23,24). These two phrases refer to the exact same reality, namely, the rule of God in

152

kingdom of God or the kingdom of heaven *is* a present reality, but is also distinct from our future hope of the new heaven and new earth, or what's commonly thought of as heaven. The kingdom of heaven has already been initiated by Jesus[278] but not yet consummated in its fullness.[279] Equally important to the reality of the kingdom of heaven are the realities that heaven and hell are future realities for our souls after the Judgment depending upon our relationship with Jesus Christ. But Rob Bell writes:

> Heaven is full of forgiven people. Hell is full of forgiven people. Heaven is full of people God loves, whom Jesus died for. Hell is full of forgiven people God loves, whom Jesus died for. The difference is how we choose to live, which story we choose to live in, which version of reality we trust. Ours or God's.[280]

In whose reality is Rob Bell trusting, his or God's? Jesus said very clearly that there are some people who will *not* be forgiven: "But if ye forgive not men their trespasses, *neither will your Father forgive* your trespasses" (Matthew 6:15); "All manner of sin and blasphemy shall be forgiven unto men: but the blasphemy against the Holy Ghost shall *not be forgiven* unto men" (Matthew 12:31). Hell is not full of forgiven people but unforgiven souls. This is not to say that God hasn't offered the gift of salvation and forgiveness of sin to all people. It is God's will that none should perish (2 Peter 3:9; 1 Timothy 2:4), but it is only in Jesus that we have redemption through his blood, even the forgiveness of sins (Colossians 1:14). Those who do not abide in Jesus do not have the forgiveness of sins. Though Rob Bell doesn't deny the existence of hell in this specific passage, he has equated heaven and hell in a way that removes the unimaginable and everlasting punishment (Matthew 25:46), destruction (2 Thessalonians 1:9), indignation, wrath, tribulation and anguish (Romans 2:8,9).

The reason Rob Bell believes and teaches what he does is very simple: he doesn't like the traditional understanding of hell. In his book

---

people's hearts.

278 Cf. Matthew 12:28; Luke 17:20,21; Romans 14:7; Colossians 1:13.

279 See 1 Corinthians 15:24-28.

280 Bell, *Velvet Elvis*, 146.

Love Wins, Rob Bell writes:

> [I]t's important that we be honest about the fact that some stories are better than others. Telling a story in which billions of people spend forever somewhere in the universe trapped in a black hole of endless torment and misery with no way out isn't a very good story.[281]

Conversely, Bell says that "everybody enjoying God's good world together with no disgrace or shame, justice being served, and all the wrongs being made right is a better story."[282] Rob Bell would prefer to have it both ways, but justice cannot be served as well as everybody enjoying God's good world together. One of man's greatest problems is that God is good and that He is love (1 John 4:16). Because He is good, we can expect that justice will be served. What if we caught a man in the act of murdering our family, turned the murderer in to the authorities, and at the trial the judge set him free because he was a "loving" judge? Is that justice? No, that judge is more vile than the criminals he sets free.[283] If justice is served, then everybody cannot enjoy God's goodness. But Bell's version of the story makes him feel better. Bell's story is just that: a story, a fable that tickles the ears. "For the time will come when they will not endure sound doctrine; but after their own lusts shall they heap to themselves teachers, having itching ears; And they shall turn away their ears from the truth, and *shall be turned unto fables*" (2 Timothy 4:3,4).

What antimatter is to physics, Brian McLaren is to Christianity. He subscribes to neither a universalist nor exclusivist understanding of

---

281 Rob Bell, *Love Wins* (New York, NY: Harper Collins, 2011), 110.
282 Ibid.
283 This is an analogy. It should be noted that vengeance belongs to the Lord and He will repay; we are not to avenge ourselves (Romans 12:19), but love our enemies, do good to those who hate us and not ask for our goods back when they are stolen (Matthew 5:27-35). Though justice will be served, and though "the saints shall judge this world," (1 Corinthians 6:2), God is willing that none should perish, but that all would repent (2 Peter 3:9). Therefore, knowing God's will, true Christians follow Christ in patience and mercy, praying for their enemies, rendering unto no man evil for evil (Romans 12:17; 1 Thessalonians 5:15, 1 Peter 3:9), eye for eye, tooth for tooth (Matthew 5:38,39).

hell. But he does oppose the traditional understanding of hell. He says:

> God loves you and has a wonderful plan for your life, and if you don't love God back and cooperate with God's plans in exactly the prescribed way, God will torture you with unimaginable abuse, forever—that sort of thing. Human parents who 'love' their children with these kinds of implied ultimatums tend to produce the most dysfunctional families.[284]

He plays on the emotions and natural sensitivities that arise from the idea of God's punishment, family disfunction and abuse in order to clandestinely slip in an irreverent presumption against the majesty and justice of God. God is love and His word warns of hell. Rather than vindicating God concerning the conventional understanding of hell, McLaren's allegation sounds more like an argument from an unbeliever or atheist. If the traditional understanding of hell is true, then McLaren brings railing accusation against God by saying that He "suffers from borderline personality disorder or some worse sociopathic diagnosis."[285] Thus, McLaren finds huge problems with the traditional understanding of hell:

> If the cross is in line with Jesus' teaching then—I won't say, the only, and I certainly won't say even the primary —but a primary meaning of the cross is that the kingdom of God doesn't come like the kingdoms of this world, by inflicting violence and coercing people. But that the kingdom of God comes through suffering and willing, voluntary sacrifice. But in an ironic way, the doctrine of hell basically says, no, that's not really true. That in the end, God gets His way through coercion and violence and intimidation and domination, just like every other kingdom does. The cross isn't the center then. The cross is almost a distraction and false

---

284 Brian McLaren, *The Last Word After That* (San Francisco: Jossey-Bass, 2003), xii.
285 Ibid.

advertising for God.[286]

But the cross is a defense of God's love and makes sense when we believe in a literal hell. Love is central to the teaching of Jesus and can be easily reconciled with the traditional understanding of hell. First, the doctrine of hell provides a loving justification for the cross of Christ: For God so loved the world that He gave His only begotten Son (John 3:16). Jesus suffered for our sakes. Second, out of love for His children, God will remove all abominable things and persons from their presence in the new creation so it and they are not plagued with sin (Revelation 21:8). McLaren is correct about the kingdom of God coming through willing, voluntary sacrifice: "We must through much tribulation enter into the kingdom of God" (Acts 14:22). But if we do not suffer now to enter the kingdom, then we will suffer later, being cast out of the kingdom, in hell. Suffering and glory are directly related (cf. Matthew 20:22-23; Luke 24:26; Romans 8:17; Philippians 1:29-30; 3:8-10; 1 Timothy 4:13; 2 Timothy 2:12; 2 Thessalonians 1:3-5), but all of those promises are conditional. Those who do not suffer with Christ have no hope of being glorified with Him.

Gehenna, Sheol, Hades and Tartaros – Place(s) Called "Hell"

Some Emergence Christians confine Hell to the place of the garbage dump outside of Jerusalem. Others like Doug Pagitt are appalled at the idea of Hell being "an actual place."[287] To them, Hell is more of a visceral concept rather than an actual place where souls are punished after death. Both Emergent viewpoints interpret hell figuratively and immanently.

Before exploring the Emergent Church views more in depth, we must note that early Christians did view Hell as *an actual place* (contrary to Pagitt's view), not merely the garbage dump outside Jerusalem, but a place of punishment for the souls of the wicked. A work known as Second Clement (100 AD) says,

---

286 Interview with Leif Hansen. *The Bleeding Purple Podcast*. January 8, 2006. Part II.
287 Todd Firel, interview with Doug Pagitt, *Way of the Master Radio*, October 22, 2007.

And Their worm shall not die, and their fire shall not be quenched, and they shall be for a spectacle unto all flesh. He speaks of that day of judgment, when men shall see those among us that lived ungodly lives and dealt falsely with the commandments of Jesus Christ. But the righteous, having done good and endured torments and hated the pleasures of the soul, when they shall behold them that have done amiss and denied Jesus by their words or by their deeds, how that they are punished with grievous torments in unquenchable fire, shall give glory to God, saying, There will be hope for him that has served God with his whole heart.[288]

Polycarp (80-167 AD) was also among the first generation of early Christians. He was a personal companion of the Apostle John. Before Polycarp's martyrdom, the proconsul said to him, "I will cause you to be consumed by fire, seeing you despise the wild beasts, if you will not repent." But Polycarp said, "You threaten me with fire which burns for an hour, and after a little is extinguished, but are ignorant of the fire of the coming judgment and of eternal punishment, reserved for the ungodly. But why do you wait? Bring forth what you will."[289]

Justin Martyr (160 AD) wrote, "Gehenna is *a place* where those who have lived wickedly are to be punished," and, "The unjust and intemperate will be punished in eternal fire."[290] Another early Christian said, "I found that Gehenna [Hell] was mentioned in the Gospel as *a place of punishment.*"[291] Also, the Treatise on the Glory of Martyrdom (255 AD) says, "*A horrible place* is it, of which the name is Gehenna [Hell]. There is an awful murmuring and groaning of bewailing souls."[292]

---

288 Clement, *Second Clement,* chapter 17.
289 *Martyrdom of Polycarp,* chapter 11.
290 Justin Martyr, *ANF,* 1.169; 1.188 in Bercot, *A Dictionary of Early Christian Beliefs,* 242.
291 Origen, *ANF,* 4.584 in Bercot, *A Dictionary of Early Christian Beliefs,* 297,298.
292 Treatise on the Glory of Martyrdom, *ANF,* 5.584 in Bercot, *A Dictionary of Early Christian Beliefs,* 297,298.

In *Love Wins*, Rob Bell explores the Hebrew word *Sheol* and the Greek words *Gehenna*, *Tartarus*, and *Hades* which are all translated "Hell" in the King James Bible.[293] More often than not, the English word "Hell" is translated from the Greek word *Gehenna*, almost exclusively by Jesus himself (as Bell points out). These words translated "Hell" in the King James Version Bible can be better understood if left untranslated in their original Greek or Hebrew form. This confusion of terms in the King James Version has led to much misunderstanding about what the Scriptures teach about the afterlife.

To the early Christians, Gehenna and Hades were two very different places.[294] Gehenna or Gehenna of fire, the word used in Jesus' teachings on hell, is of Hebrew origin and refers to the valley of Hinnom, south of Jerusalem, where the filth and dead animals of the city were cast out and burned. In fact, Jesus was the only one to teach about Hell using this word. To the early Christians, this referred to the Lake of Fire and the place of eternal punishment after the resurrection.[295]

Hinnom is first found in Joshua 15:8 and 18:6 in the layout of the lands of Judah and Banjamin. King Ahaz "burnt incense in the valley of the son of Hinnom, and burnt his children in the fire, after the abominations of the heathen whom the LORD had cast out before the children of Israel" (2 Chronicles 28:3). Also King Manasseh "caused his children to pass through the fire in the valley of the son of Hinnom: also he observed times, and used enchantments, and used witchcraft, and dealt with a familiar spirit, and with wizards: he wrought much evil in the sight of the LORD, to provoke him to anger" (2 Chronicles 33:6). In 2 Kings 23:10, righteous King Josiah, "defiled Topheth, which is in the valley of the children of Hinnom, that no man might make his son or his daughter to pass through the fire to Molech." "Topheth" means place of fire and refers to a place in the southeast end of the valley of the son of

---

293 Bell, *Love Wins*, 64-70.

294 The early Christians understood Hades, translated "hell" in the KJV, to be the intermediate state of the dead between death and the resurrection from the dead. Hades has also been translated "grave" (1 Corinthians 15:55) and Jesus also referred to it as Paradise (Luke 23:43) or Abraham's bosom (Luke 16:22,23). Cf. Matthew 11:23; 16:18; Luke 10:15; Acts 2:22-27,31; Revelation 1:18; 6:8; 20:13,14.

295 Bercot, *A Dictionary of Early Christian Beliefs*, 297.

Hinnom. There is another mention of Tophet in Isaiah 30:33 warning of a fiery judgment coming on the pro-Egypt Jews: "For Tophet is ordained of old; yea, for the king it is prepared; he hath made it deep and large: the pile thereof is fire and much wood; the breath of the LORD, like a stream of brimstone, doth kindle it." Jeremiah also prophesied of the slaughter of the idolatrous Jews in the valley of Hinnom by Nebuchadnezzar, the king of Babylon (Jeremiah 7:32; 19:2,6). Because of the idolatrous practices that were associated with the valley of Hinnom, pious Jews considered it unclean. Because garbage was constantly being thrown into the valley, the fires were continually burning and the worms continually eating. Thus, to the Jews, the valley of Hinnom, or Topheth (from which the New Testament concept of Gehenna arose) came to be understood as a place of fire, a valley of slaughter, and a place of judgment.

It has been argued by Emergents and universalists that Jesus could have been using Gehenna literally, that bodies would be destroyed in the valley of Hinnom in the 70 AD destruction. In fact, this is how Bell ultimately interprets the word: "Gehenna, the town garbage pile. *And that's it.*"[296] Hell is nothing more than a garbage dump to Bell. In addition to Bell, McLaren also suggests that Jesus' references to hell were merely referring to the 70 AD destruction of Jerusalem. He says:

> [W]e should consider the possibility that many, and perhaps even all of Jesus' hell-fire or end-of-the-universe statements refer not to postmortem judgment but to the very historic consequences of rejecting his kingdom message of reconciliation and peacemaking. The destruction of Jerusalem in A.D. 67-70 seems to many people to fulfill much of what we have traditionally understood as hell.[297]

Gehenna is the word used when Jesus said, "And if thy right eye offend thee, pluck it out, and cast it from thee: for it is profitable for thee

---

296 Bell, *Love Wins,* 69.
297 Brian McLaren. "Brian McLaren's Inferno 3: five proposals for reexamining our doctrine of hell," *Out of Ur,* May 11, 2006, http://blog.christianitytoday.com/outofur/archives/2006/05/brian_mclarens_2.html.

that one of thy members should perish, and not that thy whole body should be cast into hell" (Matthew 5:29).[298] The one time this word occurs outside of the Gospels is in James' epistle: "And the tongue is a fire, a world of iniquity: so is the tongue among our members, that it defileth the whole body, and setteth on fire the course of nature; and it is set on fire of hell" (James 3:6). Certainly there is not a literal flame on a person's tongue, but James is speaking figuratively. So others have argued that Jesus must also be speaking figuratively when referring to hell.

But there is much in favor of the traditional early Christian view of Gehenna as a place of postmortem judgment. Because of its perpetually burning fires, Jesus spoke of Ghenna as a symbol of the literal future Hell of eternal torment for the wicked after the resurrection. The picture of an unclean garbage dump where the fires and the worms never died out came to be an appropriate description of the ultimate fate of the wicked. Prior to Jesus' life and teaching, Gehenna came to be understood to the Jewish mind as the final, eternal garbage dump where all the wicked idolaters would be after the resurrection. In rabbinical Jewish literature, Gehenna was a destination of the wicked.[299]

Certainly Christ knew what Gehenna meant to the contemporary listeners of His day. The fact that Jesus utilized the rabbinic language connected with Gehenna demonstrates that He deliberately used the the term to impress the idea of eternal punishment of the wicked after the resurrection. The majority view of Gehenna was that of an eternal, conscious torment of the wicked after the resurrection.

Because Jesus spoke of hell specifically as a postmortem event, we can immediately reject the Emergent premise that hell merely referred to the destruction of Jerusalem when He spoke of Hell. McLaren's view that Hell cannot refer to "postmortem judgment" and Bell's view that Hell is merely "the town garbage pile," are irreconcilable with Jesus' words when He said, "And I say unto you my friends, Be not afraid of them that kill the body, and after that have no more that they can do. But I will forewarn you whom ye shall fear: Fear him, which

---

298 Cf. Matthew 5:22; 5:30; 10:28; 18:9; 23:15; 23:33; Mark 9:43,45,47; Luke 12:5.
299 Mishnah in Kiddushin 4.14, Avot 1.5; 5.19, 20, Tosefta t. Bereshith 6.15, and Babylonian Talmud b. Rosh Hashanah 16b:7a; b. Bereshith 28b.

after he hath killed hath power to cast into hell; yea, I say unto you, Fear him" (Luke 12:4,5). The parallel passage recorded in Matthew quotes our Lord as saying, "And fear not them which kill the body, but are not able to kill the soul: but rather fear him which is able to destroy *both soul and body* in hell" (Matthew 10:28). Taken together, these passages describe hell as much more than the destruction caused by Roman armies when Israel was besieged in 70 AD. The Roman armies could kill the body, but Jesus wanted us to know that God has power to cast into hell after death (postmortem). What makes the Emergent view even more unrealistic is that Jesus spoke about how God can cast a person's *soul* into hell, not only a person's body. This can't be referring to "the town garbage dump." It is very possible that corpses were thrown into the burning fires of the valley of Hinnom in the 70 AD destruction of Jerusalem, but there are no specific references in Josephus' account of *The Wars of the Jews.*

Aside from Jesus' use of the word Gehenna, many passages describe the weeping and gnashing of teeth which corresponds to the traditional concept of Hell. In the parable of the good fish and the bad fish, Jesus said the wicked "will be cast into the furnace of fire: there shall be wailing and gnashing of teeth" (Matthew 13:50). In the parable of the wedding feast, the king gave instruction to the servants concerning the man without wedding garments: "Then said the king to the servants, Bind him hand and foot, and take him away, and cast him into outer darkness; there shall be weeping and gnashing of teeth" (Matthew 22:13). Speaking of those who are unprepared for the coming of the Lord, Jesus said that God "shall cut him asunder, and appoint him his portion with the hypocrites: there shall be weeping and gnashing of teeth" (Matthew 24:51).

Furthermore, Paul spoke of the Second Coming of Christ saying that the Lord would come "in flaming fire taking vengeance on them that know not God, and that obey not the gospel of our Lord Jesus Christ: Who shall be punished with everlasting destruction from the presence of the Lord, and from the glory of his power" (2 Thessalonians 1:8,9). Jesus will say to the wicked, "Depart from me, ye cursed, into everlasting fire, prepared for the devil and his angels" (Matthew 25:41). Certainly spiritual beings such as the devil and his angels will not receive an earthly punishment in the garbage dump of Jerusalem, but a very real place called Gehenna, the Lake of Fire. The author of Hebrews also spoke of "eternal judgment" (Hebrews 6:2). Likewise Jesus warned that "he that shall blaspheme against the Holy Ghost hath never forgiveness, but is in danger of eternal damnation" (Mark 3:29). Paul spoke of future judgment: "Unto them that are contentious, and do not obey the truth, but obey unrighteousness, indignation and wrath, tribulation and anguish, upon every soul of man that doeth evil, of the Jew first, and also of the Gentile" (Romans 2:8,9).

Jesus spoke of the Day of Judgment saying that the wicked "shall go away into everlasting punishment: but the righteous into life eternal" (Matthew 25:46). Many are quick to interpret the "life eternal" as exactly that, but when it comes to "everlasting punishment," the Emergent Church seeks to deconstruct and redefine the terms. However, words "eternal" and "everlasting" come from the Greek word *aionios* which comes from the word *ion* or an age. *Aionios* describes that which is never to cease, everlasting, without beginning and without end.

In the parable of the wheat and the tares, Jesus said, "Let both grow together until the harvest: and in the time of harvest I will say to the reapers, Gather ye together first the tares, and bind them in bundles to burn them: but gather the wheat into my barn" (Matthew 13:30). That Day of Judgment is a day that cannot be rehearsed or put into words: "For we must all appear before the judgment seat of Christ; that every one may receive the things done in his body, according to that he hath done, whether it be good or bad" (2 Corinthians 5:10); "For if we sin willfully after that we have received the knowledge of the truth, there remaineth no more sacrifice for sins, But a certain fearful looking for of judgment and fiery indignation, which shall devour the adversaries" (Hebrews 10:26,27). Peter speaks of that Day by saying, "The Lord knoweth how to deliver the godly out of temptations, and to reserve the unjust unto the day of judgment to be punished: . . . But these, as natural brute beasts, made to be taken and destroyed, speak evil of the things that they understand not; and shall utterly perish in their own corruption . . . These are wells without water, clouds that are carried with a tempest; to whom the mist of darkness is reserved for ever" (2 Peter 2:9,12,17).

Based on today's misunderstandings of what the King James Version Bible translates into Hell, I agree with Brian McLaren that "We need to go back and take another look at Jesus' teachings about hell."[300] Perhaps the early Christians were in a better place to understand what Jesus meant. For example the *Epistle of Barnabas* (c. 70-130 AD), which many early Christians considered to be Scripture, says, "The way of darkness is crooked, and it is full of cursing. It is the way of eternal death with punishment."[301] The early Christian *Letter to Diognetus* (c. 125-200 AD) states, "You should fear what is truly death, which is reserved for those who will be condemned to the eternal fire. It will afflict those who are committed to it even to the end."[302] The primitive Christians believed Hell was much worse punishment than the temporal torments of martyrdom. The *Martyrdom of Polycarp* (135 AD) says:

> They despised all the torments of this world, redeeming themselves from eternal punishment by the suffering of a single hour. . . . For they kept before their view escape from the fire which is eternal and will never be quenched.[303]

But new Christianity is mistaken when its guru goes on to say, "For so many people, the conventional teaching about hell makes God seem vicious." He adds, "That's not something we should let stand."[304] Regardless of whether or not the conventional understanding about Hell makes God seem vicious or not, God is just, perfect and holy in all His decrees. O, McLaren, who are thou that repliest against God? (Romans 9:20) Since when do "so many people" or a majority determine truth?

---

300 Sherry Huang, "Beyond Business-as-Usual Christianity," *Beliefnet,* May, 2005, http://www.beliefnet.com/Faiths/Christianity/2005/05/Beyond-Business-As-Usual-Christianity.aspx.
301 Barnabas, *ANF*, 1.149 in Bercot, *A Dictionary of Early Christian Beliefs,* 242.
302 Letter to Diognetus, *ANF*, 1.29 in Bercot, *A Dictionary of Early Christian Beliefs,* 242.
303 Martyrdom of Polycarp, *ANF*, 1.139 in Bercot, *A Dictionary of Early Christian Beliefs,* 242.
304 Sherry Huang, "Beyond Business-as-Usual Christianity," *Beliefnet.* http://www.beliefnet.com/Faiths/Christianity/2005/05/Beyond-Business-As-Usual-Christianity.aspx

McLaren is putting his face on the face of God rather than taking the Word of God at face value.

There is a reality of God's wrath that must be taught regardless of it making God seem vicious because "narrow is the way, which leadeth unto life, and few there be that find it" (Matthew 7:14). The Bible plainly teaches that the afterlife for an unbeliever is that of anguish and torment so horrendous and terrifying that it is heretofore unimaginable to anybody. Whatever it is that the lost will experience after they die, they will have very strong regret, anguish and torment forever. Having a millstone tied around our neck and being cast into the sea or having our eyes gouged out or a limb amputated is bad enough. But Jesus said it would be better for these things to happen to us than that which is the determined fate of those who reject Jesus.

Universalism

McLaren says that Jesus used Hell to "threaten those who excluded sinners and other undesirables, showing that God's righteousness was compassionate and merciful, that God's kingdom welcomed the undeserving, that for God there was no out-group."[305] While it is true that sinners and other undesirables may be welcomed into God's kingdom, there is a condition of repentance from sins and faith in Christ. After Jesus healed a lame man, he went and found him in the temple and said, "Behold, thou art made whole: sin no more, lest a worse thing come unto thee" (John 5:14). The idea of there being "no out-group" for God suggests that McLaren is a universalist, the belief that all humankind is saved or will eventually be saved. Though McLaren has not said outright that he is a universalist, he defends the position of universalism. McLaren says,

> Tony [Campolo] and I might disagree on the details, but I think we are both trying to find an alternative to both traditional universalism and the narrow, exclusivist understanding of hell [that unless you explicitly accept and follow Jesus, you are excluded from eternal life with

---

305 McLaren, *The Last Word After That,* 74.

God and destined for hell].[306]

McLaren is anti-condemnation and anti-Hell. But he hasn't said that he is anti-universlist because universalism doesn't alienate or offend anybody. On the contrary, he says, "Universalism is not as bankrupt of biblical support as some suggest."[307] What about the undeniable biblical support for Hell? If he is supposing that nobody will be condemned to Hell, he is advocating universalism, even if he doesn't confess to be a universalist. "More important to me than the hell question, then," McLaren says, "is the mission question."[308] What is there to question? Has God really said there is a place called Hell?

McLaren adds that Tony Campolo is "presenting the inclusivist alternative" to Hell, i.e., the universalist view. When McLaren speaks of universalism, he defines it in his own words that "the work of Christ will ultimately redeem all and result in the complete unmitigated triumph of God."[309] Bell also points out the biblical phrases "all things" and "world" in certain soteriological passages to suggest that God will restore all of creation.[310]

First of all, we must give prudent care and careful attention to the use of the words "all" and "world" in Scripture. For instance, many of the passages quoted by Bell and other Emergents to lend support to universalism can be instantly refuted by properly understanding the biblical use of these words: "I, if I be lifted up from the earth, will draw *all men* unto me" (John 12:32); "restitution of *all things*" (Acts 3:21); "That in the dispensation of the fulness of times he might gather together in one *all things* in Christ" (Ephesians 1:10); "having made peace through the blood of his cross, by him to reconcile *all things* unto

---

306 Brian McLaren, "Brian McLaren's Inferno 2: are we asking the wrong questions about hell?" *Out of Ur*, May, 2006, http://www.outofur.com/archives/2006/05/brian_mclarens_1.html.
307 McLaren, *The Last Word After That*, 103.
308 Ibid., 114.
309 Ibid., 103. The biblical support McLaren gives for this view is John 12:32; Acts 3:19-21; Romans 5:12-21; 1 Corinthians 15:20-26; 2 Corinthians 5:19; Philippians 2:9-11; Ephesians 1:10; Colossians 1:16-23; 1 Timothy 2:4, 4:10; Titus 2:11; Hebrews 2:9; 2 Peter 3:9; 1 John 2:2.
310 Bell, *Love Wins*, 126-135.

himself" (Colossians 1:20). Depending on context, the phrases "all men" or "all things" very rarely mean all persons, taken individually, but some of all types. The words are generally used to signify that Christ has redeemed some Jews, some Gentiles, some rich, some poor, and has not restricted His redemption to either Jews or Gentiles. Jesus said, "And ye shall be hated of *all men* for my name's sake" (Matthew 10:22). He certainly didn't mean every individual but was referring to those apart from Christians. When Jesus said, "And *all things*, whatsoever ye shall ask in prayer, believing, ye shall receive" (Matthew 21:22), He did not mean literally all things but all righteous things that are according to the will of God.

Likewise, with the word "world": "*the whole world* has gone after him" (John 12:19); "then went *all Judea*, and were baptized of him in Jordan" (Matthew 3:5,6); "the *whole world* lieth in the wicked one" (1 John 5:19); "a decree from Caesar Augustus, that *all the world* should be taxed" (Luke 2:1). Did all the world go after Christ? Was *all Judea* baptized in Jordan? Does "the whole world," mean everybody is under the wicked one? Was the entire world taxed in the decree from Augustus? These are common figures of speech.

In Philippians 2:10,11, the eschatological fact that "every knee should bow" and "every tongue should confess" do not teach universal reconciliation. Bended knees and confessing tongues does not necessarily constitute salvation but convey the exaltation of Jesus, that the whole creation must be subject to Him and acknowledge Him as Lord. We must consider passages like this in light of the whole of Scripture, not as isolated proof texts for universalism.

It is God's will that all men be saved. This is the intent of the following three passages: "Who will have *all men* to be saved, and to come unto the knowledge of the truth" (1 Timothy 2:4); "The Lord is not slack concerning his promise, as some men count slackness; but is longsuffering to us-ward, not willing that *any* should perish, but that all should come to repentance" (2 Peter 3:9); "For therefore we both labour and suffer reproach, because we trust in the living God, who is the Savior of *all men*, specially of those that believe" (1 Timothy 4:10). Though this is God's will that all men be saved and He has "no pleasure in the death of the wicked; but that the wicked turn from his way and live" (Ezekiel 33:11), Jesus will nevertheless utter these heartbreaking words to some,

"I never knew you: depart from me, ye that work iniquity" (Matthew 7:23). God is the Savior of all men because "the grace of God that bringeth salvation hath appeared to *all men*, teaching us that, denying ungodliness and worldly lusts, we should live soberly, righteously, and godly, in this present world" (Titus 2:11,12); that is, the gift of salvation by grace through faith has been offered freely to all men, but not all men will come to God on His terms.

When Romans 5:18 speaks of judgment and condemnation coming upon "all men," certainly this is literally speaking of "all men" because judgment did come upon all men. According to the same verse, it was to the same "all men" that the free gift of justification by Christ's righteous act came. While the universalists will use this passage in their favor, it does not mean that all men are justified. That the free gift came to all men does not mean that all men accepted the free gift. That salvation has been made available to all people does not mean that all people will be saved because many will reject the free gift.

"But we see Jesus, who was made a little lower than the angels for the suffering of death, crowned with glory and honor; that he by the grace of God should taste death for *every man*" (Hebrews 2:9). Again, this is not implying universal salvation. Jesus underwent the bitter agonies of the shameful, excruciating and cursed death of the cross as the Lamb of God "which taketh away the sin of the world" (John 1:29). This is not to say that all men will have an obedient, love, faith relationship with God and be saved. Part of the putting "all things in subjection under his feet" (Hebrews 2:8) does not necessitate universal salvation but includes the punishment of everlasting destruction from the presence of the Lord (2 Thessalonians 1:9). "The LORD hath made all things for himself: yea, even the wicked for the day of evil" (Proverbs 16:4). Therefore, we must consider all passages in light of the whole of Scripture, not as isolated proof texts for universalism or any other view for that matter.

Since universalism is so popular today, we must wonder why universalism is absolutely foreign to the intertestamental and New Testament literature. Church historian Phillip Schaff states:

> Everlasting punishment of the wicked always was, and
> always will be the orthodox theory. It was held by the

Jews at the time of Christ, with the exception of the Sadducees, who denied the resurrection. It is endorsed by the highest authority of the most merciful Being, who sacrificed his own life for the salvation of sinners. . . .

Matt. 12:32 (the unpardonable sin); 26:24 (Judas had better never been born); 25:46 ("eternal punishment" contrasted with "eternal life"); Mark 9:48 ("Gehenna, where their worm dieth not, and the fire is not quenched"). In the light of these solemn declarations we must interpret the passages of Paul (Rom. 5:12 sqq.; 14:9; 1 Cor. 15:22, 28), which look towards universal restoration. The exegetical discussion lies outside of our scope, but the meaning of "aijwvnio" has been drawn into the patristic discussion, it is necessary to remark that the argumentative force lies not in the etymological and independent meaning of the word, which is limited to aeon, but in its connection with future punishment as contrasted with future reward, which no man doubts to be everlasting (Matt. 25:46).[311]

Despite two thousand years of church history, the Emergent Church prescribes to universalism. In the words of Ooze's Spencer Burke, he writes:

When I say I'm a universalist, what I really mean is that I don't believe you have to convert to any particular religion to find God. As I see it, God finds us, and it has nothing to do with subscribing to any particular religious view. . .

Universalism, as it's traditionally understood, is an attempt to offer another way of understanding the world. If you think about it, there is a certain madness to the idea that members of only one religious group can make

---

311 Philip Schaff, *History of the Church,* 1910 Edition, Vol. 2 (New York, NY: C. Scribner), chapter 12, footnote 1139.

it into heaven because they happen to know Jesus or some other religious figure.[312]

Knowing Jesus is precisely how a person will be eternally judged. "And this is life eternal, that they might know thee the only true God, and Jesus Christ, whom thou hast sent" (John 17:3). Those who just "happen to know" Jesus also happen to have eternal life. Those who *do not* "happen to know" Jesus *do not* have eternal life. Admittedly, there are some evangelicals who have come to the understanding of the universal reconciliation believing that all people will *eventually* be saved through Christ based on the passages discussed above, but Burke and other Emergents are teaching general universalism, that all people *are* already saved regardless of being in Christ or not. Burke's heresy goes even further beyond McLaren's by suggesting that a person may be justified before God apart from Jesus Christ, the "one mediator between God and men" (1 Timothy 2:5).

When deconstruction and reconstruction of the teachings of Jesus take place at such a heightened, irresponsible and unscriptural level as in the Emergent Movement, it is not difficult to understand the trouble involved in communication. For instance, in an interview with Todd Friel on Way of the Master Radio, Doug Pagitt told listeners his position on hell. Anybody can see the lack of clarity in the following exchange:

> FRIEL: Do you think there is an eternal damnation for people who are not Christians?
> PAGITT: Well, I think there's all kinds of, I mean, the damnation would sort of be that there's parts of the life and creation that seem to be counter to what God is doing and those are the things that are eliminated and removed and done away with. And so that's what I think damnation is. And so there's people who want to live out that kind of, um, want to have that good judgment, the judgment of God in their life, you know, biblical judgment that God remakes the world.
> FRIEL: Doug, hold on a second, I have no idea what you

---

312 Spencer Burke, *A Heretic's Guide to Eternity* (San Francisco, CA: Jossey-Bass, 2006), 197.

169

just said. Here's what I think hell is: eternal damnation.
God sends law-breakers to a place where there's
weeping, there's gnashing of teeth, a lake of sulfur, the
worm never dies, eternal conscious torment. Agree or
disagree?
PAGITT: Disagree.
FRIEL: What do you think Hell is?
PAGITT: I think Hell is disconnection and disintegration
with God.
FRIEL: I agree with that also.
PAGITT: I have no idea what you mean. Those sound
much more like metaphors than they do like actualities
but I don't know.
FRIEL: Well, those were the words Jesus used to
describe Hell.[313]

After all the obscurity, Pagitt finally shows his true colors as a
universalist. He says,"God is going to judge the life and repair, and
restore and heal the life of everybody in the same way."[314] Contrary to
what Pagitt is teaching, God "hath appointed a day, in the which he will
judge the world in righteousness by that man whom he hath ordained;
whereof he hath given assurance unto all men, in that he hath raised him
from the dead" (Acts 17:31). It is evident that God *will not* "judge . . .
repair, and restore and heal the life of everybody in the *same way*" as
Pagitt alleges because the Bible says, "But after thy hardness and
impenitent heart treasurest up unto thyself wrath against the day of wrath
and revelation of the righteous judgment of God; Who will render to
every man according to his deeds: To them who by patient continuance
in well doing seek for glory and honor and immortality, eternal life: But
unto them that are contentious, and do not obey the truth, but obey
unrighteousness, indignation and wrath, Tribulation and anguish, upon
every soul of man that doeth evil, of the Jew first, and also of the
Gentile; But glory, honor, and peace, to every man that worketh good, to
the Jew first, and also to the Gentile: For there is no respect of persons

313 Todd Friel, interview with Doug Pagitt, *Way of the Master Radio*, October
22, 2007.
314 Ibid.

with God" (Romans 2:5-11). The disposition of the unbeliever after the Day of Judgment is totally different than that of the Christian.

Certainly there are many opinions and views concerning various Christian doctrines within the Church, but these principles of Christ such as repentance from dead works and eternal judgment, being deconstructed and reconstructed by the Emergent Church, are the non-negotiable foundations of the Christian faith (Hebrews 6:1,2). May the Emergent leadership take heed to this message of God and the sharpness of His Word against their ideals. "If they speak not according to this word, it is because there is no light in them" (Isaiah 8:20).

Love Wins

Because of the explosion of Rob Bell's 2011 book *Love Wins* in the media and book sales, it deserves careful and thorough consideration. Bell raises many good questions in his book *Love Wins*, as does the Emergent conversation as a whole, but his greatest problem is that he often leave the questions hanging and, more importantly, don't consult the Bible for answers. For instance, Bell points to the death of a high school student and raises questions about the "age of accountability."[315] What does the Bible say?

Though children are born with a propensity toward sinful behavior, all children are God's children. It may be that children must reach a certain age or maturity before they truly know good and evil as Isaiah prophesied, "For before the child shall know to refuse the evil, and choose the good" (Isaiah 7:16). Though children behave as sinners, it is as though they do not possess a moral accountability before God and are granted an immunity from judgment if they die in their infancy. Jesus said that children belong to the Kingdom of Heaven: "Suffer little children, and forbid them not, to come unto me: for of such is the kingdom of heaven" (Matthew 19:14). Jesus also said, "Verily I say unto you, Inasmuch as ye have done it unto one of the least of these my brethren, ye have done it unto me" (Matthew 25:40). The same kind of thought in Matthew 18:5 places a child in the same status with God as a Christian (Christ's brethren) even though the child did not have the

---

315 Bell, *Love Wins*, 4.

wisdom or maturity of a Christian. Also, Jesus said, "Take heed that ye despise not one of these little ones; for I say unto you, That in heaven their angels do always behold the face of my Father which is in heaven" (Matthew 18:10). The ministry of angels is to those who belong to God. Hebrews 1:14 tells us that angels are "ministering spirits, sent forth to minister for them who shall be heirs of salvation." Thus, Jesus is placing children in the class of the saved heirs of salvation since they have guardian angels.

So at what point is a person held accountable? Condemnation and wrath come upon people at the point when they reject light and choose darkness instead by suppressing the truth in unrighteousness. "And this is the condemnation, that light is come into the world, and men loved darkness rather than light, because their deeds were evil" (John 3:19). At what point in a people's lives are they condemned or accountable and why does the wrath of God abide on them? "For the wrath of God is revealed from heaven against all ungodliness and unrighteousness of men, *who hold the truth in unrighteousness*; Because that which may be known of God is manifest in them; for God hath shewed it unto them" (Romans 1:18). It is not at a specific age such as twelve (as Bell postulates) that people are accountable, but when they receive revelation of the truth in Christ and deny it.

Again, Bell opens a can of hypotheticals about the "age of accountability" and what a person must do to be saved in this short window of time: perform a rite or ritual, take a class, be baptized, join a church, say a prayer?[316] It is very simple: "He that believeth on him is not condemned: but he that believeth not is condemned already, because he hath not believed in the name of the only begotten Son of God" (John 3:18). If people have not heard the Gospel, we can trust that God will judge them according to what they did with the amount of moral truth they did have.

Bell writes about a speaking engagement he had in San Francisco at which protestors lined the sidewalks of the theatre with the message, "Turn or Burn."[317] With Bell, I share an aversion to these types of protestors and this kind of proselytizing. "Is that what Jesus taught?"[318]

---

316 Ibid., 5.
317 Ibid., 63.
318 Ibid., 64.

Well, the message is true but that's not the message we are commanded to preach. Jesus said, "Go ye into all the world, and *preach the gospel*" (Mark 16:15). He didn't say, "Go into all the world and preach, 'Turn or Burn.'" While true, I can't wholeheartedly agree with such a message because it's not saving truth. Signs like "Turn or Burn," "God Hates You," "Don't Follow Rob Bell to Hell," etc. proclaim bad news, not the good news. The Apostle Paul rejoiced even if the Gospel was preached out of contention and not sincerely (Philippians 1:16) (but that's when it's the true Gospel that's being preached). The mere preaching of truth, even biblical truth, apart from the Gospel, will never save a soul from the grasp of Hell. The only saving truth is the Gospel of Jesus Christ. That Gospel message itself is power. And this is the powerful message that must be preached in purity and simplicity; it doesn't need any wisdom of words or craftiness of speech. The simple proclaimed Gospel stands all on its own (1 Corinthians 1:17-24). The foolishness of preaching Christ crucified is the wisdom and power of God. God destroys the wisdom of the wise by changing lives through the Gospel of Jesus, not the bad (nonetheless truthful) news about hell.

Bell makes the bold claim that "In the third century the Church fathers Clement of Alexandria (150-215 AD) and Origen (184-254 AD) affirmed God's reconciliation with all people."[319] This is historically inaccurate. Clement of Alexandria and Origen speculated that, after disciplinary punishments of Gehenna, perhaps all persons would be reconciled to God. But neither of these men *affirmed* this, as Bell states. In fact, Origen taught:

> The apostolic teaching is that the soul . . . after its departure from the world, will be recompensed according to its deserts. It is destined to obtain either an inheritance of eternal life and blessedness (if its actions will have procured this for it) or to be delivered up to eternal fire and punishments (if the guilt of its crimes will have brought it down to this).[320]

But you won't find that quote from Origen in Bell's book *Love*

---

319 Ibid., 107.
320 Origen, *ANF,* 2.240 in Bercot, *A Dictionary of Early Christian Beliefs,* 246.

Wins because it supports the traditional understanding of hell. Likewise, Rob Bell said that Clement of Alexandria affirmed God's reconciliation with all people. But Clement of Alexandria taught:

> All souls are immortal, even those of the wicked, for whom it were better that they were not deathless. For, punished with the endless vengeance of quenchless fire, and not dying, it is impossible for them to have a period put to their misery.[321]

Bell made it sound like these men taught universalism, but he said nothing about the eternal punishments mentioned by these early Christians. As we have previously covered by quoting from several early Christians writers, the early church, as a whole, did not believe in universal salvation.

Bell says he believes in a literal Hell, but then goes on for several pages about "here and now" illustrations of hell.[322] He says there is Hell now and Hell later, but does he really believe that? Bell is dogmatically undogmatic. After I read his books, it was difficult to understand what Bell actually believes. In *Love Wins*, he claims to believe in a literal Hell, yet the entirety of the book is arguing against the traditional doctrine of Hell and defending universalism. He asks, "Will all people be saved, or will God not get what God wants?"[323] Bell likens God not getting what He wants to failure. Bell goes on to say that "God does not fail"[324] implying that all people must go to heaven. Indeed, it is God's will that none perish and that all come to repentance and salvation (2 Peter 3:9; 1 Timothy 2:4). But God does not force His will upon others. For example, the Pharisees who rejected His will: "the Pharisees and lawyers rejected the counsel of God against themselves, being not baptized of him" (Luke 7:30). "For this is the will of God, even your sanctification, that ye should abstain from fornication" (1 Thessalonians 4:3), and yet, even professing Christians resist the will of God and perish in their sins. Likewise, God's will was to gather all of Jerusalem into His

---

321 Clement of Alexandria, *Ante-Nicene Fathers,* volume 2, 581.
322 Bell, *Love Wins,* 71-79.
323 Ibid., 98.
324 Ibid., 100.

kingdom, but they rejected His will as Jesus said, "O Jerusalem, Jerusalem, thou that killest the prophets, and stonest them which are sent unto thee, how often would I have gathered thy children together, even as a hen gathereth her chickens under her wings, and *ye would not!*" (Luke 23:37). This refusal does not mean that God failed! A husband whose adulterous wife forsakes him, though he did everything in his power to save their marriage, is not a failure. The husband cannot be faulted for his adulterous wife's decisions in the same way that God cannot be faulted or found a failure for the choices of people who reject Jesus. God is not helpless, not powerless, not impotent *even if people go to Hell.*

Bell continues to offer false hopes after life, this time suggesting that people will be given a second chance:

> Many have refused to accept the scenario in which somebody is pounding on the door, apologizing, repenting, and asking God to be let in, only to hear God say through the keyhole: "Door's locked. Sorry. If you had been here earlier, I could have done something. But now, it's too late."[325]

However, this scenario is identical to Jesus' parable of the ten virgins, but in the parable there are no second chances. Jesus taught, "Then shall the kingdom of heaven be likened unto ten virgins, which took their lamps, and went forth to meet the bridegroom. And five of them were wise, and five were foolish. They that were foolish took their lamps, and took no oil with them: But the wise took oil in their vessels with their lamps. While the bridegroom tarried, they all slumbered and slept. And at midnight there was a cry made, Behold, the bridegroom cometh; go ye out to meet him. Then all those virgins arose, and trimmed their lamps. And the foolish said unto the wise, Give us of your oil; for our lamps are gone out. But the wise answered, saying, Not so; lest there be not enough for us and you: but go ye rather to them that sell, and buy for yourselves. And while they went to buy, the bridegroom came; and they that were ready went in with him to the marriage: and the door was shut. Afterward came also the other virgins, saying, Lord, Lord, open to

---

325 Ibid., 108.

us. But he answered and said, Verily I say unto you, I know you not" (Matthew 25:1-12). In other words, it's too late. No second chances. Even though they had a change of heart and mind, the door was shut. Can you imagine Judas being given a second chance? Jesus said of Judas who betrayed him that it had been good for that man *if he had not been born* (Matthew 26:24).

To Rob Bell, if Hell is real, then God is "terrifying, and traumatizing, and unbearable" and "can't be loved."[326] But the Apostles who wrote the New Testament never found love toward God and God's terror antithetical. Paul was aware of the terror of the Lord when He said, *"Knowing therefore the terror of the Lord*, we persuade men" (2 Corinthians 5:11). Even Jesus feared God the Father. Jesus "in the days of his flesh, when he had offered up prayers and supplications with strong crying and tears unto him that was able to save him from death, and was heard *in that he feared*" (Hebrews 5:7). Contrary to Bell's thesis, I am one Christian who loves God, believes in eternal fire, and fears God.

To Bell, the whole idea that "God will punish people for all of eternity for sins," is an "unacceptable, awful reality."[327] No matter how unacceptable it is to Bell and other Emergents, it is nevertheless reality. Thus, Bell is exchanging biblical reality for his own reality and teaching a god of his own imagination. But the Bible says, "The fear of the LORD is the beginning of wisdom" (Proverbs 9:10). Love does win in the end, but not the kind of love without truth that Bell is advocating. "Herein is our love made perfect, that we may have boldness in the day of judgment: because as he is, so are we in this world" (1 John 4:17).

---

326 Ibid., 175.
327 Ibid., 176.

9

Contemplative Mysticism

"And he said unto them, When ye pray, say, Our Father which art in heaven, Hallowed be thy name. Thy kingdom come. Thy will be done, as in heaven, so in earth."
- Jesus (Luke 11:2)

Experiencing Mysticism

Leith Anderson (Doug Pagitt's former pastor) and president of the National Association of Evangelicals spoke on how this new 21st century Emerging Church will elevate experience over doctrine:

> The old paradigm taught that if you had the right teaching, you will experience God. The new paradigm says that if you experience God, you will have the right teaching. This may be disturbing for many who assume propositional truth must always precede and dictate religious experience.[328]

This principle of exalting experience over doctrine has become a foundation for new Christianity. Emerging leader Dan Kimball quotes

---

328 Leith Anderson, *A Church For the 21st Century* (Minneapolis, MN: Bethany House Publishers, 1992), 21.

Anderson in full in his book *The Emerging Church* repeating this "new paradigm" that teaches "if you experience God, you will have the right teaching."[329] However, this "old paradigm" was the paradigm of Jesus who said, "If ye continue in my word, then are ye my disciples indeed; and *ye shall know the truth*, and the truth shall make you free" (John 8:32). Notice that knowing the objective truth comes before the subjective experience of being made free. Truth is objectively known, but to the Emergent Church truth is experienced subjectively.

In this quest for experience, Emergents have traveled back in time to find various forms of spirituality that appeal to the senses. They have sought to make the transcendent God more immanent and relevant to postmodern people in ways that can be seen, tasted, smelled and handled. Rather than embracing that which was from the beginning, which we have heard, which we have seen with our eyes, which we have looked upon, and our hands have handled, of the Word of life (1 John 1:1), the Emergent Church has embraced mysticism.

The Emergent Church claims to be borrowing spiritual practices from ancient Christianity. But the Early Church Fathers were not involved in these mystical practices being advocated by the Emerging Church. Instead, Emergents look to Roman Catholic monastic mystics, Eastern mystics, and the Desert Fathers, who were Christian hermits, ascetics, and monks who lived mainly in the Scetes desert of Egypt beginning around the third century AD.

Author Roger Oakland concluded, "Almost without exception, leaders of the emergent conversation embrace mysticism (i.e., contemplative spirituality) in their theological playgrounds; it is the element that binds the movement together."[330] When mystical experiences are exalted to such a level, theology becomes unimportant. Peter Rollins says, "We at Ikon are developing a theology which derives from the mystics, a theology without theology to complement our religion without religion."[331] The Roman Catholic Church also created a tangibility to their religion by importing all manner of objects, icons,

---

329 Dan Kimball, *The Emerging Church* (Grand Rapids, MI: Zondervan, 2003), 190.
330 Roger Oakland, *Faith Undone* (Silveron, OR: Lighthouse Trails Publishing. 2007), 102.
331 http://www.emergingchurch.info/stories/cafe/peterrollins.

saints, and smells of incense. The Emergent Church is going in the same direction as the Catholic Church but for different reasons. While the Catholic Church did so because many illiterate pagans were being brought into the church through conquest, the Emergent Church does so because of the postmodern view of language as inadequate for communication. To them, experience is a better carrier of truth than doctrine.

Simply put, mysticism could be defined as a direct experience of the supernatural realm. Tony Jones explains: "Propositional truth is out and mysticism is in. People are not necessarily put off by a religion that does not 'make sense' – they are more concerned with whether a religion can bring them into contact with God."[332]

There are two reasons that these innovative "ancient-future" pastors are promoting mysticism. First of all, mysticism is the fruit of the Emergent Church's postmodern philosophy which rejects absolute and objective truth. Consequentially, they are adopting extra-biblical spiritual practices. Rather than knowing the truth as in the Scriptures, they seek to "experience" truth, which, according to Emergents, can exist in the midst of irreconcilable contradictions. In fact, Dwight J. Friesen says that "the more irreconcilable various theological positions appear to be, the closer we are to experiencing truth."[333] In response to this "orthoparadoxy," as Friesen calls it, mature Christians are to refute, exhort and convince those who contradict sound theological doctrine (Titus 1:9). Friesen continues, "In focusing so exclusively on our cognitive capacities, we have lost our imagination. We need mystics."[334]

Secondly, the Emergent Church is adapting to a change in the worldly culture's embrace of mystical practices. They are pragmatically adapting to the culture of unbelievers by marketing mysticism. At the Leadership Network's 1995 Re-Tooling the Church Summit, Leith Anderson said, "The rules of yesterday have been replaced." In the same presentation, one of the three specific shifts that are impacting the church

---

332 R. Scott Smith, *Truth and the New Kind of Christian: The Emerging Effects of Postmodernism in the Church* (Wheaton: IL: Crossway Books, 2005), 69.

333 Dwight J. Friesen, "Orthoparadoxy," in *An Emergent Manifesto of Hope,* eds. Jones and Pagitt, 208.

334 Ibid., 233.

was, "the quest for experience before understanding and the desire for connection to God as expressed in the increasing interest in spirituality and the supernatural."[335]

Barna's research recognized a shift in the spiritual market in the mid-1990's. Barna Research Group identified "seven issues of significance in terms of church and culture in America." The first of the seven issues was "the rejection of absolute truth vs. the ascendancy of moral relativism" and "the demise of Christian orthodoxy vs. the rise of synthetic spirituality."[336] Along with issue number one, "the ascendancy of moral relativism," is the rise of postmodernity within the church led by Emergents. Secondly, "the demise of Christian orthodoxy" and "the rise of synthetic spirituality" demonstrate a departure from Biblical truth with a substitution of mystical experiences. Furthermore, at the National Re-evaluation Forum hosted by Leadership Network, hundreds of young Emergent leaders spent four days coming up with a representation of the "church of the future." They highlighted the themes of community, experience and mysticism:

> Why is mysticism re-emerging today? The emerging culture is less dependent upon a scientific and rationalistic way of thinking and has moved to a time when people want to experience God for themselves. The mystical nature of the emerging culture is leading many churches to focus in three areas: (1) an acknowledgment of people's spirituality...the issue facing many pastors today is how to lead already spiritual people to become followers of Christ. We are entering an era when society as a whole is more spiritual in nature and yet less Christian. (2) an appreciation of mystery and wonder...Christians are recovering a sense of the mystery and awe of God. (3) a return to the

---

335 "Re-Tooling the Church. . . Summit '95," *Net Fax*, Number 20, May 29, 1995, http://media.leadnet.org/blog-content/leadnet/downloads/archives/NetFax-leadnet-org.pdf.
336 "Christian Philanthropy, America, and the World," *Net Fax*, Number 6, Novemeber 14, 1994, http://media.leadnet.org/blog-content/leadnet/downloads/archives/NetFax-leadnet-org.pdf.

creative arts.[337]

Mysticism has been described in various ways. Mysticism is misleading and irrational because an emphasis is placed on feelings, emotions, the imagination, personal dreams or visions, private illumination and interpretation or other purely subjective means. Truth cannot be sought by subjective means. Jeremiah the prophet says, "The heart is deceitful above all things, and desperately wicked: who can know it?" (Jeremiah 17:9).

While the Bible is full of mystical experiences, it is important to note that all of those experiences were initiated by God and not achieved by any human formula. A mystic, on the other hand, is someone who uses rote methods in an attempt to put himself into a trance outside of God's sanction. While the Bible does describe legitimate mystical experiences, none of them are man-initiated. For example, God initiated and facilitated Peter falling into a trance and seeing a vision in Acts 11:5. The prophet Ezekiel was among the Babylonian captives by the river of Chebar when he too saw a vision: "the heavens were opened and I saw visions of God" (Ezekiel 1:1). After the prophet Daniel sought the mercies of God in order to interpret a dream from the king of Babylon, God gave him a vision in the night (Daniel 2:19). The prophet Isaiah also saw "the Lord sitting upon a throne, high and lifted up, and his train filled the temple" (Isaiah 6:1). These holy men of God did not practice some form of mysticism for the sake of having a spiritual experience. God had a message to communicate. "For the prophecy came not in old time by the will of man: but holy men of God spake as they were moved by the Holy Ghost" (2 Peter 1:21). These mystical experiences and visions beheld by apostles and prophets were divine revelations initiated by God to men, *not by the will of man but by the will of God.*[338]

Being born of the Holy Spirit is not something that can be achieved by human means or departure from the Scriptures in exchange for the writings of Roman Catholic mystics. Jesus said that it is the Holy

---

337 "Themes of the Emerging 'Church on the New Edge,'" *Net Fax*, Number 118, March 1, 1999, http://media.leadnet.org/blog-content/leadnet/downloads/archives/NetFax-leadnet-org.pdf.
338 See also Ray Yungen, *A Time of Departing* (Silverton, OR: Lighthouse Trails Publishing, 2006), 34.

Spirit that gives life and causes a person to be born again through His word. He teaches, "It is the spirit that quickeneth; the flesh profiteth nothing: the words that I speak unto you, they are spirit, and they are life" (John 6:63). Again the Apostle Peter teaches, "Being born again, not of corruptible seed, but of incorruptible, by the word of God, which liveth and abideth for ever" (1 Peter 1:23). When the clear and intended meaning of the word of God is abandoned as authoritative and life-giving truth, being born again is almost hopeless since it is by the word of God we are born again (1 Peter 1:23). Jesus said, "That which is born of the flesh is flesh; and that which is born of the Spirit is spirit" (John 3:6). When people haven't truly been born again and aren't experiencing a true relationship with Jesus Christ, they attempt to fill that spiritual void with mystical experiences. Tony Campolo, for instance, gives instructions regarding how to have a "born-again" experience. It is a Roman Catholic formula rather than a Holy Spirit-quickening by the Word of God. Campolo says, "I learned about this way of having a born-again experience from reading the Catholic mystics, especially The Spiritual Exercises of Loyola. . . . Like most Catholic mystics, he developed an intense desire to experience a 'oneness' with God."[339] In contrast Peter the Apostle said, "And we are his witnesses of these things; and so is also the Holy Ghost, *whom God hath given to them that obey him*" (Acts 5:32).

More than Candles, Incense & Couches

Across the board, Emergent Church leaders embrace and encourage mystical practices. Brain McLaren speaks of his Franciscan friend and another Emergent leader, Fr. Richard Rohr, and he recommends his book *The Naked Now: Learning to See as the Mystics See.*[340] Tony Jones describes his spiritual journey:

I voraciously read authors and books they didn't assign in seminary: St. John of the Cross, St Theresa of Avila,

---

339 Tony Camplolo, *Letters to a Young Evangelical* (New York, NY: Perseus Books Group, Basic Books, 2006), 30.
340 Brian McLaren, *A New Kind of Christianity* (New York, NY: HarperCollins Publishers, 2010), 294.

and Pilgrim's Way. I met with other Protestants, with Roman Catholics, and with Eastern Orthodox Christians. I took a long hike in the Red Mountains of Utah with a shaman.[341]

A Shaman is a person regarded as having access to and influence in the world of spirits. Typically such people enter into a state of trance and practice divination. Jones further reveals his attraction to mysticism: "Maybe it's that there's something mystical and mysterious about these ancient rites, like we're tapping into some pre-technological, pre-industiral treasury of the Spirit."[342]

As more and more churches are exposed to and enveloped in mystical spirituality, many ancient practices such as walking the labyrinth are being implemented in worship. Though labyrinths have had a recent resurgence in evangelical churches, they are not Christian by any means. Originating in early pagan societies, a labyrinth is a maze-like structure with one path in which a participant walks through to the center during times of contemplative prayer. Often, these prayer stations are included in the labyrinth with candles, icons and pictures. The labyrinth is also called a mandala or sacred design in Buddhism. In his article titled "A-maze-ing Prayer," Dan Kimball describes his labyrinth experience at a National Pastor's Convention:

> Meditative prayer like that we experienced in the labyrinth resonates with hearts of emerging generations. If we had the room, we would set up a permanent labyrinth to promote deeper prayer. Until then, however, Graceland will continue to incorporate experiential prayer and encourage our people to stop, quiet themselves, and pray.[343]

Doug Pagitt also experiments with the mystical practice of walking the labyrinth. He writes: "The experience of walking the

341 Tony Jones, *The Sacred Way* (Grand Rapids, MI: Zondervan. 2005), 16.
342 Ibid., 17-18.
343 Dan Kimball, "A-maze-ing Prayer," *Christianity Today,* October 1, 2001, http://ctlibrary.com/9665.

labyrinth invites the body into a rhythm of moving around and moving toward the center, then back out. Dozens of people may walk the labyrinth together, some walking in, some walking out."[344] In his book entitled *Body Prayer - The Posture of Intimacy With God*, Doug Pagitt endorses more ancient and unbiblical practices: "People of faith in ancient times understood such physical acts and practices as rest and worship, dietary restrictions, and mandated fabric in their wardrobes were of great value to their faith and life."[345] It is amazing to find the Emergent leaders endorsing similar things the Apostle Paul spoke against because of the tendency to spoil and beguile believers away from the simplicity in Christ. He says, "Let no man beguile you of your reward in a voluntary humility and worshipping of angels, intruding into those things which he hath not seen, vainly puffed up by his fleshly mind, And not holding the Head, from which all the body by joints and bands having nourishment ministered, and knit together, increaseth with the increase of God. Wherefore if ye be dead with Christ from the rudiments of the world, why, as though living in the world, are ye subject to ordinances, (*Touch not; taste not; handle not; Which all are to perish with the using;*) after the commandments and doctrines of men? Which things have indeed a shew of wisdom in will worship, and humility, and neglecting of the body; not in any honor to the satisfying of the flesh" (Colossians 2:18-23).[346]

They are less concerned with truth while elevating spiritual practices. But God is interested in both. Jesus said, "The true worshippers shall worship the Father *in spirit and in truth*" (John 4:23). Not just in truth. Not just in spirit. But in spirit and in truth. Jesus said, "God is a Spirit: and they that worship him must worship him in spirit and in truth" (John 4:24). Roman Catholic Monastic Mysticism and

---

344 Doug Pagitt, *Church Re-Imagined* (Grand Rapids, MI: Zondervan. 2005), 103.

345 Doug Pagitt and Kathryn Prill, *Body Prayer - The Posture of Intimacy With God* (Colorado Springs, CO: WaterBrook Press, 2005), 3.

346 By the way, Paul was not licensing gluttony, self-indulgence, or vanity. Paul also said, "(For many walk, of whom I have told you often, and now tell you even weeping, that they are the enemies of the cross of Christ: whose end is destruction, whose God is their belly, and whose glory is in their shame, who mind earthly things.)" (Philippians 3:18,19).

Eastern Mysticism are not worship that pleases God because they are not according to truth. Mysticism claims that people will have a spiritual experience by following a certain procedure. Paul warned us not to be mesmerized by asceticism (Colossians 2:18-24).

There is an appearance of wisdom in mystical practices because they are genuine spiritual experiences that can be measured. Anybody can have a spiritual experience through mysticism, even unbelievers. While the Bible says, "Faith cometh by hearing, and hearing by the word of God" (Romans 10:17), Emergent faith comes by seeing images, touching icons, smelling incense, tasting bread and wine, hearing chants and walking the labyrinth. This sensual spirituality may make people feel good, but it is not grounded in the truth.

God is not interested in candles, incense, and couches on which the Emergent Church places much emphasis. We are told in Revelation that the incense in heaven is the prayers of the saints (Revelation 5:8). In many ways, the Emergent Church makes similar mistakes as the Eastern Orthodox Church thinking that they are going back early Christianity by embracing things like incense and icons. But they are not going back far enough for their sources because the earliest Church sources spoke against these mystical practices. Justin Martyr (160 AD) said, "God has no need of streams of blood, libations, and incense."[347] Athenagoras (175 AD) said, "The Framer and Father of this universe does not need blood, nor the odor of burnt-offerings, nor the fragrance of flowers and incense, for He is Himself perfect fragrance."[348] Lactantius (304-313 AD) said, "God is not appeased with incense . . . Rather, He is appeased by a reform of the morals."[349]

Icons and images embraced by Emergent and Eastern Orthodox churches–the primitive Church earlier prohibited these customs because they were attributed to the Gnostics (a heretical sect), and pagan Gentiles. Some even went as far as saying that demons possessed these

---

347 Justin Martyr, *ANF*, 1.166 in Bercot, *A Dictionary of Early Christian Beliefs*, 361.
348 Athenagoras, *ANF*, 2.134, 135 in Bercot, *A Dictionary of Early Christian Beliefs*, 361.
349 Lactantius, *ANF*, 7.277 in Bercot, *A Dictionary of Early Christian Beliefs*, 361.

images of the dead.[350] They based this understanding on the following Scriptures: "Wherefore, my dearly beloved, flee from idolatry" (1 Corinthians 10:14); "we walk by faith, not by sight" (2 Corinthians 5:7); "Little children, keep yourselves from idols" (1 John 5:21).

Spiritual Formation Disciplines

Again, rather than going back to the early pre-Nicene Church for spiritual formation, the Emergent movement turns toward Roman Catholic practices and medieval monastic disciplines. Emergent writer Mark Scandrette described the Emergent churches as having a "renewed interest in contemplative and bodily spiritual formation disciplines."[351] McLaren admits: "Many Christian leaders started searching for a new approach under the banner of 'spiritual formation.' This new search has led many of them back to Catholic contemplative practices and medieval monastic disciplines."[352]

The leaders of the spiritual formation movement often are Catholic mystics such as Henri Nouwen and Thomas Merton, and teachers such as Richard Foster and Dallas Willard. In the *Christianity Today* article "The Emergent Mystique," McLaren named Richard Foster as one of the "key mentors for the emerging church."[353] Quaker Richard Foster is one theologian advocating Contemplative Prayer, also known as Centering Prayer or Listening Prayer.[354] There is little difference between the mystical practices of the Emergent Church and those practiced by mystics of other religions, whether they be Roman Catholic Trappist monks, Buddhist, Hindu, or Muslims. Much like Eastern meditation practices which include breathing exercises and mantras (repeated words or phrases), the contemplative mystical silence is accomplished by the

---

350Bercot, *A Dictionary of Early Christian Beliefs,* 351,352.

351 Mark Scandrette, "Growing Pains," in *An Emergent Manifesto of Hope.* eds. Doug Pagitt and Tony Jones, 28.

352 McLaren, *A Generous Orthodoxy,* 246.

353 Andy Crouch, "The Emergent Mystique," *Christianity Today,* November, 2004, 39.

354 Foster says, "we should all without shame enroll as apprentices in the school of contemplative prayer." Richard Foster, *Celebrations of Discipline* (San Francisco, CA: Harper & Row, 1978 edition), 13.

same methods. Emergent leader Tony Jones also mentions new ways of praying and meditating by focusing on the breath and using repetitive mantras. He says:

> [S]eated comfortably in a dimly lit room with the head bowed, attend to your breathing, and then begin the prayer in rhythm with your breathing. Breath in: 'Lord Jesus Christ, Son of God' breathe out: 'have mercy on me a sinner.' Guarding the mind against all distractions, the pray-er focuses during every repetition on the meaning of the words, praying them from the heart and in the heart. . . In order to keep track of my repetitions, I use a prayer rope.[355]

Generally, practices like these known as "breath prayers" are advocated in order to pray without ceasing. However, we find applicable instruction in Luke 11 concerning prayer: "And it came to pass, that, as he was praying in a certain place, *when he ceased*, one of his disciples said unto him, Lord, teach us to pray, as John also taught his disciples" (Luke 11:1). Notice that Jesus was praying and then he ceased. First of all, this shows us that the commands to "pray without ceasing" (1 Thessalonians 5:17), and to pray "always" (Ephesians 6:18) are not necessarily literal as the mystics affirm because Jesus Himself ceased from prayer. Rather, these commands teach us to continually petition God as the persistent widow who never gave up in asking (Luke 18:1-8), a parable Jesus taught so that "men ought always to pray, and not to faint" (Luke 18:1), but not literally every minute of every day. Though Christians should pray often, we can walk with God moment by moment without being in constant and focused prayer.

Dan Kimball, author of *The Emerging Church*, also teaches different methods to reach the emerging generation: "We have neglected so many of the disciplines of the historical church, including weekly fastings, practicing the silence, and lectio divina."[356] In lectio divina, readers may randomly open their Bibles and begin reading any given verse isolated from any contextual understanding in order to create a

355 Jones, *The Sacred Way,* 17.
356 Kimball, *The Emerging Church,* 223.

mystical experience. They will repeat that verse over and over again like a mantra. The danger is that the same mystical experience may be duplicated using any other book as long as the readers were convinced that the book had some spiritual qualities. McLaren also exhorts readers to "find things to do with the Bible other than read and study it." He then adds, "If you've never learned lectio devina—an ancient approach to Scripture cherished by the Benadictines—find someone who can teach it to you."[357] Tony Campolo has also been a persistent proponent of lectio divina: "You open the Bible, read 3 or 4 verses, then center down on Jesus. Close your eyes and say, 'Jesus, tell me what you want me to learn through the scriptures I just read.'"[358]

Campolo teaches many other forms of contemplative spirituality as well such as "Centering Prayer," with the use of mantras, Campolo describes:

> In my case intimacy with Christ has developed gradually over the years, primarily through what Catholic mystics call "centering prayer." Each morning, as soon as I wake up, I take time—sometimes as much as a half hour—to center myself on Jesus. I say his name over and over again to drive back the 101 things that begin to clutter up my mind the minute I open my eyes. Jesus is my mantra, as some would say.[359]

Such an approach to spirituality is a blatant departure from Jesus who said, "But when ye pray, use not vain repetitions, as the heathen do: for they think that they shall be heard for their much speaking. Be not ye therefore like unto them: for your Father knoweth what things ye have need of, before ye ask him" (Matthew 6:7,8). Mantra mediation or sacred

---

357 Campolo and McLaren, *Adventures in Missing the Point,* 85.
358 "Role of the Church in Reaching People Today: Motivating the Church to Live Out the Great Commission — 11:00 AM Service," Garfield Memorial Church in Cleveland, OH, September 19, 2010, http://tonycampolo.org/sermons/2010/09/role-of-the-church-in-reaching-people-today-motivating-the-church-to-live-out-the-great-commission-1100-am-service/.
359 Tony Campolo, *Letters to a Young Evangelical,* 26.

word prayer qualifies as "vain repetition."

The Silence

Tony Campolo provides commentary on his contemplative prayer method of silence, one of two things he does to revitalize his passion for evangelism. He says:

> I get up in the morning a half hour before I have to and spend time in absolute stillness. I don't ask God for anything. I just simply surrender to His presence and yield to the Spirit flowing into my life. Isaiah 40:31 says, "Those who wait on the Lord will renew their strength." The next verse says, "Keep silent before me."[360]

First of all, Isaiah 40:31 and 41:1 say nothing about prayer. Secondly, in context, Isaiah 41:1 which says, "Keep silence before me," appears to be the Lord speaking to the idolatrous nations and isles that opposed God's people. Isaiah 41:1 says, "Keep silence before me, *O islands*." The chapter continues with "the isles" (Isaiah 41:5) exalting themselves over God and making idols (Isaiah 41:1-7). It is not until Isaiah 41:8 that Isaiah addresses God's people: "But thou, Israel, art my servant," in contrast to the idolatrous practices of the islands around them. In this way, taken out of context, other Old Testament Scriptures are used to by Emergents to teach this practice of "silence," but when they are more closely examined, they aren't necessarily encouraging this practice at all.[361] Neither the Old nor New Testament teaches this practice

---

360 Tony Campolo, "5 Outreach Methods and Practices," *Outreach* magazine, http://www.churchleaders.com/outreach-missions/outreach-missions-articles/139471-tony-campolo-on-outreach.html.

361 Some contemplative proponents quote Psalm 46:10, "Be still, and know that I am God." However, the context of the Psalm puts this in an entirely different frame of reference. "Come, behold the works of the LORD, what desolations he hath made in the earth. He maketh wars to cease unto the end of the earth; he breaketh the bow, and cutteth the spear in sunder; he burneth the chariot in the fire. Be still, and know that I am God: I will be exalted among the heathen, I will be exalted in the earth. The LORD of hosts is with us; the God of

of being silent in prayer. Lectio Divina causes Emergents to take Scripture out of context in support of their mystical disciplines.

While there is nothing inherently wrong with being silent before God, this type of mysticism and contemplative prayer generally leads toward emptying of the mind of all thought, a practice which characterizes meditation in many false religions rather than Christianity. For instance, Shane Hipps, teaching pastor at Rob Bell's church Mars Hill in Grand Rapids, Michigan, in his sermon entitled "Enlightenment," goes beyond the Scriptures in teaching the method of "silent prayer" and encouraging his congregation to try this practice for five minutes a day. He says:

> Silent prayer is when you go to a silent place and then you quiet the mind. And you don't say anything to God. You just be. Now, if any of you have ever tried this, you know it's totally maddening to try and just stop thinking, right?[362]

These methods sound more like New Age transcendental meditation than they do Christian spirituality. When asked how to pray, Jesus answered, "When ye pray, say, Our Father which art in heaven, Hallowed be thy name. Thy kingdom come. Thy will be done, as in heaven, so in earth" (Luke 18:1). When you pray, say! Therefore, sitting

---

Jacob is our refuge. Selah" (Psalm 46:8-11). In other words, this is an admonishment or even a rebuke from God to be still or calm and tremble no more but know that the Lord is God, He is God alone. God is our refuge, He will exalt Himself and fight our battles. The Psalm is not talking about practicing silence necessarily. Others often cite Psalm 62:5, "My soul, wait in silence for God only, For my hope is from Him" (NASB). However, this Psalm is not instructive on how to pray either. Psalm 62 is presenting God as our Savior and refuge, expecting and waiting for the salvation of our soul to come from Him. The KJV says, "My soul, wait thou only upon God; for my expectation is from him. He only is my rock and my salvation: he is my defence; I shall not be moved. In God is my salvation and my glory: the rock of my strength, and my refuge, is in God" (Psalm 62:5-7).

362 Shane Hipps, "Enlightenment, a teaching on the inner dimension of discipleship," Trinity Mennonite, October 19, 2008, http://shanehipps.com/2008/10/enlightenment/

in silence would be a direct contradiction to how Jesus taught us to pray.

Tony Jones not only advocates the use of prayer ropes made in Greek monasteries, but also devotes entire chapters of his book *The Sacred Way* to such subjects as centering prayer and *The Cloud of Unknowing* (a 14th century work by an anonymous Christian mystic on contemplative prayer). While Hipps teaches to "stop thinking," Jones describes it as "beyond thinking," when he explains:

> The basic method promoted in *The Cloud* is to move beyond thinking into a place of utter stillness with the Lord . . . the believer must first achieve a state of silence and contemplation, and then God works in the believer's heart.[363]

Whether we "stop thinking" or "move beyond thinking" in silence, the result is a subjective, relative, and irrational approach to God and truth. The Bible never encourages us to stop thinking in prayer but quite the opposite. Notice Clement of Alexandria (195 AD) practiced silent prayer, but it involved deep thought and communication with God. He said, "Prayer, then, to speak more boldly, is conversation with God. Though whispering (and consequently, not opening the lips), we speak in silence, yet we cry inwardly."[364] Deep prayer requires deep concentration and thought toward God, not the opposite. To stop thinking or move beyond thinking is a futile spiritual practice that will only draw someone further away from God. Yet this practice is very prevalent within the Emerging Church as Jones and Hipps demonstrate. Brennan Manning, American author, friar, priest, and speaker, is well-known in contemplative circles. He also writes:

> [T]he first step in faith is to *stop thinking* about God at the time of prayer. . . .
>
> [E]nter into the great silence of God. Alone in that silence, the noise within will subside and the Voice of

---

363 Tony Jones, *The Sacred Way* (Grand Rapids, MI: Zondervan, 2005), 71,72.
364 Clement of Alexandria, *ANF*, 2.534 in Bercot, *A Dictionary of Early Christian Beliefs,* 529.

Love will be heard.[365]

This "state of silence" spoken of by Emergents sounds much like the contemplative spirituality of Richard Foster, key-mentor of Emergents, who also says, "Progress in intimacy with God means progress toward silence."[366] Richard Foster tells us of the silence: "We are to live in a perpetual, inward, listening silence so that God is the source of our words and actions."[367]

Episcopalian Bishop Alan Jones, in his book *Reimagining Christianity,* also speaks about the silence in the context of "the life of contemplative prayer":

> Loved and in communion with all things, the soul is born in and out of the secret silence of God. This silence at the heart of mysticism is not only the meeting point of the great traditions but also where all hearts might meet.[368]

Again, there is nothing wrong with praying in silence. The problem arises with mysticism and the practice of silence becoming an open door to incorporating other religious mystic traditions by which "all hearts" might meet. When relative subjectivity is coupled with this "silence at the heart of mysticism . . . *where all hearts meet,*" all mystic traditions become valid, whether they be Christian, Jewish, Muslim, Buddhist or Hindu. This syncretism can be clearly documented as the outcome of those who practice mysticism in Emergence Christianity. For instance, Alan Jones, as well as Emergents like Brian McLaren and Richard Rohr, are part of the "Living Spiritual Teachers Project" along with New Agers, Buddhists and Muslims. [369] Alan Jones explains:

---

365 Brennan Manning, *The Signature of Jesus* (Sisters, OR: Multnomah, 1996, revised edition), 212, 215.

366 Ibid., 155.

367 Ibid., 166.

368 Alan Jones, *Reimagining Christianity* (Hoboken, NJ: John Wiley & Sons, 2005), 174.

369 Others include Marcus J. Borg , Wayne Dyer, Richard J. Foster, Matthew Fox, Thomas Keating, David Spangler, John Shelby Spong, Eckhart

But another ancient strand of Christianity teaches that
we are all caught up in the Divine Mystery we call God,
that the Spirit is in everyone, and that there are depths of
interpretation yet to be plumbed. . . . At the cathedral we
"break the bread" for those who follow the path of the
Buddha and walk the way of the Hindus.[370]

It should not be surprising that McLaren has endorsed this
panentheistic and inter-spiritual teaching of Alan Jones that the "Spirit is
in everyone." McLaren gave an endorsement of the same book by Jones:

It used to be that Christian institutions and systems of
dogma sustained the spiritual life of Christians.
Increasingly, spirituality itself is what sustains
everything else. Alan Jones is a pioneer in reimagining a
Christian faith that emerges from authentic spirituality.[371]

As the Emergent Church guru, McLaren has endorsed many
books which blatantly teach these anti-Christian ideas of all-inclusive
spirituality. Mysticism and contemplative practices such as "the silence"
are among the many avenues of postmodernism that lead to spiritual
plurality. To Emergence Christians, a person can be a Christian while
simultaneously being a Buddhist, Hindu, Muslim or New Ager. For
instance, Rev. Nanette Sawyer, the community pastor of Wicker Park
Grace and contributor to *An Emergent Manifesto of Hope,* states:

I am a Christian today because of a Hindu meditation
master. She taught me some things that Christians had
not. She taught me to meditate, *to sit in silence* and
openness in the presence of God. . . . I believe that all

Tolle, Desmond Tutu, Jim Wallis, Ken Wilber, Marianne Williamson. See
"Living   Spiritual   Teachers   Project,"
http://www.spiritualityandpractice.com/teachers/index.php?pg=9.
370   Alan Jones, *Reimagining Christianity* (Hoboken, NJ: John Wiley &
Sons. 2005), 89.
371 Ibid., back cover.

people are children of God.[372]

How can this statement go unchecked? All people are not the children of God: "But as many as received him [Jesus Christ], *to them* gave he power to become the sons of God, even to them that believe on his name: Which were born, not of blood, nor of the will of the flesh, nor of the will of man, but of God" (John 1:12,13). "For as many as are led by the Spirit of God, *they are the sons of God*" (Romans 8:14). Speaking exclusively to Christians, the Apostle John stated, "Behold, what manner of love the Father hath bestowed upon us, *that we* should be called the sons of God: therefore the world knoweth us not, because it knew him not. Beloved, now are *we the sons of God*, and it doth not yet appear what we shall be: but we know that, when he shall appear, we shall be like him; for we shall see him as he is" (1 John 3:1,2). Certainly, all people are children of God in the sense that God gave them life, but not in the context that Emergents force and thereby legitimize false religions and practices such as Hindu meditation. Jesus made it clear that not all people are children of God when He said to the apostate Jews, "Ye are of your father the devil, and the lusts of your father ye will do." (John 8:44).

All-inclusive Spirituality

Inevitably, subjective and relative truth leads to an all-inclusive spirituality. The Emergent Church has only sprinkled Jesus on top and called it Christian, but it is nothing of the sort. For instance, Rob Bell preaches to his congregation about practicing Yoga in conjunction with "breath prayer." Perhaps this idea was also in mind in the making of Rob Bell's *Nooma* mini-film series (Nooma comes from the Greek word *pneuma*, meaning spirit or breath). Eastern religion seems to be Bell's inspiration for in his own words, "In Yoga, one of the central tenets of Yoga is your breath needs to remain the same regardless of the pose."[373]

---

372 Nanette Sawyer in *An Emergent Manifesto of Hope,* eds. Jones and Pagitt, 45.

373 "Rob Bell Teaching Eastern Spirituality." *Muddy Streams,* January 28, 2010, http://muddystreams.wordpress.com/2010/01/28/why-is-rob-bell-teaching-eastern-spirituality/. See Bell's original sermon: http://blogs.echurchnetwork.net/Assets/UserBlog/314/052905.mp3.

Later in his sermon, Rob Bell takes deep breaths in between sentences and says that in Yoga:

> [I]t's not how flexible you are, it's not whether you can do the poses, it's not how much you can bend yourself, it's can you keep your breath consistent through whatever you are doing. And the Yoga masters say this is how it is when you follow Jesus and surrender to God. It's your breath being consistent. It's your connection with God regardless of the pose you find yourself in. That's integrating the divine into the daily.[374]

Yoga masters following Jesus? Bell's teachings are not Christian but pagan. Bell's false teachings about breath, poses, and Yoga Masters finding God are deceiving multitudes away from the simplicity in Jesus Christ. Bell speaks about Eastern practices such as meditation, silence, breath prayer, and centered prayer all in the same breath, and attempts to integrate these practices into Christianity through blatant lies:

> *Central to the Christian tradition for thousands of years have been disciplines of meditation, reflection, silence, and breathing.* It was understood that to be a healthy person and to be fully connected with God and to be fully centered, you would spend significant parts of your day in silence breathing, meditating, praying, allowing the Spirit of God to transform you and touch you. And the word *ruah* means breath, (long breath) but it also means "spirit."[375]

Yoga and the spiritual disciplines associated with it were never central to the Christian tradition. They are not in the Bible. Yoga renamed is still a Hindu practice no matter how much it is "Christianized." For example, professor Subhas Tiwari of the Hindu University at America challenges any attempts to snatch Yoga from its Hindu roots. Tiwari states that Yoga is inseparable from Hinduism:

---

374 Ibid.
375 Ibid.

> The simple, immutable fact is that yoga originated from the Vedic or Hindu culture. Its techniques were not adopted by Hinduism, but originated from it. . . . Efforts to separate yoga from its spiritual center reveal ignorance of the goal of yoga.[376]

In other words, Christian Yoga is an ultimate oxymoron. Even if Jesus' name is used, these Eastern practices will never be Christian because they cannot be extracted from their demonic origin. One Yoga teacher wrote, "Ultimately, yoga 'workouts' just may be the way that mysticism sneaks in the back door of American culture."[377]

Despite the fact that Yoga is inseparable from Hinduism, Pagitt is another avid supporter of Yoga. In fact, he devotes most of a chapter to the subject in *Church Re-Imagined* by giving specific instructions and encouraging others to practice it.[378] On a *CNN* segment called "Does God Approve of Yoga?" John MacArthur and Doug Pagitt debated about whether or not Yoga was dangerous for the Christian faith. On the television program they defined Yoga from the Merriam-Webster dictionary as a "Hindu theistic philosophy teaching the suppression of all activity of body, mind, and will in order that the self may realize its distinction from them and obtain liberation." Responding to Pagitt's defense for Christian practice of Yoga, MacArthur concluded, "That doesn't sound anything like Christianity," and also said,

> The idea of Christianity is to fill your mind with biblical truth and focus on the God that is above you, that's Christian worship. The idea of Yoga is to fill your mind with nothing except to focus on yourself and try to find the god that is inside of you. From a Christian viewpoint,

---

376 Subhas R. Tiwari, "Yoga Renamed Is Still Hindu," *Hinduism Today,* January/Febraury/March 2006, http://www.hinduismtoday.com/modules/smartsection/item.php?itemid=1456.

377 "World of Yoga." *Yoga Journal,* September/October 1994, 49.

378 See Doug Pagitt, *Church Re-Imagined* (Grand Rapids, MI: Zondervan. 2005), chapter 4, "Spiritual Formation Through Physicality."

that is a false religion.[379]

Perhaps the most troubling comments by Pagitt came after the debate. According to Pagitt, the woman "doing the filming" in Minneapolis for the CNN broadcast had a conversation with him:

WOMAN: Way to go!
PAGITT: Well, thanks. . . It's just so weird isn't' it, to hear people say stuff like that, like what he's saying?
WOMAN: That's the reason many younger people don't go to church. You know what I mean?
PAGITT: I do.
WOMAN: Because everything's so black and white, you know. A position has nothing to do with your body and spirituality, are you kidding me? [Laughter]. Seriously.
PAGITT: [sarcastically] If you want to relieve stress, go to the Word of God.
WOMAN: Yea. [More laughter].
PAGITT: Oh my goodness. . . . I apologize for him [MacArthur].[380]

This conversation is stunning and disturbing. Perhaps this woman was an unbeliever, yet Pagitt never shared the Gospel with her. Instead, he apologized for John MacArthur, mockingly repeated MacArthur's advice to go to the Word of God to relieve stress, and dismissed his biblical approach as "weird." This interview clearly demonstrates how New Christianity is not Christianity at all!

Paul pleaded with men to turn from false gods unto the living

---

379 "More on the CNN Debate 'Does God Approve of Yoga?'" YouTube video, posted by "LaneCh," March 30, 2008, http://www.youtube.com/watch?v=oVdLZlBYseg&feature=channel.
380 Ibid. See also Phil Johnson, "Biblical Propositions, Yoga Positions, and Contextualizing the Christian Message for People Who Work at CNN," *PyroManiacs,* September 21, 2007, http://teampyro.blogspot.com/2007/09/biblical-propositions-yoga-positions.html. Audio available, http://www.spurgeon.org/~phil/sounds/01pagitt.mp3.

God (Acts 14:15), but the Emergent Church is endorsing them. Isaiah the prophet spoke of apostate Israel being compromised by these eastern philosophies and practices: "Therefore thou hast forsaken thy people the house of Jacob, because they be replenished from the east, and are soothsayers like the Philistines, and they please themselves in the children of strangers" (Isaiah 2:6). Borrowing false religious practices and throwing them together into the mix of Christian worship is like the harlotry and fornication of Israel in the days of Ezekiel the prophet. Though Israel was called God's people in name, as Emergent is nominally Christian, she embraced the idolatry of the Egyptians, the Philistines, the Assyrians and the Canaanites. In the same way, the Emergent Church "playedst the harlot because of thy renown, and pouredst out thy fornications on every one that passed by" (Ezekiel 16:15). This compromise can lead to inter-spirituality.

In fact, the founder of Shalem Prayer Institute, an ecumenical organization and top contemplative prayer school in America explains, "The mystical stream is the Western bridge to Far Eastern spirituality."[381] Author Carl McColman, who studied meditation and contemplative prayer at the same Shalem Prayer Institute, acknowledges that there is no difference between Christian mysticism and the Eastern mysticism of Hinduism and Buddhism. In *The Big Book of Christian Mysticism*, he writes that ultimately, "no absolutely clear distinction can be drawn between Christian and non-Christian mysticism.[382] The author says that "Christian mystics have displayed an unusual openness to the wisdom of non-Christian philosophy and religion," and "Christian mysticism seems from the beginning to have had an intuitive recognition to the way in which mysticism is a form of unity that transcends religious difference."[383] McColman concludes:

> And the twentieth century will go down in history as the great age of inter-religious spirituality, with mystics like Thomas Merton, Bede Griffiths, Swami Abhishiktananda, Cynthia Bourgeault, and many others

---

381 Tilden Edwards, *Spiritual Friend* (New York, NY: Paulist Press, 1980), 18.
382 Carl McColman, *The Big Book of Christian Mysticism* (Charlottesville, VA: Hampton Roads Publishing Company, 2010), 63,64.
383 Ibid., 65.

expressing their Christian faith in ways that reveal the influence of wisdom traditions such as Suffism, Vedanta, or Zen."[384]

Suffism is the mysticism of Islam, Vedanta is the mysticism of Hinduism, and Zen is the mysticism of Buddhism. In reality, any "Christian faith" influenced by these mystical traditions of other religions is not really Christian. Inter-religious spirituality is the language of the Emergent Church. In fact, Emergent guru Brian McLaren endorses McColman's book:

> Before I heard about *The Big Book of Mysticism*, I had been thinking about how such a book has been needed for a long time. Now, having read it, I'm glad we waited for Carl McColman to come along and write it. It's accessible, well-informed, balanced, broad . . . just what we needed.[385]

McLaren apparently read the segment about there being no distinction between Christian and non-Christian mystics. Rather than opposing the book, he wholeheartedly endorsed the book. Also to endorse the book were other Emergents such as Franciscan priest Richard Rohr, founder of The Center for Action and Contemplation, and Phyllis Tickle, author of *The Great Emergence*.[386]

Campolo labors to make many parallels between Muslim mysticism and Christianity. He says that the Sufis "had a dimension of spirituality that included 'speaking in tongues,' which could be compared to what goes on in the present-day Pentecostalism."[387] He doesn't know

---

384 Ibid.
385 Ibid., back cover.
386 One article describes Phyllis Tickle and Richard Rohr along with McLaren and Tony Jones as "most notable leaders in the Emerging Christianity movement." See Sam Hodges, "Richard Rohr, Phyllis Tickle, Brian McLaren on bill for 'Emerging Christianity' conference," *The Dallas Morning News,* October 22, 2010, http://religionblog.dallasnews.com/archives/2010/10/richard-rohr-phyllis-tickle-br.html.
387 Tony Campolo, *Speaking My Mind* (Nashville, TN: Thomas Nelson, 2004),

what to make of the Muslim mystics who had a high regard for Jesus such as Ibn Al Arabi and Al Hallaj. He asks,

> [A] theology of mysticism provides some hope for common ground between Christianity and Islam. Both religions have within their histories examples of ecstatic union with God, which seem at odds with their own spiritual traditions but have much in common with each other. I do not know what to make of the Muslim mystics, especially those who have come to be known as the Sufis. What do they experience in their mystical experience? Could they have encountered the same God we do in our Christian mysticism?[388]

The position that mysticism provides common ground between Islam and Christianity is standing on dangerous ground. Among many demonic doctrines of Islam, the Qur'an clearly denies the Deity of Christ[389] and the crucifixion of Christ,[390] which is in direct contrast to Christianity which declares that Jesus is both God and man (John 1:1,14; Colossians 2:9) and says there is no salvation apart from the cross (Matthew 26:28, 1 Corinthians 1:18). The Bible is clear in that "Whosoever denieth the Son, the same hath not the Father: [but] he that acknowledgeth the Son hath the Father also" (1 John 2:23). Muslims reject Jesus as the crucified and risen Son of God and Savior of the world; therefore Muslims are rejecting God. "He that hath the Son hath life; and he that hath not the Son of God hath not life" (1 John 5:12). According to the Bible, Islam is a false religion and antichrist: "Who is a liar but he that denieth that Jesus is the Christ? He is antichrist, that denieth the Father and the Son" (1 John 2:22). It is therefore untenable for any Christian convert to abide in the context of a false religion such as Islam.

When a people practice mystical methods of meditation

150.
388 Tony Campolo, *Speaking My Mind* (Nashville, TN: Thomas Nelson, 2004), 149,150.
389 Qu'ran, 4:171.
390 Qu'ran, 4:157-158.

borrowed from religions which worship demons, whether they call these methods Christian or not, they are entering into a demonic spiritual realm. The terms are different but the spirituality is the same. Even Richard Foster, named by Brian McLaren as one of the "key mentors for the emerging church,"[391] stated the dangers involved in these types of spiritual practices which he and the Emergent Church are promoting:

> I also want to give a word of precaution. In the silent contemplation of God we are entering deeply into the spiritual realm, and there is such a thing as supernatural guidance that is not divine guidance. While the Bible does not give us a lot of information on the nature of the spiritual world, we do know enough to recognize that there are various orders of spiritual beings, and some of them are definitely not in cooperation with God and his way![392]

This sounds more like occultism than Christianity. Both occultism and Christianity confirm the need to hear communication of information from a supernatural source. In Christianity, the supernatural Source is God communicating through the Holy Spirit. The Holy Spirit is truth (1 John 5:6) and "will guide you into all truth: for he shall not speak of himself; but whatsoever he shall hear, that shall he speak" (John 16:13). In the occult, the source is demonic. If the Holy Spirit will guide us, we need not to worry about demonic spiritual guidance when we are seeking God in prayer unless, of course, we are participating in mystical disciplinary practices of spiritual formation borrowed from other religions which the Word of God prohibits for this very reason. Paul states, "Ye cannot drink the cup of the Lord, and the cup of devils: ye cannot be partakers of the Lord's table, and of the table of devils" (1 Corinthians 10:21). If we pray in everything with thanksgiving letting our requests be made known to God, then "the peace of God, which passeth all understanding, shall keep your hearts and minds through

---

391 Andy Crouch, "The Emergent Mystique," *Christianity Today*, November, 2004, 39.
392 Richard Foster, *Prayer: Finding the Heart's True Home* (New York, NY: HarperCollins Publishers, 1992), 157.

Christ Jesus" (Philippians 4:6,7). Thus, a praying Christian doesn't need to worry about entering into the presence of some demonic being in the spiritual realm or receiving demonic guidance because through the blood of Jesus Christ, we have "boldness to enter into the holiest" (Hebrews 10:19) where there is no unclean thing.

10

Eschatology of Hope

"Ye shall not surely die."
– The Serpent (Genesis 3:4,5)

The Early Christian Eschatology

The Almighty clearly warned Adam: "In the day that thou eatest thereof thou shalt surely die" (Genesis 2:17). "And the serpent said unto the woman, Ye shall not surely die: For God doth know that in the day ye eat thereof, then your eyes shall be opened, and ye shall be as gods, knowing good and evil" (Genesis 3:4,5). In the Garden of Eden, the serpent assured Eve that a better outcome would be the result of accepting his theology which was in blatant contradiction of God's word. In the same way, the Emergent Church is outright contradicting God's prophetic word concerning eschatological judgment by promising a better and more hopeful eschatology for sinners as the serpent did to Eve.

As I will demonstrate, new Christians explain away the New Testament verses about the last judgment, but the early Church affirmed a very literal interpretation. For instance, Athenagoras (175 AD) wrote, "We gain conviction respecting [the resurrection] from the arguments taken from providence. I am referring to the reward or punishment due to each man in accordance with just judgment, and from the end of human existence."[393] Theophilus (180 AD) said God, "will examine all things, and will judge righteous judgment, rendering merited awards to each one."[394] Tertullian (197 AD) said, "A judgment has been ordained by God according to the merits of every man."[395] Hippolytus (c. 205 AD) wrote, "Those who have done good will be justly assigned eternal bliss. To the lovers of wickedness, there will be given eternal punishment."[396]

The ante-Nicene Church all agreed upon the eschatological judgment in which there would be eternal punishments and rewards according to merits. Why did they believe this? Because Scripture clearly teaches so. The early Christians based their beliefs on the Bible—the same as Emergents do. They quoted Scriptures to support their beliefs, the same as Emergents do. The real issue is one of Bible interpretation. So the real question becomes: Whose interpretation is more likely to be correct—the early Church or the Emergent Church? Next, I will present the alternate eschatology of the Emergent Church and how it compares to relevant Bible passages.

Alternate New Eschatology

Because the Emergent Church has such a low view of sin and a universal understanding of salvation, judgment must be erased from God's word and replaced with an alternate eschatology. Tony Jones, after poking around and trying to figure out what is going on in the Emerging Church, found out that the one common conviction among Emergents was this "eschatology of hope."[397] Though the Emergent Church is an eclectic movement, most favor of an alternate eschatology of hope in

---

393 Athenagoras, *ANF*, 2.156 in Bercot, *A Dictionary of Early Christian Beliefs*, 384.

394 Theophilus, *ANF*, 2.93 in Bercot, *A Dictionary of Early Christian Beliefs*, 384.

395 Tertullian, *ANF*, 3.127 in Bercot, *A Dictionary of Early Christian Beliefs*, 384.

396 Hippolytus, *ANF*, 5.222 in Bercot, *A Dictionary of Early Christian Beliefs*, 385.

397 *An Emergent Manifesto of Hope*, eds. Tony Jones and Doug Pagitt (Grand Rapids, MI: Baker Books, 2007), 130.

which all humanity is saved.[398] Emergent eschatology is void of the final Judgment. Bono, the Emergent Church icon, says:

> There are 2,103 verses of Scripture pertaining to the poor. Jesus Christ only speaks of judgment once. It is not all about the things that the church bangs on about. It is not about sexual immorality, and it is not about megalomania, or vanity. It is about the poor. "I was naked and you clothed me. I was a stranger and you let me in." This is at the heart of the gospel.[399]

Does Jesus speak about judgment only once? Certainly Jesus and the apostles instructed us to remember the poor, but Jesus makes several statements about judgment and *the* Judgment. This judgment has much to do with people's faith and obedience toward God, whether they were righteous or wicked (see Matthew 5:22; 12:36-37; 13:40-43,49,50).

Bono says it's not about sexual immorality, but Jesus specifically addresses the sexually immoral in reference to judgment: "But the fearful, and unbelieving, and the abominable, and murderers, and whoremongers, and sorcerers, and idolaters, and all liars, shall have their part in the lake which burneth with fire and brimstone: which is the second death" (Revelation 21:8). Jesus also mentioned how fire and brimstone rained down upon the sexually corrupt city of Sodom (Luke 17:28-29). Again, Jesus speaks of judgment in relation to sexual sin when He warned the church of Thyatira: "Notwithstanding I have a few things against thee, because thou sufferest that woman Jezebel, which calleth herself a prophetess, to teach and to seduce my servants to commit fornication, and to eat things sacrificed unto idols" (Revelation 2:20). The book of Revelation continues to link sexual immorality to God's judgment and wrath: "Neither repented they of their murders, nor

---

398 Bob DeWaay's book *The Emergent Church, Undefining Christianity* (Saint Loius Park, MN: Bob DeWaay, 2009) contains an excellent critique of the Emergent movement and the topic at hand in his chapters entitled "The Road to Paradise Imagined" and "An Eschatology of Wishful Thinking."

399 Douglas Hicks, *Global Neighbors: Christian faith and moral obligation in today's economy* (Grand Rapids, MI: Wm. B. Eerdmans Publishing Co., 2008), 51.

of their sorceries, nor of their fornication, nor of their thefts" (Revelation 9:21); "Blessed are they that do his commandments, that they may have right to the tree of life, and may enter in through the gates into the city. For without are dogs, and sorcerers, and whoremongers, and murderers, and idolaters, and whosoever loveth and maketh a lie." (Revelation 22:14-15).

In *A Is For Abductive*, the authors speak of an end of entropy in the postmodern matrix wherein, "instead of being bound to past chains of cause and effects, we will feel ourselves being pulled into the future by the magnet of God's will, God's dream, God's desire."[400] They call this a "new eschatology."[401] This eschatology is new and alternative because it is not taught in Scripture.

In *Everything Must Change*, McLaren writes:

> The Jesus of one reading of the Apocalypse brings us to a grim resignation: the world will get worse and worse, and finally this jihadist Jesus will return to use force, domination, violence, and even torture—the ultimate imperial tools—to vanquish evil and bring peace.[402]

But this is not McLaren's reading of the Apocalypse. While McLaren would have us believe *his* reading of the Apocalypse, the early Christian Gregory Thaumaturgus (c. 260 AD) wrote, "Believe that everyone will be judged individually in the future and that every man will receive the just compensation for his deeds—whether they are good or evil."[403] McLaren goes on to present an alternate "Emerging" Jesus when he says:

> The Jesus of the emerging reading we have considered in the preceding chapters tells us the opposite: that good will prevail by peace, love, truth, faithfulness, and

---

400 Sweet, McLaren, and Haselmayer, *A Is For Abductive*, 113.
401 Ibid., 14.
402 Brian McLaren, *Everything Must Change* (Nashville, TN: Thomas Nelson, Inc., 2007), 146.
403 Gregory Thaumaturgus, *ANF*, 6.17 in Bercot, *A Dictionary of Early Christian Beliefs*, 385.

courageous endurance of suffering, and that domination, violence, and torture are among the things that will be overcome.[404]

McLaren sees a contradiction in eschatological judgment and Jesus' commandments not to resist an evil person (Matthew 5:39), turn the other cheek (Matthew 5:39), and love an enemy (Matthew 5:44). Disciples of Jesus are commanded to be merciful, not to take vengeance into their own hands, and to overcome evil with good. Even though Jesus forbids Christians to defend themselves with violence unto death (James 5:6), Jesus also said, "But those mine enemies, which would not that I should reign over them, bring hither, and slay them before me" (Luke 19:27). Jesus' commandments of non-resistance do not conflict with eschatological judgment of the wicked. McLaren's eschatological scenario is unbalanced and contradictory to a biblical worldview.

According to the Bible, goodness and love *do* prevail because our good and loving God prevails to dominate the world through Christ with perfect justice (Romans 9:22; 2 Thessalonians 1:3-10; 2 Peter 2:1-12). It is a righteous thing with God to recompense tribulation to those who persecute the church. Refuting McLaren's view, the Apostle Paul talks about a violent destruction of the wicked when God takes vengeance upon them in flaming fire (2 Thessalonians 1:3-10). McLaren insinuates that God's use of force and violence in judgment is unjust. He sounds much like the objector that Paul anticipates in Romans when he says, "Is God unrighteous who taketh vengeance?"(Romans 3:5). Paul answers, "God forbid: for then how shall God judge the world?" (Romans 3:6). Paul takes it for granted that God's judgment involves vengeance, a component that has been removed from Emergent eschatology. Later in his epistle to the Romans, Paul says, "Dearly beloved, avenge not yourselves, but rather give place unto wrath: for it is written, Vengeance is mine; I will repay, saith the Lord" (Romans 12:19).

According to Emergents, God will repay the wicked with peace, love, truth and faithfulness. However, it is *because* of God's peace that He will destroy those who are for war. It is *because* of God's love that He will avenge those who hated and persecuted His bride. It is *because* of

---

404 McLaren, *Everything Must Change*, 146.

God's truth and His faithfulness that He is bound to His word to do justice. Our view of God must be balanced in accordance to His goodness and severity. "Behold therefore the *goodness* and *severity* of God: on them which fell, *severity*; but toward thee, *goodness*, if thou continue in his goodness: otherwise thou also shalt be cut off" (Romans 11:22).

Appearing in *Relevant Magazine*, Rob Bell said that the Church has been "preaching horrible messages about being left behind and that this place is going to burn—absolutely toxic messages that are against the teachings of Scripture."[405] How is it that teaching the world is going to burn against Scripture? This is exactly what Scripture teaches: "But the heavens and the earth, which are now, by the same word are kept in store, reserved unto fire against the day of judgment and perdition of ungodly men. . . . But the day of the Lord will come as a thief in the night; in the which the heavens shall pass away with a great noise, and the elements shall melt with fervent heat, the earth also and the works that are therein shall be burned up" (2 Peter 3:7,10). The early Christian Mark Minucius Felix (200 AD) addressed this point nearly two thousand years ago:

> As to the burning up of the world, it is a foolish error to deny that fire will fall upon it in an unforseen way, or to deny that the world will be destroyed by fire. . . . Who would question the fact that all things that have had a beginning will perish? All created things must come to an end.[406]

In reality, to use Bell's words, the Emergent Church doctrines are "absolutely toxic messages that are against the teachings of Scripture." Mark Felix continues,

> And I am not ignorant that many, in the consciousness of what they deserve, rather desire than believe that they

---

405 "Rob Bell Tells it like it is," *Relevant Magazine*, January/February edition, 2008.
406 Mark Minucius Felix, *ANF*, 4.194 in Bercot, *A Dictionary of Early Christian Beliefs*, 238.

shall be nothing after death; for they would prefer to be altogether extinguished, rather than to be restored for the purpose of punishment. And their error also is enhanced, both by the liberty granted them in this life, and by God's very great patience, whose judgment, the more tardy it is, is so much the more just.[407]

Jurgen Moltmann's Eschatology of Hope

"We realized very early on that we weren't going to find the intellectual resources we needed in the evangelical world, so we were either going to have to create them or borrow them," Brian McLaren noted in the 2004 article "The Emergent Matrix: A New Kind of Church." From whom did the Emergent Church "borrow" these needed intellectual resources? McLaren explains,

> It turned out that a lot of us were reading the same people, who would be more respected in the mainline world, such as Walter Brueggemann, Jurgen Moltmann and Stanley Hauerwas. What happened is we started to identify ourselves as postconservative and then we found out that there was almost a parallel movement going on in the postliberal world. And the affinities that we had were very, very strong.[408]

Tony Jones calls Jurgen Moltmann his "theological muse."[409] McLaren favorably quotes Moltmann and borrows his skewed universalist eschatological view, a "new kind of eschatology" of a "new humanity." The following quotation from Moltmann is in McLaren's book *A New Kind of Christianity*:

---

407 Ibid.

408 Scott Bader-Saye, "The Emergent matrix: A New Kind of Church," *Christian Century Magazine,* November 30, 2004.

409 Tony Jones, "Are the Social Trinity and Panentheism Incommensurable?" *Theoblogy,* May 10, 2011, http://blog.tonyj.net/2011/05/are-the-social-trinity-and-panentheism-incommensurable/.

> The Message of the new righteousness which eschatological faith brings into the world says that in fact the executioners will not finally triumph over their victims. It also says that in the end the victims will not triumph over their executioners. The one [Jesus] will triumph who first died for the victims and then also for the executioners, and in so doing revealed a new righteousness which breaks through the vicious circles of hate and vengeance and which, from the victims and executioners, creates . . . a new humanity.[410]

Who is Jurgen Moltmann? A German Reformed theologian, he was born in 1926 in Hamburg. He was drafted into German military service in 1944. He recalled reading the works of Nietzsche and Goethe's poems in the miseries of war. In 1945, he surrendered to the British and was held as a prisoner of war for the next three years. In one concentration camp, Moltmann was given a New Testament which led to his Christian conversion.[411] After being released to his hometown at age 22, Moltmann studied theology to reach the survivors of his generation. Moltmann later received his doctorate after studying under professors who were followers of Karl Barth and theologians of the non-state church at the University of Gottingen.

The eschatological orientation of Marxist philosopher Ernst Bloch was the inspiration for his first major work *Theology of Hope*. Bloch established hope as the leading principle of his Marxism and emphasized the implied humanism within mystical tradition. Bloch suggested that an atheism was within the center of Christianity embodied in the belief of the death of God. Moltmann also developed an interest in Hegel, whom he referenced more times than any other author in *Theology of Hope*.[412]

The Hegelian dialectic philosophy of Thesis, Antithesis, Synthesis in relation to eschatology begins with the biblical eschatology

---

410 Jurgen Moltmann quoted in Brian McLaren, *A New Kind of Christianity* (New York, NY: HarperCollins Publishers, 2010), 206.
411 "Jurgen Moltmann." *Wikipedia*, http://en.wikipedia.org/wiki/Jürgen_Moltmann#cite_note-0.
412 Ibid.

of future judgement and destruction of the world as the Thesis. It is then synthesized into a "better" future which Moltmann demonstrated in his theology. This is where the new emerging Christians come up with their new eschatology.

In *An Emergent Manifesto of Hope*, Dwight Friesen[413] and Tony Bronsink favorably cite Jurgen Moltmann.[414] Sounding much like he is borrowing from Jurgen Moltmann's *Theology of Hope*, Jones says, "God's promised future is good, and it awaits us, beckoning us forward. We're caught in the tractor beam of redemption and re-creation and there's no sense in fighting it, so we might as well cooperate."[415]

However, Moltmann attributes his "theology of hope" to neo-Marxist and atheist Ernst Bloch. To Ernst Bloch, "atheism was the presupposition of active hope", whereas for Moltmann, Christianity "is the ground for active and passive hope." Moltmann suggests that these two contradictory world views do not have to contradict, but can work together.[416] To Moltmann and Emergents, two contradictory world views may synthesize in an Hegelian Dialectic. Moltmann believes that separation of good and evil demonstrates "fatalistic dualism."[417] The Bible foretells of two opposing outcomes for the good and the evil, but Moltmann synthesizes these aspects so that there is an eschatology of hope for all people universally.

New Age Implications

It's important to note that not only did the Serpent give Adam and Eve a false hope in an alternate eschatology by promising them they would not die, but also said, "For God doth know that in the day ye eat thereof, then your eyes shall be opened, and ye shall be *as gods*, knowing good and evil" (Genesis 3:5). In a similar way, the New Age movement teaches that everybody can become *as gods* or *is God* already. In

---

413 *An Emergent Manifesto of Hope*, eds. Tony Jones and Doug Pagitt (Grand Rapids, MI: Baker Books, 2007), 203.
414 Ibid., 68,73.
415 Ibid., 130.
416 Jurgen Moltmann, *Theology of Hope* (Minneapolis, MN: First Fortress Press, 1991), 9.
417 Ibid., 134.

conjunction with this false eschatological scenario, Emergent leaders find much in common with New Age teachings.

In *The Secret Message of Jesus*, McLaren proposes an alternate eschatology to the book of Revelation, what he calls "an alternative approach."[418] Oddly enough, McLaren's teaching is consistent with the New Age teacher Barbara Marx Hubbard.[419] She also writes of an alternate eschatology:

> In the Book of Revelation, John the Divine saw what will happen if self-centered consciousness continues. . . . In the Book of Co-Creation we see what will happen instead if the critical mass joins spiritually in love. We will experience the Gentle Path to the New Jerusalem. In the alternative to Armageddon we shall be in the upper room of our consciousness together, linked by a common thought, which will activate the God within each of us.[420]

"Co-creation" is a common term in New Age circles as demonstrated in the works of Barabara Marx Hubbard. Much like New Agers, Emergents say, "We are invited to be part of God's creative team working to see God's dream for the universe come true."[421] Doug Pagitt also says that God invites us to "join the work of God and be co-(re)creators."[422]

The connection between Brian McLaren and New Age leader Barbara Marx Hubbard does not end with their common view of an

---

418   Brian McLaren, *The Secret Message of Jesus* (Nashville, TN: Thomas Nelson, Inc., 2006), 175-180.

419   Hubbard is the President of the Foundation for Conscious Evolution. She was featured in the 2006 film *Entheogen: Awakening the Divine Within*. She is also the subject of the biography T*he Mother of Invention: The Legacy of Barbara Marx Hubbard and the Future of "YOU"* by Neale Donald Walsch, who believes in a panentheistic God. Endorsing her newest film *Visions of a Universal Humanity* are Neale Donald Walsch and Marianne Williamson, author of *A Course in Miracles*.

420   Barbara Marx Hubbard, *The Revelation: A Message of Hope for the New Millennium* (Mill Valley, CA: 1995, second edition), 86.

421   Sweet, et al, *A Is For Abductive*, 113.

422   Pagitt, *Church Re-imagined*, 185.

alternate eschatology. Hubbard is also co-founder of the World Future Society, a nonprofit educational and scientific organization devoted to creating alternate future scenarios for planet Earth. McLaren was a featured speaker at the World Future Society Annual Conference in 2008.[423]

Emergent leaders also cite New Age leader Ken Wilber as being foundational to Emergent thinking. Ken Wilber is an American author and philosopher who has written about adult development, developmental psychology, philosophy, and ecology. While Wilber does not identify himself as a Buddhist, he has been greatly impacted by and practices Buddhist meditation methods. Wilber has been categorized as a notable New Ager because of his emphasis on transpersonal view. Wilber practices transpersonal psychology ("transpersonal" psychology seeks to blend Eastern religion with modern psychology), and is also a major proponent of Buddhist mysticism.

McLaren says Wilber is one who helped him think in developmental terms in relation to the character of God.[424] Also recommending Ken Wilber's book *A Theory of Everything,* McLaren notes that Wilber's "insights" were "seeded" throughout an entire chapter of his book.[425] McLaren and other Emergents seem to be heavily influenced by Ken Wilber. In chapter 19 "Why I Am Emergent" of *A Generous Orthodoxy,* McLaren explains:

> In this chapter I am trying (with Ken Wilber's help) to make clear that I believe there is something above and beyond the current alternatives of modern fundamentalism/absolutism and pluralistic relativism. . . . This 'above and beyond' is, I believe the way of Jesus, which is the way of love and embrace. It integrates what has gone before so that something new can emerge.[426]

---

423 World Future 2008 Preliminary Program, http://www.wfs.org/MArch-April08/WF2008_preliminary.pdf.

424 McLaren, *A New Kind of Christianity* (New York, NY: HarperCollins Publishers, 2010) 273.

425 Ibid., 293.

426 McLaren, *A Generous Orthodoxy*, 287.

In the "Endnotes" section of *Velvet Elvis*, Rob Bell recommends Ken Wilber's book: "For a mind-blowing introduction to emergence theory and divine creativity, set aside three months and read Ken Wilber's *A Brief History of Everything.*"[427] These endorsements are significant in that these leaders of Emergent not only recommend Wilber's work but claim it is foundational to "emergence theory" and "the way of Jesus." In Wilber's book, we discover that Wilber is clearly teaching a New Age worldview which cannot be reconciled with Christianity. Wilber says:

> Are the mystics and sages insane? Because they all tell variations on the same story, don't they? The story of awakening one morning and discovering you are one with the All, in a timeless and eternal and infinite fashion.
>
> Yes, maybe they are crazy, these divine fools. Maybe they are mumbling idiots in the face of the Abyss. Maybe they need a nice, understanding therapist. Yes, I'm sure that would help.
>
> But then, I wonder. Maybe the evolutionary sequence really is from matter to body to mind to soul to spirit, each transcending and including, each with a greater depth and greater consciousness and wider embrace. And in the highest reaches of evolution, maybe, just maybe, an individual's consciousness does indeed touch infinity—a total embrace of the entire Kosmos—a Kosmic consciousness that is Spirit awakened to its own true nature.
>
> It's at least plausible. And tell me: is that story, sung by mystics and sages the world over, any crazier than the scientific materialism story, which is that the entire sequence is a tale told by an idiot, full of sound and fury, signifying absolutely nothing? Listen very carefully: just which of those two stories actually sounds totally insane?[428]

427 Bell, *Velvet Elvis*, 192.
428 Ken Wilber, *A Brief History of Everything* (Boston, MS: Shambhala Publications, Inc., 2000), 38,39.

The capital "K" in Kosmos and Kosmic and "S" in Spirit demonstrate Wilber's New Age understanding of God and what Christians would call the Holy Spirit. Wilber clearly presents a false evolutionary and eschatological scenario which includes all people becoming awakened to a Kosmic consciousness in which they discover their oneness with the "All."

For Christians, our hope of glory is Christ being formed in us (Galatians 4:19; Colossians 1:27) that we might be partakers of the divine nature (2 Peter 1:4). It is good to want to be like God, but the Serpent (like the New Age and Emergent movements in this respect) appeals to human pride by usurping God's role as our shepherd: "And the serpent said unto the woman, Ye shall not surely die: For God doth know that in the day ye eat thereof, then your eyes shall be opened, and ye shall be as gods, knowing good and evil" (Genesis 3:5). "Knowing good and evil" suggests having the innate power to know right and wrong and be the "god" of one's own morality. In previous chapters we have seen how this synthesis is applicable to Emergents being the arbiter of their own moral conduct without assistance from God. In this way, and more blatantly by endorsing New Age pantheism, Emergents believe they can become *as gods*.

In that day, contrary to the Serpent's false "eschatology of hope," Adam and Eve fell into the spiritual death of sin and trespass (Ephesians 2:1) which resulted in eventual physical death (Romans 6:23). Just as the Serpent's message was partly true, Emergent teachings are partly true but hopelessly false and deceptive because they are not based on the whole counsel of the Word of God. The result will be spiritual death to those who follow.

11

A Better Atonement

"For this is my blood of the new testament, which is shed for many for the remission of sins."
— Jesus (Matthew 26:28).

In *More Ready Than You Realize*, Brian McLaren described a discussion with George, a parishioner at his church, who asked, "Why did Jesus have to die?" After two weeks of consideration, McLaren answered, "a couple of weeks ago I realized that I don't know why Jesus had to die." His brother responded, "Well, neither did Jesus."[429] This is a lie. Jesus knew very well that He came, in his own words, to "give his life a ransom for many" (Matthew 20:28). At the Last Supper, Jesus said, "For this is my blood of the new testament, which is shed for many for the remission of sins" (Matthew 26:28).

I have documented in previous chapters how Emergence Christianity often rejects whatever is traditional; their view of the atonement is no exception. Today, the traditional view of the atonement held by most Protestant evangelicals is known as Penal Substitutionary Atonement. Penal Substitution refers to the doctrine that Christ's death on the cross was a full payment for sins, which satisfied both the wrath

---

429 McLaren, *More Ready Than You Realize* (Grand Rapids, MI: Zondervan, 2002), 81.

and righteousness of God, so that He could forgive sinners without compromising His own holy standard of justice. The Emergent Church rejects this model of the atonement.

As a matter of fact, as Emergents have pointed out, the primitive Christians did not believe or teach Penal Substitution either. I believe the Ransom theory or Christus Victor view of the atonement, the early Christian model, has better scriptural support than Penal Substitution. But I do not believe that the Emergent Church has rejected Penal Substitution based on biblical support or early Christian support for an alternate view, but based on the fact that they are anti-wrath.

I can understand why the wrath of God is of very little importance within the Emergent conversation because sin is de-emphasized and redefined. If people are not sinners, then there is no need for reconciliation. For example, the following is an exchange between Emergent pastor Jay Bakker and *The Christian Post*:

> I am definitely questioning the atonement and trying to discover how we can see it in a different way. . . . My experience of a loving God who's asked me to love my enemies – this isn't a God that demands something before you are accepted. I think Jesus died because Jesus was inclusive. God is inclusive. I think that the idea of God somehow being separated from us was more man's idea.[430]

Somehow God being separated from us was man's idea? The reason for the atonement and our need to be reconciled to God was because of an alienation. Isaiah the prophet said, "But your iniquities have separated between you and your God, and your sins have hid his face from you, that he will not hear" (Isaiah 59:2). Paul also explains how sin was cause of alienation from God: "This I say therefore, and testify in the Lord, that ye henceforth walk not as other Gentiles walk, in the vanity of their mind, Having the understanding darkened, *being*

---

430 Nicola Menzie, "Jay Bakker Talks Faith, Doubt and Where the Church Has Gone Wrong," *The Christian Post, February* 14, 2013, available: http://www.christianpost.com/news/jay-bakker-talks-faith-doubt-and-where-the-church-has-gone-wrong-90010/pageall.html

alienated from the life of God through the ignorance that is in them, because of the blindness of their heart: Who being past feeling have given themselves over unto lasciviousness, to work all uncleanness with greediness" (Ephesians 4:17-19). The atonement was absolutely necessary because we were alienated from God. "And you, that were sometime *alienated and enemies in your mind by wicked works*, yet now hath he reconciled in the body of his flesh through death, to present you holy and unblameable and unreproveable in his sight" (Colossians 1:21,22).

A fictitious seeker in Brian McLaren's book *The Story We Find Ourselves In*, Kerry, criticized Penal Substitutionary Atonement: "That just sounds like one more injustice in the cosmic equation. It sounds like divine child abuse. You know?"[431] Taken alone, the "divine child abuse" analogy is disturbing, but this could be expected from a non-Christian character like Kerry. McLaren also writes:

> I had always assumed that "kingdom of God" meant "kingdom of heaven," which meant "going to heaven after you die," which required believing the message of Paul's letter to the Romans, which I understood to teach a theory of atonement called "penal substitution," which was the basis for a formula for forgiveness of original sin called "justification by grace through faith."[432]

In *Reimagining Christianity*, a book endorsed by Brian McLaren, Alan Jones called Penal Substitution a vile doctrine: "The other thread of just criticism addresses the suggestion implicit in the cross that Jesus' sacrifice was to appease an angry God. Penal substitution was the name of this vile doctrine."[433] Neither does Tony Jones find Penal Substitution compelling or biblical: "I find that version of atonement theory neither intellectually compelling, spiritually compelling, nor in keeping with the

---

431 McLaren, *The Story We Find Ourselves In* (San Francisco: Jossey-Bass, 2003), 102.
432 McLaren, *A New Kind of Christianity* (New York, NY: HarperCollins Publishers, 2010), 138.
433 Alan Jones, *Reimagining Christianity* (Hoboken, NJ: John Wiley & Sons. 2005), 168

biblical narrative."[434]

Emergent pastor Jay Bakker said of Penal Substitution: "We've got this image of God who needs some sort of flesh, some sort of blood, that needs some sort of vengeance to pay for sin." Bakker sees an irreconcilable conflict between vengeance and the teachings of Jesus Christ. Bakker continued:

> In order to deconstruct the atonement theory really [it] all comes from the message of Christ, and the message of love and grace and acceptance and loving your enemies and forgiving those who persecute you. . . . The God we've seen before who smited people, or demanded that babies' heads be crushed on rocks. Christ came to say "that's not me, that's not God. Your understanding of God is an understanding of you." Jesus came and kind of turned all that stuff on its head and said "now I want you to turn the other cheek, now I want you to walk the extra mile. I hang out with tax collectors and prostitutes. I have no reputation. I don't demand my own way.[435]

Like Bakker, Steve Chalke also finds problems with harmonizing Christ's teachings with Penal Substitutionary Atonement. While the Emerging Movement is often associated with Brian McLaren in the United States, Steve Chalke is leading the Emergent conversation in the United Kingdom. In his book, *The Lost Message of Jesus,* Steve Chalke, like Brian McLaren, also spoke of Penal Substitution as child abuse.

> How then, have we come to believe that at the cross this God of love suddenly decides to vent his anger and wrath on his own Son? The fact is that the cross isn't a form of cosmic child abuse—a vengeful father,

---

434 Tony Jones, "Why Jesus Died," *Beliefnet,* April 10, 2009. available: http://blog.beliefnet.com/tonyjones/2009/04/why-jesus-died.html
435 Nicola Menzie, "Jay Bakker Talks Faith, Doubt and Where the Church Has Gone Wrong," *The Christian Post, February* 14, 2013, available: http://www.christianpost.com/news/jay-bakker-talks-faith-doubt-and-where-the-church-has-gone-wrong-90010/pageall.html

punishing his son for an offence he has not even committed. Understandably, both people inside and outside of the church have found this twisted version of events morally dubious and a huge barrier to faith. Deeper than that, however, is that such a construct stands in total contradiction to the statement "God is love." If the cross is a personal act of violence perpetrated by God towards humankind but borne by his son, then it makes a mockery of Jesus' own teaching to love your enemies and refuse to repay evil with evil. The truth is the cross is a symbol of love. It is a demonstration of just how far God as Father and Jesus as his son are prepared to go to prove that love. The cross is a vivid statement of the powerlessness of love.[436]

I discussed above how Jesus' commandments of love and non-resistance do not conflict with God's vengeance and judgment. Violent judgment does not make a mockery of Jesus' own teachings because Jesus himself said, "But those mine enemies, which would not that I should reign over them, bring hither, and slay them before me" (Luke 19:27). At least these elements of Bakker's and Chalke's arguments are unsound. Alan Jones also says that "making God vengeful, all in the name of justice, has left thousands of souls deeply wounded and lost to the Church forever."[437] To these criticisms, Paul asked the rhetorical question: "Is God unrighteous who taketh vengeance? (I speak as a man) God forbid: for then how shall God judge the world?" (Romans 3:5,6).

In his book, *Love Wins*, Rob Bell stated the following about Penal Substitution:

Many have heard the gospel framed in terms of rescue. God has to punish sinners, because God is holy, but Jesus has paid the price for our sin, and so we can have eternal life. However true or untrue that statement is

---

436 Steve Chalke, Steve, *The Lost Message of Jesus* (Grand Rapids, MI: Zondervan, 2004), 183.
437 Alan Jones, *Reimagining Christianity* (Hoboken, NJ: John Wiley & Sons. 2005), 168

theologically, what it can do is subtly teach people that Jesus rescues us from God.[438]

Some valid criticisms have been made above, though they have not been stated in very biblical terms. Did Jesus save us from God? The Penal Substitution model creates a dichotomy between the Father and the Son. The Bible does not ever say that Jesus saved us from the Father but that Jesus "gave himself for our sins, that he might deliver us from this present evil world, according to the will of God and our Father" (Galatians 1:4). The Bible says of Jesus that "He shall save his people from their sins" (Matthew 1:21), not the Father.

In a podcast interview, McLaren explained how Penal Substitutionary Atonement portrays God as requiring something of us which He is unable to do Himself.

> The traditional understanding says that God asks of us something that God is incapable of Himself. God asks us to forgive people. But God is incapable of forgiving. God can't forgive unless He punishes somebody in place of the person He was going to forgive. God doesn't say things to you—Forgive your wife, and then go kick the dog to vent your anger. God asks you to actually forgive. And there's a certain sense that a common understanding of the atonement presents God who is incapable of forgiving unless He kicks somebody else.[439]

I must confess that this is a reasonable criticism. Does God need to pour out His wrath upon somebody in order to forgive? Is that *really* forgiveness? Forgiveness is the cancelation of a debt, but Penal Substitutionary Atonement transfers the debt to somebody else, namely Jesus. In the parable of the unforgiving servant, Jesus described the kingdom of God and forgiveness like this:

Then Peter came to Him and said, "Lord, how often

---

438 Rob Bell, *Love Wins* (New York, NY: Harper Collins, 2011), 182.
439 Interview with Leif Hansen. *The Bleeding Purple Podcast*. January 8, 2006. Part II.

shall my brother sin against me, and I forgive him? Up to seven times?"

Jesus said to him, "I do not say to you, up to seven times, but up to seventy times seven. Therefore the kingdom of heaven is like a certain king who wanted to settle accounts with his servants. And when he had begun to settle accounts, one was brought to him who owed him ten thousand talents. But as he was not able to pay, his master commanded that he be sold, with his wife and children and all that he had, and that payment be made. The servant therefore fell down before him, saying, 'Master, have patience with me, and I will pay you all.' Then the master of that servant was moved with compassion, released him, and forgave him the debt.

But that servant went out and found one of his fellow servants who owed him a hundred denarii; and he laid hands on him and took him by the throat, saying, 'Pay me what you owe!' So his fellow servant fell down at his feet and begged him, saying, 'Have patience with me, and I will pay you all.' And he would not, but went and threw him into prison till he should pay the debt. So when his fellow servants saw what had been done, they were very grieved, and came and told their master all that had been done. Then his master, after he had called him, said to him, 'You wicked servant! I forgave you all that debt because you begged me. Should you not also have had compassion on your fellow servant, just as I had pity on you?' And his master was angry, and delivered him to the torturers until he should pay all that was due to him.

So My heavenly Father also will do to you if each of you, from his heart, does not forgive his brother his trespasses. (Matthew 18:21-35, NKJV)

Notice the master *forgave* the debt as an act of mercy and compassion without violating any sense of justice. By definition, the debt was canceled and the servant was released. This parable portrays the

King, who is God the Father, *forgiving* the servant without having to transfer the debt to somebody else like His Son. According to the Jesus, the debt could be reinstated if the servant did not forgive others. But according to Penal Substitutionary Atonement, the debt could not be reinstated because it was paid in full and satisfied by Jesus. That can hardly be defined as forgiving a debt, but rather taking a payment for a debt. If Jesus taught the Penal Substitution model, He would have said that the master's son paid the debt of the servant. According to Penal Substitution, only upon receiving the payment of his son on behalf of the servant could the master "forgive" the servant. But that can't be considered forgiveness because the master received a payment. If the master received the payment, then there is nothing left to forgive. The debt cannot be forgiven if it has been paid by another.

Justice is often emphasized in Penal Substitutionary Atonement. But is Penal Substitution really justice? Tony Jones criticizes, "Some people today may find it compelling that some Great Cosmic Transaction took place on that day 1,980 years ago, that God's wrath burned against his son instead of against me."[440] This is a fair summary of Penal Substitution. Likewise, Steve Chalke is correct when he characterizes Penal Substitutionary Atonement as "a vengeful father, punishing his son for an offence he has not even committed." Is it ever justice to punish an innocent person for the crimes of another? Conversely, is it *unjust* to simply forgive or cancel a debt without receiving a payment? The early Christians believed that it was in accordance with God's justice and mercy to freely forgive sin without receiving a payment. True forgiveness, by definition, is releasing the servant from the debt. This agrees with what Jesus taught.

A Ransom for Many

The Emergent Church has spent a lot of energy tearing down Penal Substitution but little time building up a scriptural case for a more plausible view of the atonement. I suspect their rejection of Penal Substitution has more to do with a repulsion for God's wrath than it does for biblical truth. Like the Emerging Church, I have found the Penal

---

440 Tony Jones, "Why Jesus Died," *Beliefnet,* April 10, 2009. available: http://blog.beliefnet.com/tonyjones/2009/04/why-jesus-died.html

Substitutionary Atonement problematic. At the same time, I believe there is a more biblical model. As Tony Jones points out,

> While some might argue otherwise, [Penal Substitutionary Atonement] was unknown before its development by Anselm of Canterbury in his 1098 book, *Cur Deus Homo* (Why a God-Man?). Therein, Anselm introduced the first substitutionary explanation of the atonement.[441]

The early Christian understanding of the atonement is known as the Ransom theory or Christus Victor. Jesus said, "The Son of man came not to be ministered unto, but to minister, and to give his life a ransom for many" (Matthew 20:28). The Bible also says, "For there is one God, and one mediator between God and men, the man Christ Jesus; Who gave himself a ransom for all, to be testified in due time" (1 Timothy 2:5,6).

A ransom is a sum of money or other payment demanded or paid for the release of a captive. The Ransom model of the atonement suggests that Jesus gave His life as a ransom to Satan. When unbelievers come to the truth, they "recover themselves out of the snare of the devil, who are *taken captive by him at his will*" (2 Timothy 2:26). Sinners have been taken captive or kidnapped by the devil, and Jesus gave His life as a ransom to redeem us. The ransom price that Satan demanded to release those taken captive by sin and death was the life of the Son of God.

A ransom is always paid to the kidnappers, not the parents of the captive. But according to Penal Substitution, Jesus ends up giving His life as a ransom to the Father and saving us from the Father. The Bible says, "For ye are bought with a price: therefore glorify God in your body, and in your spirit, which are God's" (1 Corinthians 6:20). Paul said to the Ephesian elders, "Take heed therefore unto yourselves, and to all the flock, over the which the Holy Ghost hath made you overseers, to feed the church of God, which *he hath purchased with his own blood.*" (Acts 20:28). Did Jesus purchase us from the Father when He gave His life as a ransom? The Father already owned the church. But we had sold

---

441 Tony Jones, *A Better Atonement: Beyond the Depraved Doctrine of Original Sin* (The JoPa Group, 2012) Kindle Edition, 383-385.

ourselves into bondage to Satan. Therefore, Christians have been purchased from the devil.

While Penal Substitution presents the Father reconciling *Himself to the world*, the Bible says that in Christ, the Father reconciled *the world to Himself*. "And all things are of God, who hath reconciled us to himself by Jesus Christ, and hath given to us the ministry of reconciliation; To wit, that God was in Christ, reconciling the world unto himself, not imputing their trespasses unto them; and hath committed unto us the word of reconciliation" (2 Corinthians 5:18,19).

The Ransom model portrays a release from the bondage of sin and death by the payment of a Ransom, Jesus Christ. In this way, Christ's sacrifice was substitutionary. For instance, Clement of Rome (96 AD) said, "In love has the Lord taken us to Himself. On account of the Love he bore us, Jesus Christ our Lord gave His blood for us by the will of God; His flesh for our flesh, and His soul for our souls."[442] While the early Church described Christ's sacrifice as substitutionary, they did not teach Penal Substitution. Both views teach that Jesus bore our sins and died a substitutionary death, but the Penal Substitution model understands the atonement in a very different sense. The early Christians believed that God really *forgave* our debt without requiring that debt to paid by Jesus. Mathetes (125-200 AD) described the ransom transaction of the atonement as follows:

> But when our wickedness had reached its height, and it had been clearly shown that its reward, punishment and death, was impending over us; and when the time had come which God had before appointed for manifesting His own kindness and power, how the one love of God, through exceeding regard for men, did not regard us with hatred, nor thrust us away, nor remember our iniquity against us, but showed great long-suffering, and bore with us, He Himself took on Him the burden of our iniquities, He gave His own Son as a ransom for us, the holy One for transgressors, the blameless One for the wicked, the righteous One for the unrighteous, the

---

442 Clement of Rome, *The First Epistle of Clement to the Corinthians,* chapter XLIX, ANF, volume 1, 18.

incorruptible One for the corruptible, the immortal One for them that are mortal. For what other thing was capable of covering our sins than His righteousness? By what other one was it possible that we, the wicked and ungodly, could be justified, than by the only Son of God? O sweet exchange! O unsearchable operation! O benefits surpassing all expectation! that the wickedness of many should be hid in a single righteous One, and that the righteousness of One should justify many transgressors![443]

First of all, the early Christians understood Christ's victory over Satan to be an important aspect of the atonement. Jesus ransomed us from Satan and the power of death (1 Timothy 2:5,6; 2 Timothy 2:26) rather than from an angry Father. They also emphasized Jesus's Resurrection as the victory over the grave which released the prisoners from Hades (1 Peter 3:18-20). The Resurrection was God's victory over sin and death. Origen (248 AD) asked:

But to whom did He give His soul as a ransom for many? Surely not to God. Could it, then, be to the Evil One? For he had us in his power, until the ransom for us should be given to him, even the life (or soul) of Jesus, since he (the Evil One) had been deceived, and led to suppose that he was capable of mastering that soul, and he did not see that to hold Him involved a trial of strength (thasanon) greater than he was equal to. Therefore also death, though he thought he had prevailed against Him, no longer lords over Him, He (Christ) having become free among the dead and stronger than the power of death, and so much stronger than death that all who will amongst those who are mastered by death may also follow Him (i.e. out of Hades, out of death's domain), death no longer prevailing against them. For every one who is with Jesus is unassailable by death.[444]

---

443 *The Epistle of Mathetes to Diognetus*, chapter IX, ANF volume 1, 28.
444 Origen, *Commentary on Matthew*, XVI, 8.

While the primitive Church understood Jesus's death as a sacrifice, it was an heroic sacrifice to set us free from Satan's dominion rather than to placate an angry Father. Jesus said, "No one can enter a strong man's house and plunder his goods, unless he first binds the strong man. And then he will plunder his house" (Mark 3:27). Hebrews 2:14,15 says, "Inasmuch then as the children have partaken of flesh and blood, He Himself likewise shared in the same, that through death He might *destroy him who had the power of death*, that is, the devil, and release those who through fear of death were all their lifetime subject to bondage." Irenaeus (180 AD) wrote:

> For He fought and conquered; for He was man contending for the fathers, and through obedience doing away with disobedience completely: for He bound the strong man, and set free the weak, and endowed His own handiwork with salvation, by destroying sin. For He is a most holy and merciful Lord, and loves the human race.[445]

Secondly, the early Christians understood the atonement to be a revelation of God's forgiveness of sins rather than Christ suffering the wrath of God as a payment for sin. They believed that God freely forgave those who repent. For example, Irenaeus (180 AD) wrote:

> (Because we) transgressing whose commandment became His enemies. . . . Therefore in the last times the Lord has restored us into friendship through His incarnation, having become "the Mediator between God and men;" propitiating indeed for us the Father against whom we had sinned, and canceling our disobedience by His own obedience; conferring also upon us the gift of communion with, and subjection to, our Maker. . . . He the God who is proclaimed in the Scriptures, to whom we were debtors, having transgressed His

---

445   Irenaeus, *Ante-Nicene Fathers,* Volume 1, 447-448.

commandment? Now the commandment was given to man by the Word. For Adam, it is said, "heard the voice of the Lord God." Rightly then does His Word say to man, "Your sins are forgiven you;" He, the same against whom we had sinned in the beginning, grants forgiveness of sins in the end.[446]

Finally, the early Christians believed that Jesus's blood cleanses us from sin, allowing us to be reconciled to the Father (John 1:29; Ephesians 2:13; Hebrews 9:14; 10:4,14; 13:12). "Without shedding of blood is no remission of sins," says Hebrews 9:22. Jesus said, "For this is my blood of the new testament, which is shed for many for the remission of sins" (Matthew 26:28). John the Apostle said, "But if we walk in the light, as he is in the light, we have fellowship one with another, and the blood of Jesus Christ his Son cleanseth us from all sin" (1 John 1:7). It is in this sense that Isaiah 53:5 was understood by the early Church. Barnabas (70-130 AD) wrote:

> For to this end the Lord endured to deliver up His flesh to corruption, that we might be sanctified through the remission of sins, which is effected by His blood of sprinkling. For it is written concerning Him, partly with reference to Israel, and partly to us; and [the Scripture] said thus: "He was wounded for our transgressions, and braised for our iniquities: with His stripes we are healed. He was brought as a sheep to the slaughter, and as a lamb which is dumb before its shearer."[447]

Also worth consideration is the translation of Isaiah 53 in the Septuagint (LXX), the Greek translation of the Hebrew Old Testament. More often than not, Jesus and the apostles quoted from the Septuagint when they quoted the Old Testament. The early Christians, following the example of Jesus and the apostles, also quoted from the Septuagint. The Septuagint version of Isaiah 53 agrees more with the Ransom view of the atonement as opposed to Penal Substitution. For example, in our English

---

446   Irenaeus, *Ante-Nicene Fathers,* Volume 1, 544-545
447   Barnabas, *Ante-Nicene Fathers,* Volume 1, 139.

Bible, Isaiah 53:4 says: "Surely he hath borne our griefs, and carried our sorrows: yet we did esteem him stricken, smitten of God, and afflicted." But the Bible of the early Christians, the Septuagint says: "He bears our sins, and is pained for us: yet we accounted him to be in trouble, and in suffering, and in affliction" (Isaiah 53:4, LXX). In our English Bibles Isaiah 53:10 says: "Yet it pleased the LORD to bruise him; he hath put him to grief: when thou shalt make his soul an offering for sin, he shall see his seed, he shall prolong his days, and the pleasure of the LORD shall prosper in his hand." But the Septuagint says: "The Lord also is pleased to purge him from his stroke. If ye can give an offering for sin, your soul shall see a long-lived seed" (Isaiah 53:10, LXX). Below are a couple of examples of how the early Christians quoted from Isaiah 53. Clement of Rome (96 AD) wrote:

> For Christ is of those who are humble-minded, and not of those who exalt themselves over His flock. Our Lord Jesus Christ, the Sceptre of the majesty of God, did not come in the pomp of pride or arrogance, although He might have done so, but in a lowly condition, as the Holy Spirit had declared regarding Him. For He says, "Lord, who hath believed our report, and to whom is the arm of the Lord revealed? We have declared [our message] in His presence: He is, as it were, a child, and like a root in thirsty ground; He has no form nor glory, yea, we saw Him, and He had no form nor comeliness; but His form was without eminence, yea, deficient in comparison with the [ordinary] form of men. He is a man exposed to stripes and suffering, and acquainted with the endurance of grief: for His countenance was turned away; He was despised, and not esteemed. He bears our iniquities, and is in sorrow for our sakes; yet we supposed that [on His own account] He was exposed to labour, and stripes, and affliction. But He was wounded for our transgressions, and bruised for our iniquities. The chastisement of our peace was upon Him, and by His stripes we were healed. All we, like sheep, have gone astray; [every] man has wandered in his own way; and the Lord has delivered

Him up for our sins, while He in the midst of His sufferings openeth not His mouth. He was brought as a sheep to the slaughter, and as a lamb before her shearer is dumb, so He openeth not His mouth. In His humiliation His judgment was taken away; who shall declare His generation? for His life is taken from the earth. For the transgressions of my people was He brought down to death. And I will give the wicked for His sepulchre, and the rich for His death, because He did no iniquity, neither was guile found in His mouth. And the Lord is pleased to purify Him by stripes. If ye make an offering for sin, your soul shall see a long-lived seed. And the Lord is pleased to relieve Him of the affliction of His soul, to show Him light, and to form Him with understanding, to justify the Just One who ministereth well to many; and He Himself shall carry their sins. On this account He shall inherit many, and shall divide the spoil of the strong; because His soul was delivered to death, and He was reckoned among the transgressors, and He bare the sins of many, and for their sins was He delivered."[448]

Justin Martyr (160 AD) quoted Isaiah 53:8-12 from the Septuagint version as follows:

And that the Spirit of prophecy might signify to us that He who suffers these things has an ineffable origin, and rules His enemies, He spake thus: "His generation who shall declare? because His life is cut off from the earth: for their transgressions He comes to death. And I will give the wicked for His burial, and the rich for His death; because He did no violence, neither was any deceit in His mouth. And the Lord is pleased to cleanse Him from the stripe. If He be given for sin, your soul shall see His seed prolonged in days. And the Lord is

---

448 Clement of Rome, *Ante-Nicene Fathers,* volume 1, 9.

pleased to deliver His soul from grief, to show Him light, and to form Him with knowledge, to justify the righteous who richly serveth many. And He shall bear our iniquities. Therefore He shall inherit many, and He shall divide the spoil of the strong; because His soul was delivered to death: and He was numbered with the transgressors; and He bare the sins of many, and He was delivered up for their transgressions."[449]

Even the English translation of Isaiah 53 does not explicitly say that Jesus was a substitute in the sense of suffering the wrath of God as punishment for our sins, none of the Scriptures do for that matter (all of the atonement passages can be seen through either lens). So consulting the Septuagint is not the only solution. However, it is a significantly different portrayal of the atonement. The prophet describes Jesus as our substitute in that the Father gave Him up for our sins (53:6) and He bore our sins (53:4,5,6,8,11,12). The penalty was not the wrath of God but death (53:8,12). God did not take pleasure in punishing Him but in purging Him from His stroke (53:10) and taking away the travail of His soul and show Him light (53:11), that is, vindicating Him by raising Him from the dead.

In spite of all of these ways in which the atonement is important, Tony Jones said that the cross of Christ was not necessary for sinners to be reconciled to God. In a blog post called "The Cross Is Not Necessary [Questions That Haunt]," Jones said, "No, Jesus' death was not required in order for human beings to be reconciled to God."[450] Far from the truth is Tony Jones' statement. Without Jesus' death on the cross, human beings could not be reconciled to God. The Bible says the exact opposite of Jones: "God was in Christ, reconciling the world unto himself, not imputing their trespasses unto them; and hath committed unto us the word of reconciliation" (2 Corinthians 5:19); "For it pleased the Father that in him should all fulness dwell; And, having made peace through the blood of his cross, by him to reconcile all things unto himself; by him, I

---

449   Justin Martyr, *Ante-Nicene Fathers,* volume 1, 179-180.
450   Tony Jones, "The Cross is Not Necessary, *Theoblogy,* Febrauary 27, 2013, available, http://www.patheos.com/blogs/tonyjones/2013/02/27/the-cross-is-unnecessary-questions-that-haunt/

say, whether they be things in earth, or things in heaven. And you, that were sometime alienated and enemies in your mind by wicked works, yet now hath he reconciled In the body of his flesh through death, to present you holy and unblameable and unreproveable in his sight" (Colossians 1:19-22).

In one of his articles on the doctrine of the atonement, Tony Jones concluded, "As with all theology, talk of the atonement is conjecture. God's truth is ultimately a mystery to which no human being is privy."[451] I believe there is much that the Bible tells us about the atonement; a single chapter would not be sufficient to adequately discuss this topic. I think there is an underlying reason why Emergents criticize Penal Substitution and fail to reveal the "mystery" of the atonement.

God Without Wrath

I don't believe the Emergent Church's rejection of Penal Substitution is based on a rediscovery of the ante-Nicene Church Fathers' views or compelling Scriptural arguments. The attributes of God, such as wrath, which are not compatible with a postmodern worldview have been deconstructed and redefined by Emergent leaders. The Emergent Church cannot hold to a doctrine like Penal Substitution because it involves the wrath of God. If the underlying problem for Emergents is the fact that God's wrath abides on all people who do not have obedient faith in Christ, then any doctrinal view that includes wrath is odious to them. For example, McLaren says on his blog:

> You mention the word wrath - which many people assume means "anger that leads to the punishment of eternal conscious torment." But outside of the old narrative, another possibility arises: wrath means God's displeasure that allows people to experience the consequences of their negative actions. Try that out in a reading of Romans 1 and see if you think it fits. So if we

---

451 Tony Jones, "If Jesus' Crucifixion Is the Solution, What's the Problem?" March 28, 2012, http://www.patheos.com/Resources/Additional-Resources/Jesus-Crucifixion-Is-the-Solution-Whats-the-Problem-Tony-Jones-03-39-2012

neglect the poor, there will be crime and revolutionary movements. . . . If we neglect our children, they'll feel alienated from us, hurting themselves and us. If we neglect the environment, we'll suffer erosion and global warming. If we worship idols, we'll play to our own baser instincts.[452]

Certainly God's wrath is God's "displeasure that allows people to experience the consequence of their negative actions," as McLaren stated. This idea definitely fits Romans 1: "God also gave them up to uncleanness through the lusts of their own hearts, to dishonour their own bodies between themselves. . . . God gave them up unto vile affections: for even their women did change the natural use into that which is against nature" (Romans 1:24,26).

But God's wrath is much more than giving people over to uncleanness and vile affections in this life. From the same epistle, Paul continued: "But after thy hardness and impenitent heart treasurest up unto thyself wrath against the day of wrath and revelation of the righteous judgment of God; Who will render to every man according to his deeds: To them who by patient continuance in well doing seek for glory and honour and immortality, eternal life: But unto them that are contentious, and do not obey the truth, but obey unrighteousness, indignation and wrath, Tribulation and anguish, upon every soul of man that doeth evil, of the Jew first, and also of the Gentile; But glory, honour, and peace, to every man that worketh good, to the Jew first, and also to the Gentile: For there is no respect of persons with God" (Romans 2:5-11). There remains a future day when the wicked will be rendered wrath and judgment while the righteous will be given eternal life.

In his book *Faith, Doubt, and Other Lines I've Crossed: Walking with the Unknown God,* Jay Bakker gets to the heart of what he believes about the wrath of God:

> I don't see how we can credit God with these attributes
> of holiness and justice and wrath and vengeance. I am
> not convinced by those who say we have to accept the

---

452 Brian McLaren, "Q &R: Wrath and Hell," *brian d. mclaren,* http://www.brianmclaren.net/archives/blog/q-r-wrath-and-hell.html

tension between love and wrath, grace and holiness; that we have to take this on faith, have it remain a mystery. Because Paul clearly says that while faith and hope remain, the greatest of these is love. Without love, everything else is nothing.[453]

Paul does say that "the greatest of these is love" (1 Corinthians 13:13). But love is not antithetical to God's wrath and vengeance. Paul also said, "Dearly beloved, avenge not yourselves, but rather give place unto wrath: for it is written, Vengeance is mine; I will repay, saith the Lord" (Romans 12:19). In his letter to the Romans, Paul anticipated Bakker's false dilemma about God's love and vengeance being irreconcilable: "Is God unrighteous who taketh vengeance? (I speak as a man) God forbid: for then how shall God judge the world?" (Romans 3:5-6). Paul assumes that his audience knows that God will judge the world, and that judgment involves vengeance. God is not unrighteous in taking vengeance because He *is* going to judge the world.

We cannot explain away Bible passages about the wrath of God just because they are politically incorrect. The Bible is clear: "He who believes in the Son has eternal life; but he who does not obey the Son will not see life, but the wrath of God abides on him" (John 3:36, NASB); "For this ye know, that no whoremonger, nor unclean person, nor covetous man, who is an idolater, hath any inheritance in the kingdom of Christ and of God. Let no man deceive you with vain words: for because of these things cometh the wrath of God upon the children of disobedience" (Ephesians 5:5-6); "Mortify therefore your members which are upon the earth; fornication, uncleanness, inordinate affection, evil concupiscence, and covetousness, which is idolatry: For which things' sake the wrath of God cometh on the children of disobedience: In the which ye also walked some time, when ye lived in them" (Colossians 3:5-7).

In his book, *A Better Atonement: Beyond the Depraved Doctrine of Original Sin*, Tony Jones discusses several views of the Atonement. The first and foremost problem he finds with wrath (and Penal

---

453 Jay Bakker, *Faith, Doubt, and Other Lines I've Crossed: Walking with the Unknown God* (New York, NY: Jericho Books, 2013), 14-15.

Substitutionary Atonement) is based upon *experience*, not Scripture. Jones wrote:

> The problems with this concentration on God's wrath are pluriform. First and foremost, it contradicts the experience that most of us have with God, and that a lot of us have with the Bible. Our experience of God is not of wrath, but of love. Indeed, that's how most people experience God even before they accept the idea that Christ stands between us and God. So it seems odd to first have to convince people that God's wrath burns against them, then to convince them that Jesus lovingly took on that wrath.[454]

Therefore, I suggest that the Emergent Church finds atonement alternatives to Penal Substitution because of subjective "truth." Their "experience of God is not of wrath, but of love." I ask with Paul the Apostle: "What if God, willing to shew his wrath, and to make his power known, endured with much longsuffering the vessels of wrath fitted to destruction?" (Romans 9:22). What if the Emergents experience of God's love is this endurance and patience with vessels of wrath fitted to destruction? Peter said, "The Lord is not slack concerning his promise, as some men count slackness; but is longsuffering to us-ward, not willing that any should perish, but that all should come to repentance. But the day of the Lord will come as a thief in the night; in the which the heavens shall pass away with a great noise, and the elements shall melt with fervent heat, the earth also and the works that are therein shall be burned up" (2 Peter 3:9,10). In other words, everybody has experienced God's love in many ways, but there is no escape from the fact that the Bible also warns us about His wrath upon those who suppress the truth in unrighteousness.

The Bible also says, "Much more then, being now justified by his blood, we shall be saved from wrath through him" (Romans 5:9); "And to wait for his Son from heaven, whom he raised from the dead, even Jesus, which delivered us from the wrath to come" (1 Thessalonians

---

454 Tony Jones, *A Better Atonement: Beyond the Depraved Doctrine of Original Sin* (The JoPa Group, 2012) Kindle Edition, 584-587

1:10); "For God hath not appointed us to wrath, but to obtain salvation by our Lord Jesus Christ" (1 Thessalonians 5:9). How do we understand these verses about wrath apart from Penal Substitutionary Atonement? Christians are saved from wrath because we have been forgiven of our past sins for which things sake the wrath of God originally came upon us. The blood of Christ cleanses Christians as long as they walk in the light and no longer commit sins deserving of God's wrath. Christians are no longer under the wrath of God because they are obedient to Him, not because Jesus was punished in the their place.

12

Another Jesus

" For if he that cometh preacheth another Jesus, whom we have not preached, or if ye receive another spirit, which ye have not received, or another gospel, which ye have not accepted, ye might well bear with him. "
— Apostle Paul (2 Corinthians 11:4)

The Godhood of Jesus

Emergents also present various forms of questioning and reconsidering the foundations of historic Christianity. Differing from 20th century liberals like Harry Emerson Fosdick that stated clearly what their liberal beliefs were, those within the Emergent movement will question orthodox theology or suggest foundational Christian truths are debatable and up for discussion rather than blatantly contradicting them. Rob Bell questions at length the validity of the virgin birth.[455] But then, after undermining faith in the virgin birth and sabotaging the authority of Scripture, in order to protect himself, Bell pulls back and says that he affirms the Christian faith, the virgin birth, the Trinity, the inspiration of the Bible and much more.[456] Though these approaches protect them from being labeled as false prophets, these educated scholars are well aware of

455 Rob Bell, *Velvet Elvis,* 26,27.
456 Ibid., 27.

what they are doing in questioning the Scriptures.

Tony Jones says:

> Anyway, my point in all this is that the doctrine of the Trinity is still on the table. Some people, it seems to me, would like for us to no longer debate certain "sacred" doctrines -- the Trinity, the nature of Christ, the nature of scripture, the nature of marriage etc. And these persons tend to get very jumpy when emergent-types discuss these sacrae doctrinae, especially in books and at conferences that are being taped. "This is dangerous," they say.[457]

One cannot claim to be orthodox and at the same time let sacred doctrines such as the Godhood of Jesus be open for debate. By its very nature, orthodoxy is limited to the authorized and generally accepted Christian doctrines and practices. Likewise, Doug Pagitt, though he says he believes in the Trinity, also says that the Christian understanding of the Trinity should be "on the table of reconsideration." In regard to the Trinity, Pagitt notes, "I am not saying it is wrong, but it is not complete. No view is complete. That is why all belief is progressive.[458]

Spencer Burke, who claims to be a Christian as well as a universalist and a panentheist, rejects the personhood of God: "I'm not sure I believe in God exclusively as a person anymore either."[459] Scot McKnight is a popular author and speaker on issues related to the Emerging Church. Though he has generally supported many of the movement's aims, he has, in recent years, expressed some concern about the direction of the movement. Even McKnight questions Burke's views of the Trinity:

> Is Spencer a "heretic"? He says he is, and I see no reason to think he believes in the Trinity from reading this

---

457 Tony Jones, "De Trinitate," *Theoblogy,* December 29, 2004, http://theoblogy.blogspot.com/2004/12/de-trinitate.html.
458 Ibid.
459 Spencer Burke, *A Heretic's Guide to Eternity* (San Francisco, CA: Jossey-Bass, 2006), 195.

book. That's what heresy means to me. Denial of God's personhood flies in the face of everything orthodox. To say that you believe in the creedal view of God as Father, Son, and Spirit and deny "person" is to deny the Trinitarian concept of God.

Is Spencer a "Christian"? He says he is. What is a Christian? Is it not one who finds redemption through faith in Christ, the one who died and who was raised? If so, I see nothing in this book that makes me think that God's grace comes to us through the death and resurrection of Christ. Grace seems to be what each person is "born into" in Spencer's theses in this book. That means that I see no reason in this book to think Spencer believes in the gospel as the NT defines gospel (grace as the gift of God through Christ by faith).[460]

Although the entire Emergent Church does not wholeheartedly agree with Burke's heretical positions, the Emergent guru Brian McLaren endorses Burke's book which is appropriately titled *A Heretic's Guide to Eternity*. In the foreword of the book, McLaren says that "even in a book with 'heretic' in the title, I believe any honest reader can find much truth worth seeking."[461] God forbid that McLaren is referring to denial of the Trinity, or the teaching of universalism and panenthiesm as "much truth." Apart from McLaren's own books and teachings which raise concerns, the fact that McLaren would endorse such false teaching should alarm any serious Christian.

Christian Christ or Islamic Isa

Perhaps Emergents' most egregious abuses of their voices as professing Christian leaders has been their endorsement of a Muslim document entitled "A Common Word between Us and You." Dated

---

460 Scot McKnight, "A Heretic's Guide to Eternity 4," The Jesus Creed, August 8, 2006, http://www.jesuscreed.org/?p=1319.
461 Spencer Burke, *A Heretic's Guide to Eternity* (San Francisco, CA: Jossey-Bass. 2006), x.

October 13, 2007, "A Common Word between Us and You" is an open letter from leaders of the Muslim faith to leaders of the Christian faith. It calls to work for love for God and love for neighbor as common ground and understanding among both Christian and Muslim faiths. In the short time since its release, "A Common Word" has become the world's leading interfaith dialogue initiative between Christians and Muslims.[462] In the introductory pages of the document, we find the following passage from the Qur'an (Aal 'Imran, 3:64):

> Say: O People of the Scripture! Come to *a Common Word between us and you*: that we shall worship none but God, and that we shall ascribe no partner unto Him, and that none of us shall take others for lords beside God. And if they turn away, then say: Bear witness that we are they who have surrendered (unto Him).[463]

If we consider the context of this verse in the Qur'an, we see that Muhammad is pleading with Christians whom he calls, "People of the Scripture." When Muhammad says, "We shall ascribe no partner unto Him," he is speaking against the Christian doctrine of the Trinity. Elsewhere, Muhammad says, "They do blaspheme who say God is one of three . . . for there is no Allah except one Allah."[464] In the direct context of the verse quoted in "A Common Word," the historical Jesus of the Bible is contrasted to Muhammad's Isa (Jesus) of the Qur'an. While the Bible declares Jesus to be eternal and uncreated (Colossians 1:17), the Qur'an describes Jesus as a *created* human being. Early Christians understood that Jesus was begotten but not created, but the Qur'an declares, "The similitude of Isa before God is as that of Adam; He created him from dust."[465] Thus, "A Common Word" is reiteration of Muhammad's denial of Jesus as divine substance while calling Christians to compromise the doctrine of the Trinity in order to worship Allah with

---

462 "A Common Word Between Us and You," http://en.wikipedia.org/wiki/A_Common_Word_Between_Us_and_You.
463 "A Common Word Between Us and You," (Amman, Jordan: The Royal Aal Al-Bayt Institute for Islamic Thought, 5-Year Anniversary Edition, 2012).
464 Qur'an, 5:73.
465 Qur'an, 3:59.

Muslims. Apparently Emergents have no problem with making this doctrinal compromise.

A Christian response to the letter entitled "Loving God and Neighbor Together: A Christian Response to A Common Word Between Us and You" was published in *The New York Times*. This response was endorsed by almost 300 Christian theologians and leaders including Emergent leaders like Brian McLaren and Tony Jones.[466] More problems arise when we find that the document contains statements that allude to the false belief that Muslims and Christians worship the same God, that they "share the same Divine origin." The document states:

> It is hoped that this document will provide a common constitution for the many worthy organizations and individuals who are carrying out interfaith dialogue all over the world. Often these groups are unaware of each other, and duplicate each other's efforts. Not only can A Common Word Between Us give them a starting point for cooperation and worldwide co-ordination, but it does so on the most solid theological ground possible: the teachings of the Qu'ran and the Prophet, and the commandments described by Jesus Christ in the Bible. Thus despite their differences, Islam and Christianity *not only share the same Divine Origin* and the same Abrahamic heritage, but the same two greatest commandments.[467]

---

466 Others to sign included Miroslav Volf (Founder and Director of the Yale Center for Faith and Culture, Henry B. Wright Professor of Theology, Yale Divinity School), Leith Anderson (the President of the National Association of Evangelicals), Bill Hybels (Founder and Senior Pastor of Willow Creek Community Church), Robert Schuller (Founder of Crystal Cathedral), Jim Wallis (President, Sojourners), and Rick Warren (Founder and Senior Pastor of Saddleback Church). "Loving God and Neighbor Together: A Christian Response to A Common Word Between Us and You," http://www.yale.edu/divinity/news/071118_news_nytimes.pdf.
467 The Official Website of A Common Word, http://www.acommonword.com/.

It is an atrocity that these professing Christian leaders would receive and endorse such a blasphemous document. How can the Qur'an and the Bible be of the "same Divine Origin" when the Qur'an clearly denies the Deity of Christ and the crucifixion of Christ?[468] This Muslim belief is in direct contrast to Christianity which declares that Jesus is man and also God (John 1:1,14; Colossians 2:9) and says there is no salvation apart from the cross (Matthew 26:28, 1 Corinthians 1:18). "A Common Word Between Us and You" concludes: "The basis for this peace and understanding already exists. It is part of the very foundational principles of both faiths: love of the One God."[469] The Christian response letter also refers to "God" of the "Muslim tradition" as if the Muslims worship the same "one God" as Christians. The letter does not address the profound differences between the one God of the Bible and Allah of the Qur'an. While Islam claims to worship one god, Allah can in no way be compared to the God of the Bible.

Also, the Christian response to the letter referred to God as the "All-Merciful One." Far from being a name for God of the Bible, "All-Merciful One" is a title given to Allah 57 times in the Qur'an. But nowhere in the Bible is Jehovah referred to as the "All-Merciful One" (though He is certainly merciful). The Christian respondents state, "Before we 'shake your hand' in responding to your letter, we ask forgiveness of the All-Merciful One and of the Muslim community around the world."[470]

Moreover, both the letter and the Christian response refer to Muhammad as the "Prophet Muhammad" suggesting that he and Jesus both are prophets. However, according to the biblical standard, Muhammad has been proven to be a false prophet. While both Christians

---

468 Qur'an, Surah 4:157-158 sates, "And because of their saying: We slew the Messiah Jesus son of Mary, Allah's messenger—They slew him not nor crucified, but it appeared so unto them; and lo! Those who disagree concerning it are in doubt thereof; they have no knowledge thereof save pursuit of a conjecture; they slew him not for certain. But Allah took him up unto Himself. Allah was ever Mighty, Wise.

469 http://www.acommonword.com/index.php?lang=en&page=option1.

470 "Loving God and Neighbor Together: A Christian Response to A Common Word Between Us and You." http://www.yale.edu/divinity/news/071118_news_nytimes.pdf.

and Muslims believe in the divine inspiration of Deuteronomy 18:18,19, Muslims believe the "prophet" in view is Muhammad while Christians believe it is Christ. But the following verses in Deuteronomy 18:20-22 add clarification: "But the prophet, which shall presume to speak a word in my name, which I have not commanded him to speak, or that shall speak in the name of other gods, even that prophet shall die. And if thou say in thine heart, How shall we know the word which the LORD hath not spoken? When a prophet speaketh in the name of the LORD, if the thing follow not, nor come to pass, that is the thing which the LORD hath not spoken, but the prophet hath spoken it presumptuously: thou shalt not be afraid of him." Not only did Muhammad speak in the name of other another god, but he prophesied many events which did not come to pass.[471] This fact, in addition to the Qur'an's doctrines of devils, proves that Muhammad was a false prophet. To call Muhammad a prophet is to essentially legitimize the religion of Islam. Furthermore, Paul said, "And the spirits of the prophets are subject to the prophets" (1 Corinthians 14:32). Muhammad is not subject to the true prophets of God in doctrine or in practice.

Though Christians may be in agreement with Muslims about finding common ground in not desiring strife, violence and war, it is on the basis of the Person of Jesus Christ that Christians do not kill, even love their enemies and turn the other cheek (Matthew 5:39-48). It is dishonest of the Christian response to "A Common Word" to selectively quote 1 John 4:10, "We love because [God] first loved us" while excluding the second portion of the same verse which describes how God showed His love to the world and "*sent his Son to be the propitiation for our sins.*" The love of God is uniquely expressed in Christ dying for our sins upon the cross and rising again. Islam rejects this kind of love.

The Bible is clear: "Whosoever denieth the Son, the same hath not the Father: [but] he that acknowledgeth the Son hath the Father also" (1 John 2:23). Muslims reject Jesus as the crucified and risen Son of God Savior of the world; therefore Muslims are rejecting God. Christians and Muslims do not stand together on a common ground or understanding of God or the love of God. "He that hath the Son hath life; and he that hath

---

471 For example, in Surah 30:2-4, Muhammad prophesied the defeat of the Roman Empire within 10 years (some translations say "a few years." This did not come to pass.

not the Son of God hath not life" (1 John 5:12). According to the Bible, Islam is a lie and antichrist: "Who is a liar but he that denieth that Jesus is the Christ? He is antichrist, that denieth the Father and the Son" (1 John 2:22).

Clearly, Christianity and Islam have no common word or common ground. However, it was Tony Campolo who stated that "a theology of mysticism provides some hope for common ground between Christianity and Islam" and asked about the Muslim mystics, "Could they have encountered the same God we do in our Christian mysticism?"[472] As noted earlier, Emergent guru Brian McLaren celebrates Ramadan, Muhammad's reception of the Qur'an.[473] McLaren not only has signed the response to "A Common Word," but also exalts Islam on the same level with Christianity by suggesting that Muhammad had an encounter with God. McLaren writes:

> And during his lifetime, Abraham—like Moses, Jesus, and Muhammad—had an encounter with God that distinguished him from his contemporaries and propelled him into a mission, introducing a new way of life that changed the world. . . . How appropriate that the three Abrahamic religions begin with a journey into the unknown.[474]

Emerging "Jesus"

The Emerging "Jesus" is admired by the world while the church is hated. But Jesus said, "If the world hate you, ye know that it hated me before it hated you" (John 15:18). Who is this Emergent Jesus, this Jesus that the world finds hip and cool and respects while hating His followers? Certainly it is not the historical Jesus of the Bible who said,

---

472 Tony Campolo, *Speaking My Mind* (Nashville, TN: Thomas Nelson, 2004), 149,150.
473 Brian McLaren, "Ramadan 2009: Part 1 What's going on?" Brian D McLaren, http://www.brianmclaren.net/archives/blog/ramadan-2009-part-1-whats-going.html.
474 Brian McLaren, *Finding Our Way Again* (Nashville, TN: Thomas Nelson, 2008) 22,23.

"Me [the world] hateth, because I testify of it, that the works thereof are evil (John 7:7). In *They Like Jesus But Not the Church*, Dan Kimball conducted several interviews with young people who tell him they like and respect Jesus, but they don't want anything to do with going to church and Christianity. He says these are "exciting times we live in when Jesus is becoming more and more respected in our culture by non-churchgoing people."[475]

In *A Generous Orthodoxy*, McLaren speaks of the seven different versions of Jesus he has known: the Conservative Protestant Jesus (who saves from hell through death), the Pentecostal Charismatic Jesus (who saves by giving the Holy Spirit), the Roman Catholic Jesus (who saves by rising from the dead), the Eastern Orthodox Jesus (who saves all creation by His birth), the Liberal Protestant Jesus & the Anabaptist Jesus (who saves by His teaching and example), and the Jesus of the Oppressed (who saves from injustice).[476] In doing so, McLaren implies that Jesus is only experienced in certain communities. Depending what community to which we belong, we'll experience a different Jesus, an other Jesus. And each Jesus is valid and authentic.

In a larger context, McLaren is implying that we don't really know the historical Jesus who came in the flesh and that we can't know Him. But the Apostle Paul warned: "I fear, lest by any means, as the serpent beguiled Eve through his subtilty, so your minds should be corrupted from the simplicity that is in Christ. For if he that cometh preacheth *another Jesus*, whom we have not preached, or if ye receive another spirit, which ye have not received, or another gospel, which ye have not accepted, ye might well bear with him" (2 Corinthians 11:3,4). Any *other* Jesus is *another* Jesus. This is the wonderful simplicity that is in Christ, but McLaren preaches at least seven *other* Jesuses.

Virgin Birth

Rob Bell also presents his version of the Emerging Jesus, not according to the historical Jesus:

---

475   Dan Kimball, *They Like Jesus But Not the Church* (Grand Rapids, MI: Zondervan. 2007), 37.
476   McLaren, *A Generous Orthodoxy*, Chapter 1: "The Seven Jesuses I Have Known."

What if tomorrow someone digs up definitive proof that
Jesus had a real, earthly, biological father named Larry,
and archaeologists find Larry's tomb and do DNA
samples and prove beyond a shadow of a doubt that the
virgin birth was really just a bit of mythologizing the
Gospel writers threw in to appeal to the followers of the
Mithra and Dionysian religious cults that were hugely
popular at the time of Jesus, whose gods had virgin
births? But what if as you study the origin of the word
virgin, you discover that the word virgin in the gospel of
Matthew actually comes from the book of Isaiah, and
then you find out that in the Hebrew language at that
time, the word virgin could mean several things. And
what if you discover that in the first century being "born
of a virgin" also referred to a child whose mother
became pregnant the first time she had intercourse?[477]

The virgin birth of Jesus Christ is one of the greatest and non-
negotiable doctrines of the Bible because it is linked with the
Incarnation. It is no mistake that the liberal church will contest the virgin
birth of Christ. Though Rob Bell says later that he believes in the virgin
birth, he has just given every argument against the virgin birth. This is
not edifying or helpful to immature Christian readers even if Bell
absolves himself of being at fault by later affirming the virgin birth.

To question the virgin birth is to question the very Deity of Jesus
Christ.[478] Such doubtful comments are not pious but poisonous to faith in

---

477   Bell, *Velvet Elvis*, 26,27.
478   Dr. Walter Martin addresses this very issue in refuting the Mormon
doctrine espoused by Brigham Young that God the Father had sexual relations
with Mary to conceive Jesus Christ: "Attempts to minimize the Virgin Birth of
Christ or to do away with it altogether, as some liberal theologians have
energetically tried to do, have consistently met with disaster. This is true
because the simple narratives of this momentous event recorded in Matthew and
Luke refuse to surrender to the hindsight reconstruction theories of second-
guessing critics." Walter Martin, *The Kingdom of the Cults* (Bloomington, MN:
Bethany House Publishers, 2003), 244.

Christ and will only result in spiritual decay. This sounds like the questioning serpent in the Garden of Eden, "Yea, hath God said" (Genesis 3:1). Has God said that Jesus was born of a virgin? Has God really said that "that which is conceived in her is of the Holy Ghost" (Matthew 1:20)? The Gospel record informs us clearly that Joseph and Mary did not have sexual relations until she had brought forth her firstborn Son, Jesus (Matthew 1:23-25).

For those Christians who may have read Bell's arguments against the virgin birth and their weak consciences were wounded, we should take the time now to refute them. Bell's argument that the word "virgin" in the Hebrew Old Testament "could mean several things" is a common objection to the Gospel brought up by Jewish anti-missionaries. Messianic apologist Michael Brown addresses this very issue by demonstrating how the Hebrew word *'alma* (from the prophecy of Isaiah 7:14 quoted by Matthew) does not specifically mean "virgin." In fact, there is no word in the Hebrew language that always and only means "virgin" This linguistic issue is probably what Bell is getting at. However, the Septuagint, the Greek translation of the Hebrew Old Testament, translated the Hebrew word *'alma* in Isaiah 7:14 with the Greek *parthenos* (normally rendered "virgin") more than two hundred years prior to the lifetime of Jesus Christ. Brown adds:

> [W]hile the evidence is not entirely clear, it is possible that the Septuagint rendering indicated this expectation that the birth spoken of in Isaiah 7:14 would be virginal (and, hence, supernatural), just as the Hebrew could point to the unusual nature of the birth . . . it became apparent that the 'alma of whom the prophet spoke, this unnamed maiden, was in fact a parthenos—a virgin— bearing the very Son of God. If a different word had been used (e.g., a specifically designated woman/wife, rather than just "the 'alma"), then a later virginal conception would have been impossible. The miraculous nature of the sign ultimately becomes clear in light of its fulfillment, whatever the original expectations and overall understanding might have been.

Centuries after Isaiah's day, this uniqueness came to the fore, quite possibly reflected in the Septuagint's parthenos, and then certainly reflected in Matthew's Greek text. So, the deepest meaning of the prophecy became apparent as the fullness of time dawned.[479]

The early Christian Origen (185-255 AD) asks this important question in regard to interpreting "young female" instead of "virgin" in the Old Testament prophecy of Isaiah 7:14: "What kind of sign would that have been, if it were merely a young woman—not a virgin—giving birth to a child?"[480] Tertullian (197 AD) also directed the following comment toward the Jews, "You are refuted by the fact that something that is a daily occurrence—the pregnancy and giving birth of a young female—cannot possibly be anything of a sign."[481]

But Bell is not only disputing the Old Testament prophecy of the virgin birth but also the clear teaching of the New Testament: "Now the birth of Jesus Christ was on this wise: When as his mother Mary was espoused to Joseph, before they came together, she was found with child of the Holy Ghost" (Matthew 1:18). Bell says that "Gospel writers threw in to appeal to the followers of the Mithra and Dionysian religious cults." This is a common argument from skeptics. An intelligent person like Rob Bell should have known better than to advocate such nonsense.

Concerning Mithraism, the late Dr. Ronald Nash sates: "Mithra was supposedly born when he emerged from a rock."[482] So unless this rock was a virgin, there is no virgin birth for Mithra. The available accounts of Dionysus' birth indicate that Dionysus was not born of a virgin. In the best known myth, Dionysus was born through an affair between Zeus and a princess.[483] In another version of the myth, Zeus

---

479 Michael Brown, *Answering Jewish Objections to Jesus Volume Three* (Grand Rapids, MI: Baker Books, 2003) 31.

480 Origen, *ANF*, 4.411 in Bercot, *A Dictionary of Early Christian Beliefs,* 671.

481 Tertullian, *ANF*, 3.161 in Bercot, *A Dictionary of Early Christian Beliefs*, 671.

482 Ronald Nash, *The Gospel and the Greeks* (Phillipsburg, NJ: P & R Publishing, 2003), 144.

483 Barry Powell, *Classical Myth*, 3rd ed. (Upper Saddle River, NJ:

mated with his daughter Persephone and she bore Dionysus.[484] Dr. Edwin Yamauchi, professor of history at Miami University confirms,

> There's no evidence of a virgin birth for Dionysus. As the story goes, Zeus, disguised as a human, fell in love with the princess Semele, the daughter of Cadmus, and she became pregnant. Hera, who was Zeus's queen, arranged to have her burned to a crisp, but Zeus rescued the fetus and sewed him into his own thigh until Dionysus was born. So this is not a virgin birth in any sense.[485]

Apparently it wouldn't bother Rob Bell if he found out Jesus wasn't born of a virgin as the Bible clearly says. Bell is essentially saying that if we get rid of the virgin birth, we don't really lose anything. Rob Bell is not bound to the historical Jesus as presented in Scripture but can settle with a yet *another* Jesus of his own image. If Bell could continue to be a Christian aftler he found out Jesus wasn't born of a virgin, then what kind of Christian is he?

Notice how different Bell's writings sound in comparison to the apologetic defenses of the primitive church. Ignatius (105 AD) wrote, "He was truly born of a virgin."[486] Justin Martyr (160 AD) wrote, "We even affirm that He was born of a virgin."[487] Clement of Alexandria (195 AD) wrote, "The Son of God—He who made the universe—assumed flesh and was conceived in the virgin's womb."[488] This new kind of Christianity being taught by Bell is not in agreement with the Apostolic

---

Prentice Hall: 2001), 250.

484   Mark Morford and Robert Lenardon, *Classical Mythology*, 7th ed. (New York, NY: Oxford University Press, 2003), 364.

485   Lee Strobel, *The Case for the Real Jesus* (Grand Rapids, MI: Zondervan, 2007), 180.

486I   Ignatius, *ANF* 1.86 in Bercot, *A Dictionary of the Early Christian Beliefs*, 670.

487   Justin Martyr, *ANF* 1.170 in Bercot, *A Dictionary of the Early Christian Beliefs*, 670.

488   Clement of Alexandria, *ANF* 2.509 in Bercot, *A Dictionary of the Early Christian Beliefs*, 670.

and primitive church. Tertullian (207 AD) said, "Whoever wishes to see Jesus, the Son of David, must believe in Him through the virgin's birth."[489] So why does Rob Bell question this essential doctrine? In 180 AD, Irenaeus said, "The heretics . . . do not acknowledge His incarnation. Others ignore the arrangement of a virgin and maintain that He was begotten by Joseph."[490]

To question the virgin birth and Incarnation is a violent assault on the Gospel, that Jesus "being in the form of God, thought it not robbery to be equal with God" (Philippians 2:6), that Jesus "was the Word, and the Word was with God, and the Word was God" (John 1:1), that Jesus "is the image of the invisible God" (Colossians 1:15), that in Jesus "dwelleth all the fulness of the Godhead bodily" (Colossians 2:9), that Jesus is, as Thomas said, "My Lord and my God" (John 20:28). Jesus is "God with us" (Matthew 1:23).

---

489   Tertullian, *Ante-Nicene Fathers*, volume 3, 411.
490   Irenaeus, *Ante-Nicene Fathers*, volume 1, 547.

13

Another Gospel

*"But I fear, lest by any means, as the serpent beguiled Eve through his
subtilty, so your minds should be corrupted from the simplicity that is in
Christ."*
– Paul (2 Corinthians 11:3)

Paul the Apostle spoke to his congregations with the following warnings:
"For if he that cometh preacheth another Jesus, whom we have not
preached, or if ye receive another spirit, which ye have not received, or
another gospel, which ye have not accepted, ye might well bear with
him" (2 Corinthians 11:4); "I marvel that ye are so soon removed from
him that called you into the grace of Christ unto another gospel: Which is
not another; but there be some that trouble you, and would pervert the
gospel of Christ" (Galatians 1:6,7). Essentially, there are only two
Gospels: the true Gospel and *everything else*. Anything *other* than the
Gospel of Jesus Christ is *another gospel*. If it can be clearly
demonstrated that Emergent has changed the Gospel, then we can safely
conclude that their message is one of these *other gospels* which Paul
warned against.

Rob Bell makes clear that the Emergent movement is changing
theology. Bell seeks to reform the way the Christian life is defined, lived
and explained, especially concerning "the beliefs about God, Jesus, the
Bible, salvation, the future. We must keep reforming the way the

251

Christian faith is defined, lived and explained."[491] Tony Jones stated the Emergent Church Movement is about "changing theology" and that "the message of the gospel changes."[492] This sounds nothing like Jude's exhortation to "earnestly contend for the faith which was once delivered unto the saints" (Jude 1:3). Theology, by definition, is the study of the nature of God who does not change. It is written, "I am the LORD, I change not" (Malachi 3:6) and "Jesus Christ the same yesterday, and to day, and for ever" (Hebrews 13:8). Nor can the message of the Gospel ever be changed, hence the term "the everlasting gospel" in Revelation 14:6.

Repentance

Many believe themselves "saved" when they have no idea *from what* they have been saved. Before preaching the good news of the Gospel of Jesus Christ, we must first lay a foundation of sin and repentance. Before preaching the Gospel, the Apostle Paul begins his letter to the Romans first addressing humankind's utter sinfulness. The Bible defines sin the following way: "Whosoever committeth sin transgresseth also the law: for sin is the transgression of the law" (1 John 3:4). But the Emergent Church in many ways has redefined sin and the need for turning away from sin.

During his "The God's Aren't Angry" tour, Rob Bell said, "Anytime someone makes you feel guilty about how you are living, that is part of the old system (pre-Christ)."[493] Here, Bell is administering a spiritual novocain and numbness to sin by nullifying one of the primary works of the Holy Spirit to convict the world of sin (John 16:8). What

---

491   Bell, *Velvet Elvis*, 12.
492   Tony Jones. "A New Theology for a New World," A workshop for the 2004 Emergent Convention in San Diego, CA. The audio recording of this seminar can be purchased through PSI, Inc. at 1-800- 808-8273 or via the web at: http://sf1000.registeredsite.com/%7euser1006646/miva/merchant.mv? Screen=BASK&Store_Code=YS-   SD&Action=ADPR&Product_Code=NS05-057CD&Attributes=Yes&Quantity=1.
493   Jesse Johnson, "Rob Bell: The gods Should Be Angry," Pulpit Magazine, November 21, 2007, http://www.sfpulpit.com/2007/11/21/rob-bell-the-gods-should-be-angry.

Rob Bell calls the "old system" is the foundation of the principles of Christ. In speaking about foundations in the Christian life, the writer of Hebrews wrote, "Therefore leaving the principles of the doctrine of Christ, let us go on unto perfection; not laying again the foundation of *repentance from dead works*, and of faith toward God" (Hebrews 6:1). Before people can recognize their need of the Savior, they must know that they are guilty before God: "Now we know that what things soever the law saith, it saith to them who are under the law: that every mouth may be stopped, and all the world may become guilty before God" (Romans 3:19). Unbelievers should feel guilty for the sins they have committed. The title of Bell's tour, "The God's Aren't Angry," is misleading and Bell's plea for people to realize that God is not angry with them is a tremendous disservice. The Bible says, "God is angry with the wicked every day" (Psalm 7:11). "He that believeth on the Son hath everlasting life: and he that believeth not the Son shall not see life; but *the wrath of God abideth on him*" (John 3:36).

Rob Bell defines repentance as "what happens when your eyes are opened and you see what has already been done."[494] What? This cannot be what John the Baptist meant when he said, "Repent ye: for the kingdom of heaven is at hand" (Matthew 3:2), or Jesus when He said, "Repent: for the kingdom of heaven is at hand" (Matthew 4:17), or the Apostle Peter when he said, "Repent, and be baptized every one of you in the name of Jesus Christ for the remission of sins, and ye shall receive the gift of the Holy Ghost" (Acts 2:38). Repentance is sincere regret or remorse about one's wrongdoing of sin and turning *from* sin to righteousness through obedience of faith in Christ, but Bell redefines it and thereby excludes the problem of sin altogether.

Rob Bell has often presented a self-affirming gospel while Jesus' good news is self-denial. Rob Bell says:

> God has an incredibly high view of people. God believes that people are capable of amazing things. I have been told that I need to believe in Jesus. Which is a good thing. But what I am learning is that Jesus believes in me. I have been told that I need to have faith in God.

---

494   Ibid.

Which is a good thing. But what I am learning is that
God has faith in me.[495]

This language creates comfortability in sin and leaves the reader
with the impression that God needs something from us when in reality
it's not about us. "I am the vine, ye are the branches," the Lord Jesus said;
"He that abideth in me, and I in him, the same bringeth forth much fruit:
for *without me ye can do nothing*" (John 15:5). It's about Jesus. The self-
affirming message is the exact opposite of what Jesus taught. He said, "If
any man will come after me, let him deny himself, and take up his cross
daily, and follow me" (Luke 9:23), and "whosoever doth not bear his
cross, and come after me, cannot be my disciple" (Luke 14:27). In its
first century context, the "cross" represents total death to self because
people who carry their cross have accepted their fate of execution. The
Romans could nail condemned criminals to a cross against their will, but
only a person who voluntarily carried their cross accepted their own
death, embraced public humiliation and rejection, and denied all
ambitions of life. This self-denial parallels the Christian life in which we
are dead to our sinful and corrupt nature of self.

Perhaps Eugene Peterson's Message Bible translation is an
Emergent favorite because it appeals to the carnal, the worldly and
unregenerate by allowing them to continue in sin while thinking
themselves to be saved.[496] For example, when the KJV says in Romans
8:35, "Who shall separate us from the love of Christ? shall tribulation, or
distress, or persecution, or famine, or nakedness, or peril, or sword?" *The
Message* Bible says, "Do you think anyone is going to be able to drive a
wedge between us and Christ's love for us? There is no way! Not trouble,
not hard times, not hatred, not hunger, not homelessness, not bullying
threats, not backstabbing, *not even the worst sins listed in Scripture*."
While sin is absent from the list Paul gives of that which can separate us
from God, Eugene Peterson says that not even the worst sins listed in

---

495   Bell, *Velvet Elvis*, 134.
496   For instance, Emergent icon Bono's favorite version of the Bible is The
Message. We read: "Yes, Bono takes a knee and recites a few lines from Eugene
Peterson's paraphrase of Psalm 116 (the version of the Good Book promoted by
Bono and known as The Message)." "Tebow, Bono & Jesus," Interference,
January 10, 2012, http://www.u2interference.com/15343-tebow-bono-jesus/.

Scripture can separate us from God. Conversely, the prophet Isaiah says, "But your iniquities have separated between you and your God, and your sins have hid his face from you, that he will not hear" (Isaiah 59:2).

Again, *The Message* takes Psalm 25:10, "All the paths of the LORD are mercy and truth unto such as keep his covenant and his testimonies" and translates, "From now on every road you travel will take you to God." Every road will take you to God? Certainly this is the epitome of Postmodern subjective and relative truth which ends with plurality, but Jesus said, "I am the way, the truth, and the life: no man cometh unto the Father, but by me" (John 14:6) and "strait is the gate, and narrow is the way, which leadeth unto life, and few there be that find it" (Matthew 7:14). The Emergent Church denies the exclusivity of Christ: "For there is one God, and one mediator between God and men, the man Christ Jesus" (1 Timothy 2:5) and "Neither is there salvation in any other: for there is none other name under heaven given among men, whereby we must be saved" (Acts 4:12).

Where is the Gospel?

What is lacking from Emergent theology is the proclamation of the Gospel of Jesus Christ. Jesus taught that He was the embodiment of truth and the only way to God: "I am the way, the truth, and the life: no man cometh unto the Father, but by me" (John 14:6). But Rob Bell states that the "way of Jesus is the best possible way to live."[497] When asked to present the Gospel on Twitter (which is 140 characters), Rob Bell responded:

> I would say that history is headed somewhere. The thousands of little ways in which you are tempted to believe that hope might actually be a legitimate response to the insanity of the world actually can be trusted. And the Christian story is that a tomb is empty, and a movement has actually begun that has been present in a sense all along in creation. And all those times when your cynicism was at odds with an impulse within you

---

497   Bell, *Velvet Elvis*, 20.

that said that this little thing might be about something bigger—those tiny little slivers may in fact be connected to something really, really big.[498]

Where is the Gospel? In Bell's convoluted and pitifully lacking presentation of the Bible's glad tidings, there is no mention of Jesus as the Son of God, the life of Christ, His death for our sins, repentance and forgiveness, the freedom from sin, the atonement, or salvation. Consider Paul's "Twitter" of the Gospel in fewer words than Bell: "Christ died for our sins according to the scriptures; And that he was buried, and that he rose again the third day according to the scriptures" (1 Corinthians 15:3,4). In even fewer words, Paul says, "For I am not ashamed of the gospel of Christ: for it is *the power of God unto salvation to every one that believeth*" (Romans 1:16). Either Bell has rejected the Gospel of Jesus Christ or he doesn't know what the Gospel is.

The Gospel is the good news that leads to salvation. Peter said that Christians "are kept by the power of God through faith unto salvation ready to be revealed in the last time" (1 Peter 1:5). While Bell presents the truth of an empty tomb, he preaches no repentance, forgiveness, or deliverance from sin. He has left those first-time hearers of "the Gospel" without hope and without a choice but to continue as shackled and chained slaves in bondage to sin and death. Jesus came to actually save us from our sins (Matthew 1:21).

Yes, Bell mentioned an empty tomb, which is true, but what are the implications of this empty tomb? God has "appointed a day, in the which he will judge the world in righteousness by that man whom he hath ordained; whereof he hath given assurance unto all men, in that he hath raised him from the dead" (Acts 17:31). "Therefore we are buried with him by baptism into death: that like as Christ was raised up from the dead by the glory of the Father, even so we also should walk in newness of life. For if we have been planted together in the likeness of his death, we shall be also in the likeness of his resurrection: Knowing this, that our old man is crucified with him, that the body of sin might be destroyed, that henceforth we should not serve sin. For he that is dead is freed from sin. . . . For *sin shall not have dominion over you*: for ye are not under

---

498   Mark Galli, "The Giant Story," *Christianity Today*, April 22, 2009, http://www.christianitytoday.com/ct/2009/april/26.34.html?start=3.

the law, but under grace." (Romans 6:4-7,14). This message is the power of God unto salvation. This story is the good news. It's not the good news about anything and everything, that "history is headed somewhere" and "those tiny little slivers may in fact be connected to something really, really big." It's the good news that JESUS IS LORD!

Preaching

Many in the Emergent Church are not advocating better preaching or more effective preaching but reject preaching altogether. Doug Pagitt teaches:

> I'm writing with the assumption that most of you who are reading this book have concluded what I have: Preaching doesn't work—at least not in the ways we hope. If it did, pastors wouldn't reach with such anticipation for new books about preaching; we'd already be following the established, tried-and-true methods laid in the huge array of available preaching resources.[499]

Pagitt refers to preaching as a form of communication he calls "speaching." He believes that preaching or "speaching" will not get people connected with God. He continues: "If you know how to listen, you can hear the rumblings that confirm that preaching, as we know it, is a tragically broken endeavor."[500] Perhaps preaching, as many evangelicals know it, is truly a broken endeavor because the Gospel is not being preached. But to dismiss preaching altogether because of this sort of pragmatism would be a rebellious neglect of what Scripture commands. Rather than re-inventing or re-imagining the act of preaching (as Pagitt's book titles suggest), we ought to rediscover what the Bible says about preaching.

The Bible says that the message of the Gospel itself is power: "I determined not to know any thing among you, save Jesus Christ, and him

---

499   Doug Pagitt, *Church Re-Imagined: The Spiritual Formation of People in Communities of Faith* (Grand Rapids, MI: Zondervan, 2003), 225.
500   Ibid.

crucified" (1 Corinthians 2:2). The mere preaching of truth, even biblical truth, apart from the Gospel, will never save a soul from the grasp of hell or change lives. The only saving truth is the biblical Gospel of Jesus Christ. This powerful message must be preached in purity and simplicity; it doesn't need any wisdom of words or craftiness of speech. The simple proclaimed Gospel stands all on its own. "For Christ sent me not to baptize, but to preach the gospel: not with wisdom of words, lest the cross of Christ should be made of none effect. For the preaching of the cross is to them that perish foolishness; but unto us which are saved it is the power of God. For it is written, I will destroy the wisdom of the wise, and will bring to nothing the understanding of the prudent. Where is the wise? where is the scribe? where is the disputer of this world? hath not God made foolish the wisdom of this world? For after that in the wisdom of God the world by wisdom knew not God, it pleased God by the foolishness of preaching to save them that believe. For the Jews require a sign, and the Greeks seek after wisdom: But we preach Christ crucified, unto the Jews a stumbling block, and unto the Greeks foolishness; But unto them which are called, both Jews and Greeks, Christ the power of God, and the wisdom of God" (1 Corinthians 1:17-24).

The foolishness of preaching Christ crucified is the wisdom and power of God. God destroys the wisdom of the wise by changing lives through the Gospel. Adulterers, prostitutes, fornicators, and those who are in bondage to pornography and lust find themselves with new desires and in love with Jesus. Rapists, pedophiles, homosexuals, murderers, and psychopaths hear the Gospel and find themselves in their right mind sitting at the feet of Jesus. Thieves and liars repent and have faith in Jesus. Alcoholics dry up and drug addicts are set free without any therapy or rehab. The depressed find a peace that passes understanding without a psychologist. The Emergent Church would have us abandon preaching altogether because it's not changing lives. But if preaching isn't changing lives, then the Gospel isn't being preached.

Offensive it may seem and foolish it may be, but God has chosen the act of preaching as a means to salvation. We are saved by grace through faith (Ephesians 2:8), and faith cometh by hearing, and hearing by the word of God (Romans 10:17). How then shall they call on him in whom they have not believed? How shall they believe in him of whom they have not heard? How shall they hear without a preacher? (Romans

10:14)

Not only are Emergents preaching a false gospel, but they altogether condemn the preaching of the true Gospel. In *Preaching Re-Imagined*, Doug Pagitt wrote, "The value of our practices—including preaching—ought to be judged by their effects on our communities and the ways in which they help us move toward life with God."[501] This sort of pragmatism when it comes to Gospel proclamation is unacceptable, especially if nobody responds to the simple good news.

In his Bullhorn video, Rob Bell presents a Christian evangelist as some sort of sicko conservative out-of-touch street preacher in a collared shirt and tie, printing copies of Gospel tracts in a poorly lit room as the creepy soundtrack sets the mood. Next we see Rob Bell in his hip and casual clothes sitting on bus bench in the heart of the city. Bell says, "Bullhorn guy, I don't think it's working. All the yelling and the judgment and the condemnation. I don't think it's working. I actually think it's making things worse. I don't think it's what Jesus had in mind."[502]

These Emergents have altogether abandoned the biblical model of preaching the Gospel and replaced it with cultural relevance. Paul's question nearly two thousand years ago is just as relevant today for the Emergent Church: "how shall they hear without a preacher?" For professing Christians to dissuade the preaching of the Gospel, I'd question their salvation because "the preaching of the cross is to them that perish foolishness; but unto us which are saved it is the power of God" (1 Corinthians 1:18). The preaching of the Gospel is God's tool to save those who believe. "It pleased God by the foolishness of preaching to save them that believe" (1 Corinthians 1:21). We are commanded by the Lord himself in the Great Commission to "preach the gospel to every creature" (Mark 16:15). We preach Christ crucified, unto the Jews a stumbling block, and unto the Greeks foolishness; But unto them which are called, both Jews and Greeks, Christ the power of God, and the wisdom of God (1 Corinthians 1:23,24).

So how is it that the Emergents want to abolish street preaching? Granted, many street preachers can be unreasonable, unloving, and

---

501   Doug Pagitt, *Preaching Re-Imagined* (Grand Rapids, MI: 2005), 18,19,28.
502   Bullhorn 009 - Rob Bell, dir. by Santino Stoner (Storefront Pictures, 2006).

unapproachable, but even in this case we should be like Paul and praise God that the Gospel is preached. "Some indeed preach Christ even of envy and strife; and some also of good will: The one preach Christ of contention, not sincerely, supposing to add affliction to my bonds: But the other of love, knowing that I am set for the defense of the gospel. What then? notwithstanding, every way, whether in pretense, or in truth, Christ is preached; and I therein do rejoice, yea, and will rejoice" (Philippians 1:15-18). Yet this is *not* the attitude of the Emerging Church that wants to silence the preaching of Gospel.

Social Gospel Gone Green

In many Emergent books, the emphasis is shifted from the priority of preaching the Gospel to environmentalist priorities such as "rescuing nature from an exploitive urban industrial society."[503] Perhaps one of the most ridiculous statements comes from Campolo who says, "I am also obliged to do what Jesus said: save the whales."[504] There is nothing inherently wrong in being an environmentally conscious "green" Christian; all Christians should be faithful stewards of the Earth. But when saving the environment from destruction becomes priority over saving souls from sin, there is a serious problem. McLaren describes this "new way" as follows:

> Even if only a few would practice this new way, many would benefit. Oppressed people would be free. Poor people would be liberated from poverty. Minorities would be treated with respect. Sinners would be loved, not resented. Industrialists would realize that God cares for sparrows and wildflowers—so their industries should respect, not rape, the environment.[505]

Certainly these injustices are concerns for Christians, but solving the world's problems is not our priority. The Great Commission given by Jesus to His disciples was: "Go ye into all the world, and preach the

---

503   Campolo and McLaren, *Adventures in Missing the Point*, 187.
504Ibid., 191.
505   McLaren, *A Generous Orthodoxy*, 111.

gospel to every creature. He that believeth and is baptized shall be saved; but he that believeth not shall be damned" (Mark 16:15,16). By "every creature," Jesus did not mean animals, but those who could potentially be baptized and saved.

Paul said, "For it is written in the law of Moses, Thou shalt not muzzle the mouth of the ox that treadeth out the corn. *Doth God take care for oxen?* Or saith he it altogether for our sakes? For our sakes, no doubt, this is written: that he that ploweth should plow in hope; and that he that thresheth in hope should be partaker of his hope" (1 Corinthians 9:9,10). It is not oxen and asses God is concerned about, but this is written for our sakes. But the Emergent Church *is concerned* about oxen.

Jesus said, "Behold the fowls of the air: for they sow not, neither do they reap, nor gather into barns; yet your heavenly Father feedeth them. Are ye not much better than they? (Matthew 6:26). Jesus' point was that God cares for these lesser things in the creation like birds and lilies. So how much more will he care for people? People are much better than birds and lilies, so they are not to worry about God feeding and clothing them. But the Emergent Church is giving priority to birds, lilies and whales over people.

The Emergent zeal is characterized by immanence rather than transcendence. Members of the Emergent movement often place a high value on social activism by emphasizing "here and now" while neglecting the weightier matters of eternal salvation. Mark Scandrette, an Emergent writer and teacher, characterizes the Emergent Church phenomenon as

> significant interest in "community," communal living, and renewed monastic practices . . . revitalized interest in the social dimensions of the gospel of Jesus, including community development, earth-keeping, global justice, and advocacy.[506]

Dan Kimball says:

Our faith also includes kingdom living, part of which is

---

506   Mark Scandrette, "Growing Pains," in *An Emergent Manifesto of Hope*, eds. Tony Jones and Doug Pagitt, 28.

the responsibility to fight locally and globally for social justice on behalf of the poor and needy. Our example is Jesus, who spent His time among the lepers, the poor and the needy.[507]

Absolutely Jesus showed compassion on the poor and needy, but neither Jesus nor the apostles fought for social justice, the environment, political tyranny, eradication of poverty and illiteracy or the elimination of deadly diseases or other social ills. Jesus taught, "My kingdom is not of this world: if my kingdom were of this world, then would my servants fight, that I should not be delivered to the Jews: but now is my kingdom not from hence" (John 18:36). Concerning the poor, Jesus did not foresee any elimination of poverty; He said, "For the poor always ye have with you; but me ye have not always" (John 12:8). We should not neglect the poor; we should give and minister to those in poverty. But our priority and emphasis in every ministry ought to be preaching the Gospel and teaching people to obey all things Jesus commanded.

In an endnote to chapter one of *The Secret Message of Jesus*, Brian McLaren writes of the subtitle he wished to have used, "The Secret Message of Jesus: His surprising and Largely Untried Plan for a Political, Social, Religious, Artistic, Economic, Intellectual, and Spiritual Revolution."[508] He asks,

> What if Jesus' secret message reveals a secret plan? What if he didn't come to start a new religion—but rather came to start a political, social, religious, artistic, economic, intellectual, and spiritual revolution that would give birth to a new world?[509]

McLaren's audacious claim cannot stand against the Scriptures. Are we to believe that after two thousand years of Christian history, the Church somehow missed the message of Jesus? To the Emergent, the emphasis of the Christian mission is not to save sinners from their sins and from a lost and dying world which God is going to destroy, but to

---

507   Kimball, *The Emerging Church*, 224.
508   McLaren, *The Secret Message of Jesus*, 229, n. 1.
509   Ibid., 4.

save the whole planet Earth in a social and environmental way. But God's idea of recycling is very different than the environmentalists' view (See 2 Peter 3:7,10-13). These notions of redemption for everybody including unbelievers as well as birds and the planet Earth are foreign to the Bible. The very definition of redemption, being saved from sin, limits the concept of redemption to sinful human beings.

What Must We Do to Be Saved?

Emergence Christians are redefining what it means to be a Christian. Donald Miller says, "If we hold that Jesus wanted us to 'believe' certain ideas or 'do' certain things in order to be a Christian, we are holding to heresy."[510] What? Teaching such heresy will cause many people to die and go to hell. Jesus wanted us to both "believe" certain ideas and to "do" certain things in order to be a Christian. It was Jesus who said, "If ye believe not that I am he, ye shall die in your sins" (John 8:24). In other words, people aren't Christians and will die in their sins if they do not believe that Jesus is the Messiah.[511]

Jesus concluded the Sermon on the Mount by saying: "Therefore whosoever heareth these sayings of mine, and *doeth them*, I will liken him unto a wise man, which built his house upon a rock: And the rain descended, and the floods came, and the winds blew, and beat upon that house; and it fell not: for it was founded upon a rock. And every one that heareth these sayings of mine, and *doeth them not*, shall be likened unto a foolish man, which built his house upon the sand: And the rain descended, and the floods came, and the winds blew, and beat upon that house; and it fell: and great was the fall of it" (Matthew 7:24-27). According to Jesus, we must do what He said in order to be a Christian.

---

510   Donald   Miller,   "Searching   for   God   Knows   What," http://www.donaldmillerwords.com/searching.php.
511   The Bible explains very clearly, "He that believeth on him is not condemned: but he that believeth not is condemned already, because he hath not believed in the name of the only begotten Son of God" (John 3:18); "He that believeth on the Son hath everlasting life: and he that believeth not the Son shall not see life; but the wrath of God abideth on him" (John 3:36); "He that believeth and is baptized shall be saved; but he that believeth not shall be damned" (Mark 16:16).

We know that Jesus is relating the building of a house to a person's salvation based on the immediate context of the previous verses about doing the will of the Father (Matthew 7:21-23) and concluding, "Therefore whosoever heareth these sayings of mine, and doeth them . . ." (Matthew 7:24). Jesus is addressing those who have heard His words. The wise man is the one who hears the words of Jesus and does them (Matthew 7:24), whose Christian life will endure and not fall apart, whereas the foolish man is the one who hears the sayings of Jesus and does not do them (Matthew 7:26), whose life will fail. Thus, contrary to Donald Miller's teaching, obedience (doing certain things) is a condition for our salvation by God's grace through faith (believing certain things). The gift of salvation is no less a gift simply because it's conditioned on faith and obedience.

The Emerging Church generally believes that the modern church cannot connect with the postmodern mind and culture. Though the term "missional" characterizes Emergent evangelism, these leaders stray from the biblical model of missions and evangelism. McLaren asks,

> Is getting individual souls into heaven the focal point of the gospel? I'd have to say no, for any number of reasons. Don't you think that God is concerned about saving the whole world? . . . . It is the redemption of the world, the stars, the animals, the planets, the whole show.[512]

Certainly redemption, whether we call it salvation from sin or "getting individual souls into heaven," is at least *a* focal point of the Gospel if not *the* focal point of the Gospel. Sadly, McLaren shifts the focus to planetary, animal, and universal salvation, which is definitely *not* a focal point of the Gospel. Jesus Christ is the focus of the Gospel. Even His name means "Jehovah is salvation." "Thou shalt call his name JESUS: for he shall save his people from their sins" (Matthew 1:21). Jesus said, "For the Son of man is come to seek and to save that which was lost" (Luke 19:10). This point is the reason and purpose for which Christ came: salvation from sin. It has to be the primary focal point.

---

512   McLaren, *A New Kind of Christian*, 129.

Many of us Christians can share the aversion to the modern form of Christian salvation that's merely an inoculation of the "sinner's prayer" which takes people out of the line to hell and gives them a ticket to heaven even though there are no life changes. McLaren rightly acknowledges that the phrase "accept Christ as your personal Savior" or even "personal Savior" are not phrases found in the pages of the Bible. He notes that modern ideas of salvation are often past tense and accompanied with church rituals including altar calls and invitations.[513] We can come in agreement with the Emergent conversation that this is an unbiblical and powerless form of Christianity. But rather than redefining the mission of the church in terms of social and planetary salvation in history as the Emergent Church at times has done, we should seek to be ever consistent with the Biblical view and importance of individual salvation from sin and hell. Our very knowledge of salvation is given through the remission of sins (Luke 1:77).

In *Adventures in Missing the Point*, McLaren Campolo note how ancient Jews missed the point of salvation by considering it to be only about politics here and now, and the modern Christians missed the point by thinking salvation is only about escaping hell when we die.[514] In McLaren's approach to salvation, "being rescued from fruitless ways of life here and now, to share in God's saving love for all creation, in an adventure called the kingdom of God," he includes the "here and now" aspect but the future tense is totally abandoned.[515] Of course salvation is not *all about* escaping hell when we die, but it is certainly our hope (Romans 8:24). We are "kept by the power of God through faith unto salvation ready to be revealed in the last time" (1 Peter 1:5). While he brings out how the ancient Jews and modern Christians missed the point about salvation, he misses the point as well by teaching a similarly unbalanced and flawed view. Salvation has been accomplished (Luke 19:9), is continuous today (2 Corinthians 6:2) and hoped for in the future (Romans 8:24).

I agree with Bell that the Gospel is being diminished and reduced by Christianity today to "a question of whether or not a person

---

513   McLaren, and Campolo, *Adventures in Missing the Point,* 19.
514   McLaren and Campolo, *Adventures in Missing the Point,* 25.
515   Ibid.

will "get into heaven," a ticket to heaven or merely forgiveness.[516] He says that "the good news is better than that."[517] Indeed the Gospel is better than a ticket to heaven, but Bell is mistaken in expanding the Gospel to something it is not. He adds to the Gospel by teaching that Jesus "is saving everybody"[518] when, in fact, the New Testament frequently affirms a distinction between those who are being saved and those who are perishing.[519] They have missed the point themselves by neglecting what the Bible tells us about being rescued form sin. Through the blood and intercession of Jesus Christ, through the grace of God and the Holy Spirit, we are saved from the bondage, the power, the condemnation and the penalty of sin. "Being now justified by his blood, we shall be saved from wrath through him" (Romans 5:9). "Take heed unto thyself, and unto the doctrine; continue in them: for in doing this thou shalt both save thyself, and them that hear thee" (1 Timothy 4:16).

Speaking to Christian recipients of his letter, Paul spoke about the present and continuous aspect of salvation: "Moreover, brethren, I declare unto you the gospel which I preached unto you, which also ye have received, and wherein ye stand; By which also ye are saved, if ye keep in memory what I preached unto you, unless ye have believed in vain" (1 Corinthians 15:1,2). Again, McLaren inappropriately applies this present salvation to the entire planet Earth and not just Christians. He writes:

> I am a Christian because I believe that, in all these ways, Jesus is saving the world. By "world" I mean planet Earth and all life on it, because left to ourselves, un-judged, un-forgiven, and un-taught, we will certainly destroy this planet and its residents. And by "the world"

---

516   Bell, *Love Wins*, 178.

517   Ibid., 179.

518   Ibid., 155.

519   For example, "For the preaching of the cross is to them that perish foolishness; but unto us which are saved it is the power of God" (1 Corinthians 1:18); "For we are unto God a sweet savour of Christ, in them that are saved, and in them that perish: To the one we are the savour of death unto death; and to the other the savour of life unto life. And who is sufficient for these things?" (2 Corinthians 2:15,16).

I specifically mean human history, because again, it was
and is in danger, grave danger, ultimate danger, self-
imposed danger, and I don't believe anyone else can
rescue it. [520]

Thus, to the Emergents, when the Bible says that "God so loved
the world" (John 3:16), that Jesus came to "save the world" (John 12:47),
they understand "the world" as all of humanity as well as plants, animals,
planets and stars. Rob Bell informs us:

Salvation is the entire universe being brought back into
harmony with its maker. This has huge implications for
how people present the message of Jesus. Yes, Jesus can
come into our hearts. But we can join a movement that is
as wide and as big as the universe itself. Rocks and trees
and birds and swamps and ecosystems. God's desire is to
restore all of it. . . .

So this is reality, this forgiveness, this reconciliation, is
true for everybody. Paul insisted that when Jesus died on
the cross, he was reconciling "all things, in heaven and
on earth, to God." All things, everywhere. This reality
then isn't something we make come true about ourselves
by doing something. It is already true. Our choice is to
live in this new reality or cling to a reality of our own
making.[521]

No, in reality this reconciliation is not already true for
everybody. In the same verse quoted by Rob Bell, the Apostle says to
Christians, not unbelievers: "And all things are of God, who hath
reconciled us to himself by Jesus Christ, and hath given to us the
ministry of reconciliation" (2 Corinthians 5:18). So they are Christians,
not everybody in the world, that have been reconciled. Next Paul says,
"To wit, that God was in Christ, reconciling the world unto himself, not
imputing their trespasses unto them; and hath committed unto us the

---

520   McLaren, *A Generous Orthodoxy*, 97.
521   Bell, *Velvet Elvis*, 109-110, 146.

word of reconciliation" (2 Corinthians 5:19). This is not to say that the world, all things, everywhere, have been reconciled. If the entire world had been reconciled, then there would be no need for the "word of reconciliation" to be committed to us Christians. That this reconciliation is not true for everybody as Rob Bell insisted is further evidenced in the next verse: "Now then we are ambassadors for Christ, as though God did beseech you by us: we pray you in Christ's stead, be ye reconciled to God" (2 Corinthians 5:20). There would be no reason for Christians to beseech others to be reconciled to God if they have already been reconciled.

God has initiated and offered reconciliation, but receiving it is conditional based on the necessities of repentance and faith in Christ. For this reason Paul testified both "repentance toward God, and faith toward our Lord Jesus Christ" (Acts 20:21). Furthermore, "the righteousness which is of faith speaketh on this wise, Say not in thine heart, Who shall ascend into heaven? (that is, to bring Christ down from above:) Or, Who shall descend into the deep? (that is, to bring up Christ again from the dead.) But what saith it? The word is nigh thee, even in thy mouth, and in thy heart: that is, the word of faith, which we preach; That if thou shalt confess with thy mouth the Lord Jesus, and shalt believe in thine heart that God hath raised him from the dead, thou shalt be saved" (Romans 10:6-9).

In the preface of *Love Wins*, Rob Bell reveals his motive for writing the book, namely, because "a staggering number of people have been taught that a select few Christians will spend forever in a peaceful, joyous place called heaven, while the rest of humanity spends forever in hell."[522] This belief, he says, is "misguided and toxic."[523] But is this belief truly misguided and toxic or is it the truth? Why is it that a staggering number of Christians believe that only a "select few" will be saved while many will be damned? Because Jesus said so. His disciples asked him explicitly, "Lord, are there few that be saved?" to which Jesus responded, "Strive to enter in at the strait gate: for many, I say unto you, will seek to enter in, and shall not be able" (Luke 13:23,24). In the parallel passage, Jesus said, "Enter ye in at the strait gate: for wide is the gate, and broad is the way, that leadeth to destruction, and many there be which go in

---

522   Bell, *Love Wins*, viii.
523   Ibid.

threat: Because strait is the gate, and narrow is the way, which leadeth unto life, and few there be that find it" (Matthew 7:13,14).

It is interesting that Jesus describes the wide gate and broad way as a path that leads to destruction (Matthew 7:13,14), but Rob Bell likens the Christian faith to a "wide stream we're swimming in," and "The Christian faith is big enough, wide enough, and generous enough to handle that vast range of perspectives."[524] Rob Bell asks how a person ends up being one of the few if there are truly a select few that are saved.[525] Chance? Luck? Random Selection? Bell neglects to provide a biblical answer for his question. The Bible declares: "For by grace are ye saved through faith; and that not of yourselves: it is the gift of God: Not of works, lest any man should boast" (Ephesians 2:8,9). It has nothing to do with chance, luck, or random selection, but has everything to do with a person's relationship to Jesus Christ. "Which Jesus?" Bell later asks.[526] Good question. The biblical Jesus Christ is the answer. With Him we must have an obedient-love-faith relationship with God by His grace. But "the phrase 'personal relationship' is found nowhere in the Bible."[527] True, this is an extra-biblical phrase, yet it accurately sums up what is required for salvation (See John 15). Jesus explains that we can have a relationship with Him through obedience. If we obey Him, then we know that we truly love Him and believe in Him. Jesus said, "Ye are my friends, if ye do whatsoever I command you" (John 15:14).

Bell sarcastically responds to good works by saying, "All we have to do is accept and confess and believe, aren't those verbs? And aren't verbs actions? . . . How is any of that grace? How is that a gift?"[528] However, meeting conditions is not earning merit. God's grace is unmerited but not unconditional. I couldn't answer Bell's question any more directly than the Apostle Paul: "The righteousness of God which is by faith of Jesus Christ unto all and upon all them that believe: for there is no difference: For all have sinned, and come short of the glory of God; Being justified freely by his grace through the redemption that is in Christ Jesus: Whom God hath set forth to be a propitiation through faith

---

524   Ibid., 110.
525   Ibid., 2.
526   Ibid., 7.
527   Ibid., 10.
528   Ibid., 11.

in his blood, to declare his righteousness for the remission of sins that are past, through the forbearance of God; To declare, I say, at this time his righteousness: that he might be just, and the justifier of him which believeth in Jesus. Where is boasting then? It is excluded. By what law? of works? Nay: but by the law of faith" (Romans 3:22-27). We are saved by grace through faith, but faith is not a meritorious work according to Paul. Neither is obedience meritorious for salvation: "When ye shall have done all those things which are commanded you, say, We are unprofitable servants: we have done that which was our duty to do" (Luke 17:10). Salvation is by grace and cannot be earned. But a gift is no less a gift simply because it is conditioned on faith and obedience. God is selective in His giving, and He chooses to give salvation to those who love and obey Him. Absolutely salvation and heaven are "dependent on something I do?"[529] Bell leaves all these important questions unanswered.

Salvation belongs to God and is in the Lord Jesus Christ (2 Timothy 2:10). "Truly in vain is salvation hoped for from the hills, and from the multitude of mountains: truly in the LORD our God is the salvation of Israel" (Jeremiah 3:23). It is in Jesus Christ alone that "we have redemption through his blood, the forgiveness of sins, according to the riches of his grace" (Ephesians 1:7). "Neither is there salvation in any other: for there is none other name under heaven given among men, whereby we must be saved" (Acts 4:12). Our redemption is therefore dependent upon us abiding in Jesus Christ. "Let that therefore abide in you, which ye have heard from the beginning. If that which ye have heard from the beginning shall remain in you, ye also shall continue in the Son, and in the Father" (1 John 2:24).

The things necessary for salvation are a changed heart (Jeremiah 31:31-33), the witness of the Holy Spirit (Romans 8:16), obedience (John 14:15), sanctification (1 Corinthians 6:9-11), and love (John 13:35). If all Christians practiced the Sermon on the Mount for an entire day, the whole world would be turned upside down (Acts 17:6). These attributes and qualities of salvation are stressed throughout the entire Bible, but the Emergent Church places more importance on social justice and saving the environment. Rather than Emergent turning the world upside down, the world has turned Emergent upside down.

---

529   Ibid.

14

The Kingdom of God

"Repent ye: for the kingdom of heaven is at hand"
- Jesus (Matthew 3:2)

McLaren recalls being asked what the Gospel is according to Jesus and not having a sufficient answer. A "well-known Evangelical theologian" then turned McLaren's attention to the Gospel of the Kingdom of God. McLaren recalls:

> Like a lot of Protestants, for many years I "knew" what the gospel was. I "knew" that the gospel was the message of "justification by grace through faith," distorted or forgotten by those pesky Catholics, but rediscovered by our hero Martin Luther through a reading of our even greater hero Paul, especially his magnum opus, the Letter to the Romans. If Catholics were called "Roman Catholics" because of their headquarters in Rome, we could have been called "Roman Protestants," because Paul's Roman letter served as our theological headquarters. As its avid students, we "knew" without question what it was about. To my embarrassment, though, about fifteen years ago I stopped knowing a lot of what I previously knew. A

271

lunchtime meeting in a Chinese restaurant unconvinced and untaught me.

My lunch mate was a well-known Evangelical theologian who quite rudely upset years of theological certainty with one provocative statement: "Most Evangelicals haven't got the foggiest notion of what the gospel really is." He then asked me how I would define the gospel, and I answered as any good Romans Protestant would, quoting Romans. He followed up with this simple but annoying rhetorical question: "You're quoting Paul. Shouldn't you let Jesus define the gospel?" When I gave him a quizzical look, he asked, "What was the gospel according to Jesus?" A little humiliated, I mumbled something akin to "You tell me," and he replied, "For Jesus, the gospel was very clear. The Kingdom of God is at hand. That's the gospel according to Jesus, right?" I again mumbled something, maybe "I guess so." Seeing my lack of conviction, he added "Shouldn't you read Paul in light of Jesus, instead of reading Jesus in light of Paul?"[530]

Certainly many Christians have neglected the Gospel of the Kingdom of God on account of viewing the Gospel and Paul's writings through the lens of Luther's Reformation rather than the doctrine of Jesus. While the Reformation led the church out of the Roman Catholic Church's apostasy, it failed to emphasize the Kingdom of God. Aside from whatever the view of the Kingdom of God is according to the Emergent Church or this unnamed evangelical theologian with whom McLaren spoke, I agree that this Gospel of the Kingdom of God is the Gospel according to Jesus and the entire New Testament.

Clothed in camel's hair and wearing a leather belt, John the Baptist was a striking prophet with this startling message: "Repent ye: for *the kingdom of heaven is at hand*" (Matthew 3:2). This is the clear message that John the Baptist, Jesus' predecessor was heralding.

---

530   Brian McLaren, *A New Kind of Christianity* (New York, NY: HarperCollins Publishers, 2010), 137-138.

What did Jesus preach? From the time John was cast into prison, "Jesus began to preach, and to say, Repent: for the kingdom of heaven is at hand" (Matthew 4:17). The moral imperative of repentance must not be overlooked in both John's and Jesus' the preaching the Kingdom of God. Jesus said, "I must preach the kingdom of God to other cities also: for therefore am I sent" (Luke 4:43). We read in Matthew 4:17 and 23: "From that time Jesus began to preach, and to say, Repent: for the kingdom of heaven is at hand. . . And Jesus went about all Galilee, teaching in their synagogues, and preaching the gospel of the kingdom, and healing all manner of sickness and all manner of disease among the people." The disciples likewise Jesus instructed, "As ye go, preach, saying, The kingdom of heaven is at hand" (Matthew 10:7).

What did Jesus command His disciples to preach? "Then he called his twelve disciples together, and gave them power and authority over all devils, and to cure diseases. And he sent them to preach the kingdom of God" (Luke 9:1,2). Jesus also said, "Let the dead bury their dead: but go thou and preach the kingdom of God" (Luke 9:60). Did Jesus' glad tidings of the Kingdom change after His death and resurrection? No, Jesus showed Himself alive after his passion by many infallible proofs, "being seen of them forty days, and speaking of the things pertaining to the kingdom of God" (Acts 1:3). Were the early disciples faithful to preach the message of the Kingdom of God which Jesus instructed them to preach? "But when they believed Philip preaching the things concerning the kingdom of God, and the name of Jesus Christ, they were baptized, both men and women" (Acts 8:12).

What about the Apostle Paul? The Apostle "went into the synagogue, and spake boldly for the space of three months, disputing and persuading the things concerning the kingdom of God" (Acts 19:8). This message of the Kingdom of God was Paul's message documented throughout the book of Acts. We read in the very last lines of the book of Acts: "And Paul dwelt two whole years in his own hired house, and received all that came in unto him, Preaching the kingdom of God, and teaching those things which concern the Lord Jesus Christ, with all confidence, no man forbidding him" (Acts 28:30,31).

Therefore, we *should* read Paul in light of Jesus as this evangelical theologian suggested to McLaren. However, by doing so, I think we will come to a much different conclusion about the Kingdom of

God than that of the Emergent Church. This Gospel according to Jesus is no different than the Gospel of Paul. First of all, Paul speaks of the Gospel of the grace of God and the Gospel of the Kingdom of God interchangeably proving that Paul's good news was the synonymous with Jesus' good news of the Kingdom of God. Paul said, "But none of these things move me, neither count I my life dear unto myself, so that I might finish my course with joy, and the ministry, which I have received of the Lord Jesus, to testify the gospel of the grace of God. And now, behold, I know that ye all, among whom I have gone preaching the kingdom of God, shall see my face no more" (Acts 20:24,25). It is evident from Paul's previous statement that he received this message from the Lord Jesus himself. He declared, "But I certify you, brethren, that the gospel which was preached of me is not after man. For I neither received it of man, neither was I taught it, but by the revelation of Jesus Christ" (Galatians 1:11,12). Paul's good news was the same good news that he received by the revelation of Jesus. The Lord appeared to Paul at Corinth and encouraged him to continue preaching the Gospel that he gave him: "Then spake the Lord to Paul in the night by a vision, Be not afraid, but speak, and hold not thy peace: For I am with thee, and no man shall set on thee to hurt thee: for I have much people in this city. And he continued there a year and six months, teaching the word of God among them" (Acts 18:8-11).

What about the early Christians? The primitive Christians also preached the Gospel of the Kingdom of God. Clement of Rome (96 AD) explained how the Gospel of the Kingdom was that one and only Gospel handed down from Jesus and the apostles. He wrote:

The apostles have preached the Gospel to us from the Lord Jesus Christ; Jesus Christ [has done so] from God. Christ therefore was sent forth by God, and the apostles by Christ. Both these appointments, then, were made in an orderly way, according to the will of God. Having therefore received their orders, and being fully assured by the resurrection of our Lord Jesus Christ, and established in the word of God, with full assurance of the Holy Ghost, they went forth proclaiming that the kingdom of God was at hand.[531]

The Kingdom of God was a present reality to the early Christians, not just a theoretical idea. To become a citizen of Christ's kingdom was often a death sentence. Justin Martyr (160 AD) wrote,

> And when you hear that we look for a kingdom, you suppose, without making any inquiry, that we speak of a human kingdom; whereas we speak of that which is with God, as appears also from the confession of their faith made by those who are charged with being Christians, though they know that death is the punishment awarded to him who so confesses. For if we looked for a human kingdom, we should also deny our Christ, that we might not be slain; and we should strive to escape detection, that we might obtain what we expect. But since our thoughts are not fixed on the present, we are not concerned when men cut us off; since also death is a debt which must at all events be paid.[532]

Emerging Kingdom

What is the Kingdom of God to new Emerging Christians? McLaren defines the Kingdom of God as "God's new benevolent society . . . a new way of life, a new way of peace that carried good news to people of every religion."[533] McLaren says, "the kingdom-oriented term 'Christ' means 'liberating king,' the one who will free God's people from oppression, confront and humble their oppressors, and then lead both into a better day."[534] The Bible says that "Messiah" being interpreted is "Christ" (John 1:41). Indeed, Jesus was the promised deliverer and Savior prophesied in the Old Testament. But He did not come to deliver God's people from their oppressors and then lead the oppressed and the oppressors into a better day as McLaren proclaimed. Again, McLaren's

---

531 Clement of Rome, *Ante-Nicene Fathers*, volume 1, 16.
532 Justin Martyr, *Ante-Nicene Fathers,* volume 1, 166.
533 McLaren, *A New Kind of Christianity*, 138-139.
534 Ibid.

view of the Kingdom consists of the poor and oppressed being set free and liberated, minorities being treated fairly and industrialists caring for the environment.[535]

Like McLaren, many people within the Emergent movement express concern for what they consider to be the practical manifestation of the Kingdom of God on earth, by which they mean saving the planet and changing society. U2's lead singer Bono becomes the ultimate Emergent Christian in this sense. Campolo writes:

> Bono is using his wealth and celebrity status to do just that: increase the kingdom of God in the here and now. Even back in 1982 he was part of the Live Aid and Band-Aid concerts, whose earnings helped Ethiopians suffering through famine. . . .

> He now works fiercely to change the policies of governments and of organizations like the World Bank and the International Monetary Fund—in order that funding for public health, education, and essential social services will *increase* rather than decrease.[536]

But does Bono preach the Kingdom of God? Jesus *did* miraculously feed the hungry and heal the sick but this was primarily to confirm *His message* of the Gospel of the Kingdom of God,[537] a message that Bono and Emergent are not preaching. Certainly the Kingdom of God will impact society and turn the world upside down but not in the

---

535   McLaren, *A Generous Orthodoxy*, 111.

536   Campolo, *Adventures in Missing the Point*, 50.

537   Jesus said, "Believest thou not that I am in the Father, and the Father in me? the words that I speak unto you I speak not of myself: but the Father that dwelleth in me, he doeth the works. Believe me that I am in the Father, and the Father in me: or else believe me for the very works' sake. Verily, verily, I say unto you, He that believeth on me, the works that I do shall he do also; and greater works than these shall he do; because I go unto my Father" (John 14:10-12). The Gospel of Mark concludes, "And they went forth, and preached everywhere, the Lord working with them, and confirming the word with signs following" (Mark 16:20).

ways Emergent is advocating. Liberating oppressed and impoverished people, loving and respecting sinners are good deeds not to be neglected. Absolutely Jesus showed compassion on the poor and needy, but neither Jesus nor the apostles politicized the Gospel or prioritized social justice to save the environment or eradicate poverty and illiteracy. These are not the priorities of the Gospel of the Kingdom of God. Campolo continues:

> Politicians with views as diverse as Bill Clinton and Jesse Helms have taken Bono seriously and joined him in successful efforts to reduce Third World debts. He has persuaded wealthy countries to lend their financial muscle to addressing the AIDS crisis in Africa, thus saving tens of thousands from death.[538]

Again, this is not the kind of "saving" that Jesus preached. In fact, Jesus called His disciples out of political involvement to follow Him, but Tony Jones argues that "Jesus was interested in . . . the machinations of human politics."[539] Jones says that "the emergents are activists—even political activists."[540] Jesus didn't try to garner support from King Herod, Governor Pontius Pilate or Caesar Augustus in order to reduce poverty or address leprosy. The Gospel of Matthew states: "Thou shalt call his name JESUS: for he shall save his people *from their sins*" (Matthew 1:21). It is not a liberalized postmodern social gospel, but the Gospel of Christ is "the power of God unto salvation to every one that believeth" (Romans 1:16).

The Emergent idea of people being "saved" from poverty, famine, and oppression rather than sin sounds more like the contemporary Jewish anticipation of a politically-charged kingdom in Jesus' day. They believed the King would deliver them from Roman oppression and usher in a worldly kingdom. But Jesus had no interest in establishing a physical kingdom with the nation of Israel: "When Jesus therefore perceived that they would come and take him by force, to make him a king, he departed again into a mountain himself alone" (John 6:15). The inauguration of this kingdom is not to come at a future time

---

538   Campolo, *Adventures in Missing the Point*, 50.
539   Jones, *The New Christians,* 82.
540   Ibid.

but was in the midst of Jesus' contemporaries as demonstrated by the power of God over sin and spiritual principalities of wickedness in high places whereas the Emergent view of the Kingdom of God consists of social justice rather than individual salvation from sin.

The Kingdom of God was not the physical king or dominion that many of the Jewish sects were looking for, but Jesus said to Pilate, "My kingdom is *not of this world*: if my kingdom were of this world, then would my servants fight, that I should not be delivered to the Jews: but now is my kingdom not from hence" (John 18:36). Paul also defined how the Kingdom of God is "not meat and drink," that is, not physical in nature, "but righteousness, and peace, and joy in the Holy Ghost" (Romans 14:17). The Bible says of Christians that God has "delivered us from the power of darkness, and hath translated us into the kingdom of his dear Son" (Colossians 1:13). For the kingdom of God is not in word, but in power (1 Corinthians 4:20).

What is the true Gospel message of Kingdom of God? The Gospel of the Kingdom is the good news about the Kingdom of God, namely, that Jesus is Lord and the time was fulfilled for His kingdom to be established.[541] A kingdom is simply a domain ruled over by a king. Jesus inaugurated this spiritual kingdom in which He rules and reigns as Lord in the hearts of His people. His Kingdom transcends this world's divisions and boundaries of continents and countries because His citizens are Christians scattered throughout the world. But the Emergent Church does not acknowledge such boundaries in the Kingdom of God by including people from all religions.

Consistently, Emergents view the Kingdom of God as all-inclusive to both Christians and unbelievers. McLaren defines the message of the Kingdom of God as "calling all people together into one unified new humanity."[542] McLaren says, "Maybe God's plan is an opt-out plan, not an opt-in one. If you want to stay out of the party, you can.

---

541 "The Lord knoweth them that are his. And, Let every one that nameth the name of Christ depart from iniquity" (2 Timothy 2:19); "Wherefore come out from among them, and be ye separate, saith the Lord, and touch not the unclean thing; and I will receive you" (2 Corinthians 6:17).
542 YouTube video, posted by "TheOOZEtv," March 15, 2010, http://www.youtube.com/watch?v=zPJRoG5uSr4&feature=related.

Nobody will force you to enjoy it."[543] According to McLaren's view, everybody is *already* in the Kingdom, but they can "opt-out" if they so choose, whereas the Bible says it is actually the other way around, that people are in darkness and must be translated into the Kingdom of God (Colossians 1:13). Jesus said, "Verily, verily, I say unto thee, Except a man be born of water and of the Spirit, he cannot enter into the kingdom of God" (John 3:5). Thus, people cannot opt-out of the Kingdom of God if they haven't even entered the Kingdom of God through the new birth. Jesus said, "That which is born of the flesh is flesh; and that which is born of the Spirit is spirit. Marvel not that I said unto thee, Ye must be born again. The wind bloweth where it listeth, and thou hearest the sound thereof, but canst not tell whence it cometh, and whither it goeth: so is every one that is born of the Spirit" (John 3:6-8). Yet the Emergent Church hijacks Jesus' teaching and suggests instead that all religions are in the Kingdom of God. This view is inevitable with a postmodern view of subjective and relative truth accompanied with spiritual plurality and the doctrine of universalism. For instance, Samir Salmanovic writes in *An Emergent Manifesto of Hope*:

> Is our religion the only one that understands the true meaning of life? Or does God place his truth in others too? Well, God decides, and not us. The gospel is not *our* gospel, but the gospel of the kingdom of God, and what belongs to the kingdom of God cannot be hijacked by Christianity. God is sovereign, like the wind. He blows wherever he chooses.[544]

The Bible makes clear distinctions between those who are *in* and those who are *out* of the Kingdom of God. Jesus also likened the Kingdom to wheat and tares of which He said the reapers would be told, "Gather ye together first the tares, and bind them in bundles to burn them: but gather the wheat into my barn" (Matthew 13:30). He also made the following clear distinction: "the good seed are the children of the

---

543   Brian McLaren, *The Last Word After That* (San Francisco, CA: Jossey-Bass, 2005), 138.
544   Samir Salmanovic, "The Sweet Problem of Inclusiveness," in *An Emergent Manifesto of Hope*, eds. Pagitt and Jones, 194.

kingdom; but the tares are the children of the wicked one. . . The Son of man shall send forth his angels, and they shall gather *out* of his kingdom all things that offend, and them which do iniquity; And shall cast them into a furnace of fire: there shall be wailing and gnashing of teeth" (Matthew 13:38,41,42). These verses do not stop Tony Jones from stating:

> Some of my Christian friends made it clear that Jews could not possibly be involved in Kingdom of God work because they did not profess belief in Jesus. To emergents, this kind of thinking binds God's work to the church and implies that outside the lives of professed Christians, God is handicapped.[545]

But Jesus specifically addressed whether or not unbelieving Jews would be a part of His Kingdom. Unfortunately, many of the the Jews to whom the Kingdom was originally promised rejected their Messiah Jesus and forfeited their inheritance in the Kingdom of God. Jesus said, "Many shall come from the east and west, and shall sit down with Abraham, and Isaac, and Jacob, in the kingdom of heaven. But the children of the kingdom shall be cast out into outer darkness: there shall be weeping and gnashing of teeth" (Matthew 8:11,12). In a parable about the Messiah coming to the nation of Israel, Jesus said, "A certain nobleman went into a far country to receive for himself a kingdom, and to return. And he called his ten servants, and delivered them ten pounds, and said unto them, Occupy till I come. But his citizens hated him, and sent a message after him, saying, We will not have this man to reign over us" (Luke 19:12-14). As a result of the Kingdom being generally rejected by all but the remnant of national Israel, Jesus spoke about the transfer of the Kingdom of God to a "nation bringing forth the fruits thereof." Jesus said: "Did ye never read in the scriptures, The stone which the builders rejected, the same is become the head of the corner: this is the Lord's doing, and it is marvelous in our eyes? Therefore say I unto you, *The Kingdom of God shall be taken from you*, and given to a nation bringing forth the fruits thereof" (Matthew 21:42-43). God is far from being

---

545   Jones, *The New Christians,* 156.

"handicapped," but His Kingdom, like any other Kingdom, has boundaries.

Though the Emergent definition of the Kingdom of God is off the mark, I do commend them for bringing focus upon this aspect of the Gospel as well as its "here and now" implications. One writer on *Emergent Village* blog adequately summarizes the Emergent position: "The kingdom of God is now. Right now."[546] Many evangelicals believe that such an understanding of the Kingdom of God is at odds with premillennialism, but most early Church writers were premillennialists while they also believed in the Kingdom of God here and now. Where the Emergent Church differs with the early Church is their neglect to teach *both* aspects of the Kingdom of God. Even responsible amillennialists will acknowledge the "already/not yet" aspects of the Kingdom of God. Indeed, Jesus taught us to pray, "Thy kingdom come. Thy will be done *in earth* as it is in heaven" (Matthew 6:10). When Jesus was demanded of the Pharisees when the Kingdom of God should come, he answered them, "The Kingdom of God cometh not with observation: Neither shall they say, Lo here! or, lo there! for, behold, the Kingdom of God is within you" (Luke 17:20,21). Jesus said the Kingdom had come upon them and was in their midst. He also said, "If I cast out devils by the Spirit of God, then the kingdom of God *is come unto you*" (Matthew 12:28). Jesus acknowledged in a mysterious way that the Kingdom of God had already come.

Yet Scripture also reveals how the Kingdom will come in its fullness after all enemies are put under Christ's feet. There is a future time when "all things shall be subdued unto him, then shall the Son also himself be subject unto him that put all things under him, that God may be all in all" (1 Corinthians 15:28). The Kingdom of God exists in this earth but it does not have full dominion being in conflict with the kingdom of darkness until the end of the age (see Matthew 13:24-30,38-43). Thus, in one sense the Kingdom has already come. In another sense, we anticipate its fullness. Origen (245 AD) wrote:

That person is already in the kingdom of the heavens

---

546   Janel Apps Ramsey, "The Kingdom of God," Emergent Village, February 22, 2012, http://www.patheos.com/blogs/emergentvillage/2012/02/the-kingdom-of-god/.

who lives according to the virtues. Accordingly, the saying, "Repent, for the kingdom of heaven is at hand," refers to deeds and disposition–not to a certain time. Christ, who is all virtue, has come. For this reason, He says that the kingdom of God is within His disciples–not here or there. [547]

Cyprian (250 AD) wrote concerning the Kingdom of God:

Dearest brethren, Christ himself may be the kingdom of God, whom day by day we desire to come. . . . The kingdom of God may be understood to be Himself, since in Him we will reign. But we do well in seeking the kingdom of God–that is, the heavenly kingdom. For there is also an earthly kingdom. But he who has already renounced the world, is already greater than its honors and its kingdom.[548]

The Emergent Church embraces all the positive aspects of the Kingdom of God in a literal fashion whereas the negative aspects (discussed at length in earlier chapters of this book) which are directly associated with the Kingdom are nullified by the postmodern relativistic culture. For instance, concerning the topics of hell, universalism and final judgment, Jesus said the following in relation to the Kingdom: "Strive to enter in at the strait gate: for many, I say unto you, will seek to enter in, and shall not be able. When once the master of the house is risen up, and hath shut to the door, and ye begin to stand without, and to knock at the door, saying, Lord, Lord, open unto us; and he shall answer and say unto you, I know you not whence ye are: Then shall ye begin to say, We have eaten and drunk in thy presence, and thou hast taught in our streets. But he shall say, I tell you, I know you not whence ye are; depart from me, all ye workers of iniquity. There shall be weeping and gnashing of teeth, when ye shall see Abraham, and Isaac, and Jacob, and all the

---

547   Origen, *ANF*, 9.458 in Bercot, *A Dictionary of Early Christian Beliefs*, 387.
548   Cyprian, *ANF*, 5.451 in Bercot, *A Dictionary of Early Christian Beliefs*, 388.

prophets, in the kingdom of God, and you yourselves thrust out. And they shall come from the east, and from the west, and from the north, and from the south, and shall sit down in *the kingdom of God*" (Luke 13:24-29).

By and large, the Emergent Church dissuades Christians from preaching the Gospel, but this was the primary method of communicating the Kingdom of God in the early church (see Acts 20:25; 28:23; 28:31). Furthermore, concerning the severity of sin, particularly homosexuality, the Apostle Paul warns: *"Know ye not that the unrighteous shall not inherit the kingdom of God?* Be not deceived: neither fornicators, nor idolaters, nor adulterers, nor effeminate, nor abusers of themselves with mankind, Nor thieves, nor covetous, nor drunkards, nor revilers, nor extortioners, shall inherit the kingdom of God"* (1 Corinthians 6:9,10); "Now the works of the flesh are manifest, which are these; Adultery, fornication, uncleanness, lasciviousness, Idolatry, witchcraft, hatred, variance, emulations, wrath, strife, seditions, heresies, Envyings, murders, drunkenness, revellings, and such like: of the which I tell you before, as I have also told you in time past, that they which do such things *shall not inherit the kingdom of God*" (Galatians 5:19-21)

Sadly, the Emergent Church is speaking the language of many young Christians who are newly discovering the neglected truth of the Gospel of the Kingdom of God, only to devour them as prey with their subsequent false teaching concerning the Kingdom.

In conclusion, the Emergent Church teaching deserves commendation in its attempt to bring this important aspect of the Gospel, the Kingdom of God, back into focus and relevance here and now in a very practical way, but condemnation for its lawlessness against Christ's kingdom. Any good that may come from their efforts are far outweighed by their tremendous disservice to the world and the church in re-defining the Kingdom's King by preaching another Jesus, re-defining its laws by disregarding the King's commandments, and re-defining its subjects or citizens by including everybody from all religions in the Kingdom.

ABOUT THE AUTHOR

Elliott Nesch has a passion to edify the body of Christ by teaching the Word of God and producing Christian documentary films. He has been a disciple of Jesus since 2003 when God gloriously and radically saved him from a lifestyle of sin. He is also the founder of Holy Bible Prophecy (HBP), an online ministry devoted to Bible teaching, Christian apologetics, spiritual discernment, and Christ-centered revival. Elliott, his wife Harmony and their six children currently reside in Roseburg, Oregon.